THE FUTURE OF MANAGEMENT EDUCATION

To remain relevant, management education must reflect the realities that influence its subject matter, management, while at the same time addressing societal needs and expectations. Faced by powerful drivers of change, many of which are amplified by the immense turbulence caused by the COVID-19 pandemic in early 2020, an assessment of where management education stands and where it is going is timely.

This book brings together management education scholars, practitioners, and stakeholders to identify trends and to critically analyze key challenges from their respective perspectives. They consider the requirements for providing relevant management education in the future and explore changes and opportunities around themes such as responsibility, sustainability, innovation, competitive strategy, and technological change. The different perspectives of the authors contribute distinct insights and form a fascinating kaleidoscope of reflections on the present and predictions and prescriptions for the future of management education.

The result is a comprehensive volume that will be essential reading for scholars and administrators committed to the growth and development of management education. It also will be of keen interest to management educators as well as management learners who will shape and be shaped by the management education of the future.

Martin R. Fellenz is Associate Professor in Organisational Behaviour and Director for Adjunct Faculty at Trinity Business School, Trinity College Dublin, Ireland, and Adjunct Professor of Leadership and Organizational Behaviour at IMD, Switzerland.

Sabine Hoidn is Senior Lecturer in Management and Education and the Head of the Student-Centered Learning Lab at the University of St. Gallen, Switzerland, as well as the Chair of the AOM Management Education and Development Division in 2021.

Mairead Brady is Associate Professor in Marketing and Technology and Director of Joint Honours Degrees at Trinity Business School, Trinity College Dublin, Ireland. She is the 2022 Program Chair of the Management and Education Division of the Academy of Management Conference and is Chair Elect for 2024.

Routledge Advances in Management Learning and Education

Series Editors - Mikael Holmqvist and Alan Irwin

The role of managers in society is significant and not without controversy. A key aspect in understanding contemporary management is the education of its practitioners. This series brings together scholars from around the globe to examine and analyse the development of management education from various perspectives.

Elite Business Schools
Education and Consecration in Neoliberal Society
Mikael Holmqvist

The Future of Management Education
Martin R. Fellenz, Sabine Hoidn, and Mairead Brady

THE FUTURE OF MANAGEMENT EDUCATION

*Edited by Martin R. Fellenz, Sabine Hoidn,
and Mairead Brady*

Routledge
Taylor & Francis Group

LONDON AND NEW YORK

Cover image: © Chinnapong

First published 2022
by Routledge
4 Park Square, Milton Park, Abingdon, Oxon OX14 4RN

and by Routledge
605 Third Avenue, New York, NY 10158

Routledge is an imprint of the Taylor & Francis Group, an informa business

© 2022 selection and editorial matter, Martin R. Fellenz, Sabine Hoidn, and Mairead Brady; individual chapters, the contributors

British Library Cataloguing-in-Publication Data
A catalogue record for this book is available from the British Library

Library of Congress Cataloguing-in-Publication Data
Names: Fellenz, Martin R., editor. | Hoidn, Sabine, editor. | Brady, Mairead, editor.
Title: The future of management education / edited by Martin R. Fellenz, Sabine Hoidn and Mairead Brady.
Other titles: Future of management education (Routledge)
Description: Abingdon, Oxon ; New York, NY : Routledge, 2022. | Series: Routledge advances in management learning and education | Includes bibliographical references and index.
Identifiers: LCCN 2021051490 (print) | LCCN 2021051491 (ebook) | ISBN 9780367559724 (hardback) | ISBN 9780367559717 (paperback) | ISBN 9781003095903 (ebook)
Subjects: LCSH: Management--Study and teaching (Higher) | Business education.
Classification: LCC HD30.4 .F87198 2022 (print) | LCC HD30.4 (ebook) | DDC 658.0071/1--dc23/eng/20211020
LC record available at https://lccn.loc.gov/2021051490
LC ebook record available at https://lccn.loc.gov/2021051491

ISBN: 978-0-367-55972-4 (hbk)
ISBN: 978-0-367-55971-7 (pbk)
ISBN: 978-1-003-09590-3 (ebk)

DOI: 10.4324/9781003095903

Typeset in Bembo
by MPS Limited, Dehradun

CONTENTS

PART V
Conclusion 245

THE EDITORS

Martin R. Fellenz is Associate Professor in Organizational Behaviour and Director for Adjunct Faculty at Trinity Business School, Trinity College Dublin, Ireland. He is also Adjunct Professor for Leadership and Organizational Behaviour at IMD, Switzerland. An experienced management educator, he has received many institutional, national and international awards and recognitions for his teaching and regularly contributes to executive education programs at leading international business schools. His research focuses on leadership development, organizational change and transformation, and professional and management education and development.

Sabine Hoidn is a Senior Lecturer in Management and Education and the Head of the Student-Centered Learning Lab at the University of St. Gallen as well as the current Chair of the AOM Management Education and Development Division. Her research focuses on student-centered management and higher education teaching, learning and curriculum as well as on learning organizations with her latest co-edited *The Routledge Handbook on Student-Centred Learning and Instruction in Higher Education* published in 2020. She regularly presents at scientific conferences, publishes in peer-reviewed international journals, acts as a scientific adviser and expert panel member for European bodies such as PPMI and ECA in the area of (higher) education and serves on the editorial board of journals such as *JME, MTR, JHRE*, and *EJHE*. She teaches graduate and undergraduate classes in management and education and conducts professional development lectures and workshops for faculty worldwide. She received a PhD in business education from the University of St. Gallen, and the venia legendi in educational science, especially higher education (PD) from the University of Zurich.

Mairead Brady is Associate Professor in Marketing and Technology and Director of Joint Honours Degrees at Trinity Business School, Trinity College Dublin, Ireland. Her research and teaching focuses on the intraorganizational challenges for marketing managers and the adoption of digital technologies into marketing practices, with a second stream of research exploring the adoption of technologies and particularly artificial intelligence within higher education. She co-authors the leading Marketing Management (2019) textbook with Philip Kotler, Kevin Keller, Malcolm Goodman, and Torben Hansen and has developed a Marketing Planning simulation with Pearson Education. She was elected to the leadership track of the Management Education and Development Division of the Academy of Management Conference, as program chair in 2022 and Chair in 2024. Her work has been published in more than 100 refereed journal articles, books, book chapters and conference papers including the *Journal of Business and Industrial Marketing, Psychology and Marketing, International Journal of Technology Marketing, British Journal of Educational Technology, Services Industries Journal, Journal of Marketing Management,* and *Management Decision.*

CONTRIBUTORS

Kleio Akrivou is a Professor of Business Ethics and Moral Development, at Henley Business School, the University of Reading in the UK and visiting scholar at the University of Navarra, Pamplona, Spain. Her PhD is on adult moral development at Case Western Reserve University, USA. Following work in adult development in the modern humanistic traditions, Kleio studied classical moral philosophy researching a revised anthropology for better understanding human beings, action, and growth to enrich modern frames of reference. Accordingly, she published different works applying personalist virtue ethics, linked with the study of practical wisdom and the theory of self and human action. Her current research and work continues on these, emphasizing transcendental anthropology and personalist virtue ethics to inform business ethics, ethical education and moral development.

Douglas B. Allen is Associate Professor of Management and former Director of the International MBA program at the University of Denver Daniels College of Business. He received his BS Sociology from the University of Zimbabwe, his MBA from the Harvard Business School and his PhD from the University of Michigan Business School. He has served as a visiting professor at Renmin (People's) University in Beijing and Tongji University in Shanghai. He has consulted with Fortune Global 500 companies and has published articles on China, globalization, human resource management, cross-cultural and diversity issues as well as technology issues related to education. Earlier, he worked at Chrysler World Headquarters as a Human Resource Management Specialist and at the Bahá'í National Center as an International Placement Specialist. He is co-author (with Dwight Allen) of the book: Formula 2+2: The Simple Solution for Successful Coaching.

Rob B. Briner is Professor of Organizational Psychology at Queen Mary University of London and co-founder and Scientific Director of the Center for Evidence-Based Management. His research focuses on several topics including well-being, emotions, ethnicity, and the psychological contract. Beyond his academic roles Rob has written for and presented to practitioners on many aspects of HR and organizational psychology and is now involved in several initiatives aimed at developing evidence-based practice. He has received several awards for his work in this area including the British Psychological Society Division of Occupational Psychology Academic Contribution to Practice Award in 2014 and topped HR Magazine's Most Influential Thinker list in 2016. In 2019, he was given a Lifetime Achievement Award by HR Magazine.

Alexandra Bristow is Senior Lecturer in Organizational Behavior at the Open University. She previously worked at the Universities of Lancaster (where she completed her PhD), Surrey and Birmingham. Her interests are in the field of critical management studies and education and include academic work, identities and careers; business schools and universities and their role in society; and issues of power, politics, resistance, and learning. She has published in a range of journals including Academy of Management Learning and Education, Ephemera, Leadership, Management Learning, Organization, and Organization Studies.

Stephanie Bryant is executive vice president and chief accreditation officer of AACSB International where she recently oversaw the creation and implementation of AACSB's 2020 Guiding Principles and Standards for Business Accreditation. Prior to AACSB she spent 23 years in higher education leading business schools in strategy and innovation and has published over 30 academic articles, co-authored two accounting textbooks, and served on numerous academic journal editorial boards. At AACSB she oversees global accreditation strategy and policy for over 870 accredited schools. She holds a PhD in accounting from Louisiana State University.

Alessandra Capezio is Associate Professor in Organization Behavior at the Research School of Management of The Australian National University, Canberra. She is a fellow of Center for Evidence-Based Management and is an international proponent and educator of evidence-based practice in management and leadership. Her primary research focus is on critical thinking, evidenced-based decision-making and practice in organizations, dysfunctional workplace behaviors, the "dark" side of organizational behavior, careers, emotion, and self-regulation at work. Alessandra's research has been published in top-tier journals including Journal of Management, Human Relations, Journal of Vocational Behavior, Journal of Management Studies, Journal of Construction & Engineering Management, Journal of Business Ethics, and Journal of Career Assessment.

Leonardo Caporarello PhD is a Professor of Practice of Leadership and HR at SDA Bocconi School of Management (Milan, Italy), where he is also the Deputy Dean of Lifelong Learning. Leonardo is also the Delegate Rector for elearning at Bocconi University (Milan, Italy) and Director of BUILT (Bocconi University Innovations in Learning and Teaching). He has a long and wide experience in designing, coordinating, and teaching graduate and executive education programs – onsite, online, blended. Currently, Leonardo is the Vice President for Education (ItAIS), and member of the Advisory Board of the "e-Learning & Innovative Pedagogies." Leonardo has recently received the following awards: Best Professor 2020, Teaching Award, Rotman School of Management; Top 50 Global Thought Leaders & Influencers on Change Management, 2020; Top 100 Leaders in Education, 2019, Global Forum for Education and Learning.

Patrick Cullen has extensive experience in business education. He held a range of positions at AACSB International from 2010 to 2020, most recently vice president for strategy and innovation. Prior to AACSB, he was the lead researcher on the Future of MBA Education project at Harvard Business School and co-author of the book "Rethinking the MBA: Business Education at a Crossroads." He holds a PhD in management from the Judge Business School, University of Cambridge.

John G. Cullen lectures in Maynooth University School of Business where he has served as Director of Undergraduate Teaching & Learning. He has also served as the Associate Dean of the Faculty of Social Sciences and Interim Dean of Graduate Studies. His pedagogical research focuses on sustainable and socially responsible management learning and education. He is an Associate Editor of the Journal of Management Education and a member of the editorial boards of the Academy of Management Learning & Education and Human Relations.

Patrick L'Espoir Decosta is an Associate Professor of Marketing. Patrick's research interests include tourism marketing, consumer behavior and evidence-based education. He is also interested in ways to integrate evidence-based practice and methods in management curriculum development and teaching. Patrick's work has appeared in leading academic journals including Annals of Tourism Research, Journal of Travel Research, Tourism Management, International Marketing Review and Journal of Retail and Consumer Services. Patrick's contribution to practice includes an advisory role as Director of Quality Assurance to the Centre of Evidence-Based Management in the Netherlands, a nexus where he links theory with practice and research-led education.

Bill Foster is a Professor of Management at the Augustana Campus of the University of Alberta. His primary research interests include rhetorical history, social memory studies, service learning, and business ethics. He has been published in journals such as Journal of Management, Strategic Management Journal, Human Relations, Business History, and Journal of Business Ethics. He is the former Editor-in-Chief of Academy of Management Learning and Education and serves on the Editorial Review Boards of Organization Studies, Academy of Management Review, Journal of Management Studies, Journal of Management Education, and Business History. He has taught courses in organizational behavior, ethics, strategy, sustainability, marketing, and management. His teaching style is Socratic and is focused on engaging students through various techniques such as experiential learning, service learning, case studies, and classroom discussion.

Cynthia V. Fukami (Cindi) is a Professor in the Department of Management at the Daniels College of Business, University of Denver. She earned her PhD in Organizational Behavior from Northwestern University's Kellogg Graduate School of Management. Her current disciplinary research is focused on identities for professional employees. Along with her disciplinary work, Cindi has been a prominent contributor to the literature on the scholarship of teaching and learning. She co-edited (with Steven J. Armstrong) the SAGE Handbook of Management Learning, Education and Development, and currently serves as Associate Editor of the Journal of Management Education.

Manuel Joaquín Fernández González is a doctor of pedagogy, leading researcher at the Scientific Institute of Pedagogy of the Faculty of Education, Psychology and Art of the University of Latvia. After completing a postdoctoral research founded by the ERDF about character and virtue education at school in Latvia (2017–2020), he currently holds an individual grant from the Latvian Academy of Sciences for pursuing his research in this field. He is an expert in social sciences (education sciences) of the Latvian Council of Science and holds the MA "Character Education" by the Jubilee Centre for Character and Virtues of the Department of Education and Social Justice of the University of Birmingham.

Paul Hibbert is Dean of Arts & Divinity and Professor of Management at the University of St Andrews and an Honorary Professor at the University of Auckland Business School. His research is principally concerned with reflexive, relational and collaborative processes of organizing and learning. He is the Editor of Academy of Management Learning & Education and is the former Chair of the Management Education and Development Division of the Academy of Management. He sits on the editorial boards of the Journal of Management Education, Management Learning, and Organizational Research Methods. He is a Fellow of the British Academy of Management, the Chartered Management Institute, and the Higher Education Academy.

Anna Holland is Deputy Director of Learning and Teaching and a Senior Teaching Fellow in Management for the Centre of Management Education at Surrey Business School. An experienced teacher in adult learning and higher education, Anna has extensive knowledge and experience of designing and delivering blended learning journeys for a range of subjects and levels. Anna has led the design, implementation and delivery of Active Digital Design – Surrey Business School's hybrid learning strategy in response to COVID-19. An alumni of the Executive MBA and PG Cert in Management Education at Surrey Business School, Anna has shared her expertise at national events and workshops and works as a consultant in curriculum design.

Ulrich Hommel is an internationally recognized expert of accreditation, quality management, risk management and strategic leadership in higher education, and a prolific writer on business school topics. He has served in various leadership capacities at EFMD Global Network over a period of more than 12 years, including Director of Quality Services, Director of Business School Development and Director of Research & Surveys. He is currently the Director of the Quality Assurance Academy of EFMD Global Network. Ulrich Hommel has completed more than 20 years of service as Professor of Finance at EBS University & Law in Wiesbaden (Germany), which included appointments as Dean, Rector and Managing Director. His academic research focuses on risk management, restructuring and entrepreneurial financing, all topics that mirror his interests in higher education. Ulrich holds a PhD in Economics from the University of Michigan, Ann Arbor, and has been awarded a Dr. abil in Business Administration by WHU. Within XOLAS, Ulrich Hommel contributes particularly to the creation of knowledge and intelligence solutions and helps business schools to enhance their risk management capabilities; he develops restructuring solutions for clients and spearheads the development of XOLAS' financial advisory capabilities.

Juliane E. Iannarelli has held a range of positions at AACSB International from 2004 to 2020, most recently as senior vice president and chief knowledge officer. Her extensive experience with business education includes roles related to accreditation, data reporting and benchmarking, diversity and inclusion, industry news and research, and thought leadership. Juliane holds a master's degree in international business from the University of Florida.

David Lefevre is director of the Edtech Lab at the Imperial College Business School which he helped form in 2004. This team launched Imperial's first online module in 2005, Imperial's first online degree program (the Global Online MBA program) in 2015, the first blended degree program in 2017 and now delivers a portfolio of 225 online modules per year. In 2020, the team played a pivotal role in managing the School's response to the disruption caused by the COVID-19 pandemic. Throughout this work, the primary focus has been on matters relating to quality in online education and what constitutes an optimal student experience. In 2005, David was co-founder of the Imperial College eLearning spin-out firm Epigeum (now part of the Oxford University Press) and in 2018 co-founded Insendi, another Imperial College spin-out which has offered a learning experience platform focusing on high quality online education.

Ricardo Murcio is a Research Professor in the Human Factor department at IPADE Business School. He holds an MBA from IPADE and a PhD in Government and Organizational Culture from the University of Navarra. He has previously worked in decision-making positions in the hospitality and education industries, and as a consultant for family-based businesses in Mexico. He recently published Person-Centered Leadership: A Proposal from Carlos Llano (EUNSA, 2020).

Olivier Ratle is a Senior Lecturer in Organization Studies at the University of the West of England, where he teaches research philosophies and methods, theories of organisations and organizational change. His research is about the politics of knowledge production in management studies, and about academic work in the contemporary University and Business School. With his co-authors Alexandra and Sarah, he has published extensively on the predicament of early-career academics, touching upon the themes of identity, resistance, career strategies, experiences of time and work rhythms, violence, and the terror of performance regimes.

Clare Rigg is Professor of Leadership and Management and Associate Dean (Research) at the University of Suffolk, UK. Her academic career has prioritised teaching and research that is close to practice and is concerned to enable students to make a critical impact in their organisations and communities. Her work has been published in a range of journals including British Journal of Management, Entrepreneurship and Regional Development, Leadership, Journal of Management Education, Management Learning, and Public Management Review. She is Associate Editor, Academy of Management Learning & Education.

Christine Rivers is Co-director for Centre of Management Education (CME) at University of Surrey, Surrey Business School and is an accredited Executive Coach and Consultant. Through CME Christine plays an integral role in shaping the future of Management Education as a scholarly profession. She also leads the first credit-bearing PG Cert in Management Education, and consults and collaborates with professional bodies, business schools and higher education institutions in the area of staff development and blended learning design. Christine's expertise and knowledge of developing staff and designing meaningful blended learning experiences has been instrumental in supporting the transition of Surrey during COVID-19.

Sarah Robinson is Professor in Management and Organization Studies at Adam Smith Business School, Glasgow University. She has worked at the Open University Business School and Lancaster University School of Management, where she also completed her PhD. Her interests include organizational and management learning, issues of power, resistance and identity within professions, critical management studies, and the application of Bourdieu's sociology to Organization Studies. Her publications include work in *Academy of Management Learning and Education, Organization Studies, Human Relations, British Journal of Management, Organization, Business History*, and *Management Learning*.

Germán Scalzo is a Professor of Business Ethics at Universidad Panamericana (Mexico). He earned his PhD in Government and Organizational Culture from the University of Navarra (Spain). He has published numerous articles, chapters and books on the relationship between economics, business and ethics through an anthropological and philosophical lens. His current research includes personalist virtue ethics and the logic of gift.

Kiran Trehan is Pro-Vice Chancellor for Partnerships and Engagement at The University of York and Director of the Centre for Women's Enterprise, Leadership, Economy & Diversity. Professor Trehan is a key contributor to debates on leadership, enterprise development and diversity in small firms and business. She has led a number of leaderships, enterprise and business support initiatives and has extensively published a number of journal articles, policy reports, books, and book chapters in the field. She has received invitations as Guest Editor from reputable international journals (Human Relations, Management Learning, International Small Business Journal), as well as national and international advisory roles that shape debates and policy in diversity and enterprise.

Koen Vandenbempt is the Dean of the Faculty of Business and Economics of the University of Antwerp (Belgium) and is furthermore a non-executive director of the Antwerp Management School (Belgium). He has held various leadership positions in the past (among them Associate Dean for Internationalization, Academic Director of the eMBA Program, Chairman of the Department of Management), both at the University of Antwerp and the Antwerp Management School. Koen is also a Visiting Professor at universities and business schools in the US, Russia, and India. Koen Vandenbempt's work focuses on strategic change in organizations (mainly in industrial and technical settings) and in different industry contexts. In this capacity, he often works together with companies on change projects and/or is involved in management training sessions in the context of change. He is and has been involved as an independent director of companies in different industries (IT solution provider to the creative industries; Diamond Certification; Diamond federation; Higher Education).

Dennis P. Wittmer is a professor in the Management Department of the Daniels College of Business at the University of Denver. He currently teaches courses related to ethical leadership, business ethics, organizational ethics, developing business to serve the social good, as well as AI and the future of work. His research spans various areas: ethical sensitivity and ethical decision making, ethical work climates, public-private sector differences related to moral development and ethical work climates, and cultural differences related to behavioral economics and ethics. More recently his work has been focused on pedagogical issues related to teaching business ethics, including the teaching of virtue ethics, the role of service learning in ethics courses, teaching team-taught transdisciplinary courses, designing curriculum to strengthen practical wisdom, and the future of management and work related to AI and robotics. Dennis enjoys skiing, biking, hiking, fishing, and all of the outdoors activities Colorado has to offer!

Geoffrey Wood is DanCap Private Equity Chair of Innovation and Head of DAN Management at Western University in Canada, and Visiting Professor at Trinity College, Dublin. Previously, he served as Dean and Professor of International Business, at Essex Business School and before then as Professor of International Business at Warwick Business School, UK. He has authored/co-authored/edited twenty books, and over two hundred and twenty articles in peer reviewed journals. He holds honorary positions at Griffith and Monash University in Australia. Geoff's research interests centre on the relationship between institutional setting, corporate governance, firm finance, and firm level work and employment relations. He is a Fellow of the Academy of Social Sciences, and a Fellow of the British Academy of Management, and is also in receipt of an Honorary Doctorate in economics from Aristotle University, Greece. Geoffrey Wood is Editor in Chief of the Academy of Management Perspectives, Official Journal of the Academy of Management (US), as well as of Human Resource Management Journal. He is Co-editor of the Annals of Corporate Governance, editor of the Chartered ABS Journal Ranking list, and International Reviewer of the ABDC Journal Guide.

PART I

The Changing Context of ME

1

"MAY YOU LIVE IN INTERESTING TIMES": CONSIDERING THE FUTURE OF MANAGEMENT EDUCATION

Martin R. Fellenz, Mairead Brady, and Sabine Hoidn

Introduction

Worldwide there are more than 13,000 business schools offering degrees (Williams, 2011) to millions of enrolled students. Many of them also offer non-degree management education (ME) to many more learners, which includes the commercially important segment of executive education (CABS, 2017). Business degrees are the most popular choice among all academic disciplines. In 2018, business degrees awarded in the USA accounted for 19.5% ($n = 386,201$) of all bachelor's degrees conferred (NCES, 2019). In the same year more than 400,000 bachelors and masters degrees in management and administration and/or business were awarded across the EU-27 (Eurostat, 2018). In addition to such formal higher education settings, management learners also receive formal ME in many other professional, vocational, and corporate educational settings. This scope and variety of ME highlights the value it is held in by students, employers, and other stakeholders.

Yet to remain relevant, ME must address both societal needs and expectations and the realities that influence its subject matter, management (Ghoshal, 2005; Khurana, 2007; Murillo & Vallentin, 2016; Spender, 2016). In the context of immense turbulence that has characterized the time since the outbreak of the COVID-19 pandemic in early 2020, an assessment of where ME stands and where it is going is timely. Even without the global pandemic, ME stands at the crossroads of significant changes that require innovative responses (see Bachrach et al., 2017; Peters, Smith, & Thomas, 2018; Thomas, Lee, Thomas, & Wilson, 2014; Üsdiken, Kipping, & Engwall, 2021).

The drivers of change are multifaceted, and include changing local, regional, and global markets for ME; evolving business models resulting in changing

DOI: 10.4324/9781003095903-2

requirements for management learners' skillsets and mindsets; increasingly diverse and complex social and cultural contexts; shifting societal expectations; speed, complexity, and variety of technological development; evolving and new roles for ME stakeholders in the face of emerging new players and new forms of competition; expanding policy, regulatory, and accreditation influences; and issues related to environmental and sustainability concerns. These factors have recently been over-shadowed by the global COVID-19 pandemic and its direct impact on the provision of ME worldwide, particularly as rolling lockdowns, travel restrictions and education system closures have forced an increased reliance on remote and digitalized delivery of teaching and learning. Many of the pandemic-induced changes will be temporary, some will be permanent, and others have accelerated or amplified existing trends and developments that will profoundly alter ME.

In this context, ME, in general, and business schools as the traditionally most visible actors in the ME space in particular, face questions about their future. It remains to be seen to what degree current models of ME practice may be sustainable, and how the changing modes of ME and of competition among existing and new players in this arena will drive business schools to change and adapt. It is also unclear which existing approaches will prove to be fit for the emerging expectations and requirements for success, and which will not and if not what may take their place.

Against this backdrop this edited volume considers a range of issues that reflect the dynamic and complex context in which ME currently exists and continues to evolve. The individual chapters contribute to our understanding of relevant dynamics in a variety of ways. Some identify and discuss aspects of ME that are in flux and identify trends that are influencing ME's future. Others alert us to somewhat less visible aspects of the complex dynamics shaping ME that are likely to come to the forefront over time as important factors that influence the where, how, what, and who: where and how management will be learnt and taught, what content or orientations will be central to ME, and who will design and teach – and who will learn about – management in the future. Individually and collectively, the contributions in this book provide insight and direction for those interested in ME at the level of individual learners and educators, at the strategic level of business schools and their current and emerging competitors, and at the level of markets and the ME industry as a whole. They provide a timely exploration of likely and possible scenarios, probe current practices as to their continued relevance and sustainability, and present arguments about how ME can, will or should develop into the future.

The book is structured as follows: the first part focuses on the changing context of ME, the second on evolving prospects and perspectives followed by the third part on innovative practices in teaching and learning practices, and the concluding part exploring the dynamics of accreditation and other external regulatory influences on ME. The overall picture that is emerging is one of increasingly complex interactions and multi-layered dynamics that make specific predictions about the future difficult, maybe even impossible. Yet such predictions are not the only valuable outcome of an exploration of the future of ME. This edited text also provides description of current trends, explanation of visible changes, exploration of less visibly, almost tectonic shifts in the underlying fabric of the ME ecosystems, as well as more normative statements about what should (or should not) become center stage in the ME of the future. All of these offer valuable insights, which inform and may aid developments in the ME domain.

Pandemic-Induced Change and the Wider Themes of ME Evolution

To frame these critical considerations it is useful to briefly outline some of the recent, pandemic-influenced changes, and to briefly consider them separately before framing them in the context of the overarching themes that outline the factors influencing the future development of ME that are identified and discussed across the different contributions. At the time of writing, among the most visible issues with the most profound implications for ME related to the ongoing pandemic are (1) social distancing and global travel restrictions which have placed limitations on ME learner mobility both domestically but also impacting on the international ME markets, and (2) the resulting changes to delivery formats through the forced technological pivot experienced across ME through the immense acceleration of technology adoption in the delivery of ME (Brammer & Clark, 2020; Greenberg & Hibbert, 2020).

These two particular issues are closely connected to the wider themes that mark the dynamics influencing the future evolution of ME. The next parts will briefly discuss these two pandemic related issues and then broaden the view to preview wider themes of ME evolution.

International ME Markets and ME Learner Mobility

Even though worldwide only about 2% of all students are international students (Altman & Bastian, 2020), higher education in European, Oceanian, and North American countries is an internationalized industry. As an OECD average, foreign students comprise 9%, 21%, and 29% of newly enrolling students in bachelor, masters, and doctoral programs, respectively, and, as an extreme example, foreign student account for more than a quarter of total funding for Australian universities (Hurley & Van Dyke, 2020). In 2018, English-speaking countries such as the USA (987,000), the UK (452,000), Australia (445,000), and Canada (225,000) attracted large numbers of international students, with other countries such as Germany (312,000), Russia (262,000), France (230,000), Japan (183,000), and China (178,000) also important destination countries (OECD, 2020).

The largest home countries of international students are China, India, and Korea (OECD, 2020).

The relative proportion of international students in business disciplines is considerably higher than the general average with, for example, 61% and 43% of master's students enrolling in business schools in Australia and the UK in 2018, respectively, coming from abroad (OECD, 2020). About a third of international students in the UK study business (CABS, 2016), and between 2015 and 2018 nearly seven out of ten business and management master's graduates in the UK were international students (ICEF Monitor, 2019).

The widespread COVID-19 related travel restrictions and the pandemic's impact on the willingness to travel has significantly affected enrolment in business schools in 2020. Many internationally oriented business schools as well as those national ME markets that are particularly focused on attracting international students (Wood, this volume), such as the UK and Australia, were particularly hard hit by the impact of the pandemic (Hurley & Van Dyke, 2020; Jayasuriya, 2021). The effect of the pandemic on longer-term mobility patterns among ME students remains to be seen, but the financial impact on those providing ME primarily or even exclusively to international students is likely to be severe (*The Economist*, 2020). Overall, the predictions are that, especially in segments catering to international students, the impact of the pandemic on ME and ME providers will be significant for the short term or even the long term through shifting and reduced student cohorts, reduced revenues, and serious financial implications (Drayton & Waltmann, 2020; Korn, Belkin, & Chung, 2020; Maslen, 2020; *The Economist*, 2020).

This impact is likely to spread beyond business schools especially in higher education institutions that have used their business schools as cash cows to finance other activities (McKie, 2018). An outcome could be that particularly university-based business schools may find their status affected and their ability to invest back into their own activities severely curtailed as their host universities suffer general financial difficulties as a result of the pandemic's impact on student numbers and university revenues. Both university-based business schools and their independent competitors will likely feel significant financial and competitive pressures that may lead to many of them being taken over, forced to merge or engage in close strategic collaborations, or go out of business altogether (Drayton & Waltmann, 2020; Rosowsky, 2020; Schifrin & Tucker, 2021).

The Technological Pivot in ME

The adoption of educational technologies as a significant element of ME provision significantly accelerated in response to the mobility and congregation restrictions and shutdowns of education systems across all levels in most countries worldwide in response to the COVID-19 pandemic (Brammer & Clark, 2020; Goyal, Daipuria, & Jain, 2021; Teräs, Suoranta, Teräs, & Curcher, 2020;

UNESCO, 2020). The previously relatively slow adoption of digital educational technologies, the incorporation of blended educational designs, and the step to offer ME programs that are largely or even exclusively delivered online have all seen significantly accelerated developments that are unlikely to be reversed or reversed fully (see Lefevre & Caporarello, this volume).

This technological pivot has transformed ME within the space of a single year in ways and at a speed inconceivable before the outbreak of the pandemic. Technology adoption and concomitant educational redesign, along with the broad-based involvement of (and required skill-building by) ME faculty, now provide a very different platform for future development of technologically enabled, enhanced, and transformed ME.

Predictions of transformations of ME state that technology will play an increasingly central role even in segments such as executive education where the move to online has been comparatively slow (Kohan, 2020; Sawhney, 2021). For this sector, Sawhney predicts growth at the bottom end of the segment through comparatively low-cost options, and at the high end of the market through high quality and premium-priced in-person programs. This latter segment will likely be concentrated among a small number of prestigious providers, and he warns of the danger of getting caught in a competitive niche not aligned with the resources, capabilities, and reputation of the ME provider.

The Wider Themes of ME Evolution

Such developments and the resulting competitive dynamics will play out in the complex context of an evolving ME ecosystem where new players emerge (see Hommel & Vandenbempt, this volume) in the context of changing ME designs and delivery approaches (see Lefevre & Caporarello, this volume; Rivers & Holland, this volume) in a sector significantly disrupted and changed by an increasingly unbundled value chain that offers opportunities to new entrants and different types of ME providers. At the same time, the legacies of the past will strongly influence both the actions of individual players in the ME markets through limitations and opportunities rooted in existing and re-formed identities (see Hibbert & Foster, this volume) and by existing models of selecting and rewarding individual faculty primarily for research rather than educational contributions (see Wood, this volume; Rattle, Bristow & Robinson, this volume).

Individual management learners and their expectations are also evolving and becoming more diverse, which has significant implications for the content and delivery of ME (Akrivou et al., this volume; Fukami et al., this volume; Trehan & Rigg, this volume). Legitimacy for ME vis-à-vis expectations of individual management learners and other stakeholders such as employers can be improved by appealing to the quality and utility of the material taught (see Briner et al., this volume; Bryant et al., this volume; Cullen, this volume; Landfester & Metelmann, 2020; Rubin & Dierdorff, 2009; Rubin & Morgeson, 2013).

Similarly, at a macro level public expectations regarding the sustainability and societal contributions of business schools (Bryant, Cullen, & Iannarelli, this volume; Cullen, this volume) are increasing the pressure on ME providers to gain and retain legitimacy. These pressures are highly visible in the degree to which business schools are engaged in accreditation and ranking-relevant activities (Adler & Harzing, 2009; Alajoutsijärvi, Kettunen, & Sohlo, 2018; Bachrach et al., 2017; Hommel & Vandenbemp, this volume; Wedlin, 2011; Wilkins & Huisman, 2012) and other legitimating activities such as symbolic and verbal actions, lobbying, and mimicry (Fiset & Al Hajj, 2021; Kothiyal, Bell, & Clarke, 2018; Üsdiken et al., 2021; Zhang, Zheng, & Xi, 2020). The focus on ethics and CSR, central to much of the actions of business schools and the rhetoric on their role in society in the first two decades of this century (Adler, 2002; Pettigrew & Starkey, 2016; Rasche & Gilbert, 2015), has been joined by a distinct reorientation toward issues related to environmental and sustainability topics (Millar & Price, 2018; Slager, Pouryousefi, Moon, & Schoolman, 2020). In this area, there is a marked increase in both substantive and virtue-signaling activities of business schools in relation to their environmental and sustainability activities and credentials (Burchall, Kennedy, & Murray, 2015; García-Feijoo, Eizaguirre, & Rica-Aspiunza, 2020; Gill, 2021; Miotto, Blanco-González, & Díez-Martín, 2020; Snelson-Powell, Grosvold, & Millington, 2020).

Overall, the drivers of change affecting ME are numerous. The complex dynamics arising out of the only partly visible – and mostly only partially understood – interplay between and among them present a most interesting and intriguing object of study. To those charged with steering business schools through these white-water conditions, these dynamics may present as a set of almost intractable challenges. To business school faculty and other ME educators, they will provide a context of increased uncertainty that offers new opportunities but likely also many challenges and tribulations. To management learners they appear to offer more choice and flexibility, innovative teaching, and multiple, often technology-based, delivery options but also increased risk as the relative quality and fit of traditional and emerging educational offerings will be difficult to determine. Lastly, to those who observe or those who research this area there is a wealth of avenues for exploration and a rich and fertile research domain.

Undoubtedly, the next years will see significant challenges to the hegemony of business schools as a whole, and to the reputation and market position of individual schools, as the value chain of ME is unpacked by new competitors and new forms of competition emerge.

The future developments in important segments such as executive education remain unclear (Jack, 2020). Existing business school accreditation and ranking approaches will continue to be debated, with endogenous (see Bryant et al., this volume) and exogenous (see Hommel & Vandenbemp, this volume) changes likely to accelerate. Technological developments and innovative technology deployment may enable management learners to develop into more discerning users and customers of ME.

As an example, such emancipated, self-directed management learners will be increasingly able to, and – as their maturity and confidence grows – increasingly demand to self-curate their educational experiences in terms of both content and process. This development, like so many others, has already begun in many professional contexts and is supported by both employers switching their recruitment focus away from traditional degrees toward skill credentials (Jack, 2021) and self-directed learners that have started to see such micro-credentials (Finocchietti & Lokhoff, 2021) as additions or even alternatives to traditional degree-based education (see Acree, 2016; Milligan & Kennedy, 2017; Rottmann & Duggan, 2021).

Management faculty and other management educators will have to adapt their skillsets and – maybe a more profound challenge – their mindsets to operate in a more complex and volatile industry. With all this uncertainty there is no doubt that exciting times lay ahead for ME!

References

Abreu-Pederzini, G. D., & Suárez-Barraza, M. F. 2020. Just let us be: Domination, the postcolonial condition, and the global field of business schools. *Academy of Management Learning & Education*, 19(1): 40–58.

Acree, L. 2016. *Seven lessons learned from implementing micro-credentials.* Raleigh, NC: Friday Institute for Educational Innovation at the NC State University College of Education.

Adler, N. J., & Harzing, A. 2009. When knowledge wins: Transcending the sense and nonsense of academic rankings. *Academy of Management Learning & Education*, 8: 72–95.

Adler, P. S. 2002. Corporate scandals: It's time for reflection in business schools. *Academy of Management Executive*, 16: 148–149.

Alajoutsijärvi, K., Kettunen, K., & Sohlo, S. 2018. Shaking the status quo: Business accreditation and positional competition. *Academy of Management Learning & Education*, 17(2): 203–225.

Altman, S. A., & Bastian, P. 2020. *DHL global connectedness index 2020: The state of globalization in a distancing world.* Bonn, Germany: Deutsche Post DHL Group.

Bachrach, D. G., Bendoly, E., Beu Ammeter, D., Blackburn, R., Brown, K. G., Burke, G., Callahan, T., Chen, K. Y., Day, V. H., Ellstrand, A. E., Erekson, O. H., Gomez, J. A., Greenlee, T., Handfield, R., Loudder, M. L. , Malhotra, M., Petroni, K. R., Sevilla, A., Shafer, S., Shih, M. & Voss, D. (2017). On academic rankings, unacceptable methods, and the social obligations of business schools. *Decision Sciences*, 48(3): 561–585.

Brammer, S., & Clark, T. (2020). COVID-19 and management education: Reflections on challenges, opportunities, and potential futures. *British Journal of Management*, 31(3): 453.

Burchall, J., Kennedy, S., & Murray, A. 2015. Responsible management education in UK business schools: Critically examining the role of the United Nations Principles for Responsible Management Education as a driver for change. *Management Learning*, 46: 479–497.

CABS. 2016. *UK business schools and international student recruitment: Trends, challenges and the case for change*. London: Chartered Association of Business Schools.

CABS. 2017. *The impact of executive education: A review of current practice & trends*. London: Chartered Association of Business Schools.

Drayton, E., & Waltmann, B. 2020. Will universities need a bailout to survive the COVID-19 crisis? *IFS Briefing Note BN300*. The Institute for Fiscal Studies.

Economist. 2020. Uncanny university: Covid-19 could push some universities over the brink. *The Economist*. Accessed May 4, 2021, at https://www.economist.com/briefing/2020/08/08/covid-19-could-push-some-universities-over-the-brink

Eurostat. 2018. (educ_uoe_grad02), Tertiary education statistics. https://ec.europa.eu/eurostat/statistics-explained/index.php/Tertiary_education_statistics#Fields_of_education

Finocchietti, C., & Lokhoff, J. 2021. The promise of micro-credentials? The road to recognition. *University World News*, February 27, 2021. Accessed May 4, 2021, at https://www.universityworldnews.com/post.php?story=20210224114309588

Fiset, J., & Al Hajj, R. 2021. Mission Statement Content and the Signaling of Institutional Performance: An Examination of Non-US International Business Schools. *Academy of Management Learning & Education* (in press).

García-Feijoo, M., Eizaguirre, A., & Rica-Aspiunza, A. 2020. Systematic review of sustainable-development-goal deployment in business schools. *Sustainability*, 12(1): 440.

Ghoshal, S. 2005. Bad management theories are destroying good management practices. *Academy of Management Learning and Education*, 4(1): 75–91.

Gill, M. J. 2021. High flying business schools: Working together to address the impact of management education and research on climate change. *Journal of Management Studies*, 58(2): 554–561.

Goyal, J. K., Daipuria, P., & Jain, S. 2021. An alternative structure of delivering management education in India. *Journal of Educational Technology Systems*, 49(3): 325–340.

Greenberg, D., & Hibbert, P. 2020. From the editors – Covid-19: Learning to hope and hoping to learn. *Academy of Management Learning & Education*, 19(2): 123–130.

Hurley, P., & Van Dyke, N. 2020. *Australian investment in education: Higher education*. Melbourne: Mitchell Institute.

ICEF. 2019. UK's business schools highly reliant on international postgraduate students. *ICEF Monitor*. Accessed May 4, 2021, at https://monitor.icef.com/2019/10/uks-business-schools-highly-reliant-on-international-postgraduate-students/#:~:text=A%20new%20report%20from%20the,UK%20universities%20were%20international%20students

Jack, A. 2020. Executive education must retool for the post-pandemic world. *Financial Times*. Accessed May 4, 2021, at https://www.ft.com/content/a88e72ae-8356-11ea-b872-8db45d5f6714

Jack, A. 2021. Employers shift focus from education to skills. *Financial Times*, May 3, 2021. Accessed May 4, 2021, at https://www.ft.com/content/4e610474-9c93-4e47-a042-915d2222cc4b

Jayasuriya, K. 2021. COVID-19, markets and the crisis of the higher education regulatory state: The case of Australia. *Globalizations*, 18(4): 584–599. 10.1080/14747731.2020.1815461

Khurana, R. 2007. *From higher aims to hired hands: The social transformation of American business schools and the unfulfilled promise of management as a profession*. Princeton, NJ: Princeton University Press.

Kohan, E. B. 2020. Yes, Exec Ed programs can deliver value online: Pedagogical approaches to elevate the impact of remote executive education. *Inspiring Minds, Harvard Business Publishing.* Accessed April 26, 2021, at https://hbsp.harvard.edu/ inspiring-minds/yes-exec-ed-programs-can-deliver-value-online/?cid=web %7Cwebinar-recording-page%7C2021-03-4-webinar-recording-page-what-lies-beyond-the-future-of-executive-education%7Cnone%7Cwebinar%7Ceducator %7Cinspiring-minds-article%7Cmar2021

Korn, M., Belkin, D., & Chung, J. 2020. Coronavirus pushes colleges to the breaking point. Forcing "hard choices" about education. *The Wall Street Journal,* April 30, 2020. Accessed May 4, 2021, at https://www.wsj.com/ articles/coronavirus-pushes-colleges-to-the-breaking-point-forcing-hard-choices-about-education11588256157? mod=searchresults&page=1&pos=1

Kothiyal, N., Bell, E., & Clarke, C. 2018. Moving beyond mimicry: Developing hybrid spaces in Indian business schools. *Academy of Management Learning & Education,* 17(2): 137–154.

Landfester, U., & Metelmann, J. 2020. Back to the roots: Why academic business schools should re-radicalize rationality. *Academy of Management Learning & Education,* 19(3): 345–365.

Maslen, G. 2020. Universities face disastrous fall in income due to COVID-19. *University World News,* April 22, 2020. Retrieved April 2, 2021, from https://www. universityworldnews.com/post.php?story= 202004221408487

McKie, A. 2018. UK universities "bleeding their business schools dry." *Times Higher Education Supplement.* Accessed April 28, 2021, at https://www.timeshighereducation. com/news/ukuniversities-bleeding-their-business-schools-dry

Millar, J., & Price, M. 2018. Imagining management education: A critique of the contribution of the United Nations PRME to critical reflexivity and rethinking management education. *Management Learning,* 49(3): 346–362.

Milligan, S. M., & Kennedy, G. 2017. To what degree? Alternative micro-credentialing in a digital age. In R. James, S. French, & P. Kelly (Eds.), *Visions for Australian tertiary education:* 41–53. Melbourne, VIC: The University of Melbourne: Melbourne Center for the Study of Higher Education.

Miotto, G., Blanco-González, A., & Díez-Martín, F. 2020. Top business schools legitimacy quest through the Sustainable Development Goals. *Heliyon,* 6(11): e05395.

Murillo, D., & Vallentin, S. 2016. The business school's right to operate: Responsibilization and resistance. *Journal of Business Ethics,* 136: 743–757.

NCES. 2019. *Digest of education statistics.* National Center for Education Statistics. Accessed April 2, 2021, at https://nces.ed.gov/programs/digest/d19/tables/dt19_322.10.asp

OECD. 2020. *Education at a glance 2020: OECD indicators.* Paris: OECD Publishing. 10.1787/69096873-en

Peters, K., Smith, R. R., & Thomas, H. 2018. *Rethinking the business models of business schools: A critical review and change agenda for the future.* Bingley, UK: Emerald.

Pettigrew, A., & Starkey, K. 2016. From the guest editors: The legitimacy and impact of business schools – key issues and a research agenda. *Academy of Management Learning & Education,* 15: 649–664.

Rasche, A., & Gilbert, D. U. 2015. Decoupling responsible management education: Why business schools may not walk their talk. *Journal of Management Inquiry,* 24(3): 239–252.

Rosowsky, D. 2020. Where does higher education go next? *Forbes,* September 5, 2020. Accessed May 4, 2021, at https://www.forbes.com/sites/davidrosowsky/2020/09/05/ where-does-higher-education-go-next/

Rottmann, A. K., & Duggan, M. H. 2021. Micro-credentials in higher education. In J. Keengwe (Ed.), *Handbook of research on innovations in non-traditional educational practices*: 223–236, Hershey, PA: IGI Global.

Rubin, R. R., & Morgeson, F. P. 2013. Reclaiming quality in graduate management education. In B. C. Holtom & E. C. Dierdorff (Eds.), *Disrupt or be disrupted: A blueprint for change in management education*: 297–345. San Francisco, CA: Jossey-Bass.

Rubin, R. S., & Dierdorff, E. C. 2009. How relevant is the MBA? Assessing the alignment of required curricula and required managerial competencies. *Academy of Management Learning and Education*, 8(2): 208–223.

Sawhney, M. (2021). *What lies beyond: The future of executive education*. Harvard Business Publishing Webinar. Accessed April 26, 2021, at https://hbsp.harvard.edu/webinars/what-lies-beyond-the-future-of-executive-education/?cid=email%7Celoqua%7C2021-04-20-the-faculty-lounge%7C339003%7Cfaculty-lounge-newsletter%7Cnewsletter-subscribers%7Cvarious%7Capr20212397&acctID=8350900

Schifrin, M., & Tucker, H. 2021. College financial grades 2021: Will your alma mater survive Covid? *Forbes*. Accessed May 4, 2021, at https://www.forbes.com/sites/schifrin/2021/02/22/college-financial-grades-2021-will-your-alma-mater-survive-covid/

Slager, R., Pouryousefi, S., Moon, J., & Schoolman, E. D. 2020. Sustainability centres and fit: How centres work to integrate sustainability within business schools. *Journal of Business Ethics*, 161(2): 375–391.

Snelson-Powell, A. C., Grosvold, J., & Millington, A. I. (2020). Organizational hypocrisy in business schools with sustainability commitments: The drivers of talk-action inconsistency. *Journal of Business Research*, 114: 408–420.

Spender, J. C. 2016. How management education's past shapes its present. *BizEd*. Accessed April 2, 2021, at https://bized.aacsb.edu/articles/2016/03/how-management-education-past-shapes-present

Teräs, M., Suoranta, J., Teräs, H., & Curcher, M. 2020. Post-Covid-19 education and education technology 'solutionism': A seller's market. *Postdigital Science and Education*, 2(3): 863–878.

Thomas, H., Lee, M., Thomas, L., & Wilson, A. 2014. *Securing the future of management education: Competitive destruction of constructive innovation?* Bingley, UK: Emerald.

UNESCO. 2020. *Distance learning solutions*. United Nations Educational, Scientific and Cultural Organization. ttps://en.unesco.org/covid19/educationresponse/solutions

Üsdiken, B., Kipping, M., & Engwall, L. 2021. Professional school obsession: An enduring yet shifting rhetoric by us business schools. *Academy of Management Learning & Education* (in press).

Wedlin, L. 2011. Going global: Rankings as rhetorical devices to construct an international field of management education. *Management Learning*, 42(2): 199–218.

Wilkins, S., & Huisman, J. 2012. UK business school rankings over the last 30 years (1980–2010): Trends and explanations. *Higher Education*, 63(3): 367–382.

Williams, J. R. 2011. Vision for the future. *BizEd*, AACSB. Accessed April 2, 2021, at https://bized.aacsb.edu/articles/2011/09/vision-for-the-future

Zhang, X., Zheng, X., & Xi, Y. 2020. How governmental agencies legitimize organizations: A case study on Chinese business schools from 1977 to 2014. *Academy of Management Learning & Education*, 19(4): 521–540.

2

THE GLOBAL MARKET FOR MANAGEMENT EDUCATION

Geoffrey Wood

The Boom Years of Management Education

The period from 1990 to well into the 2000s saw a boom in management education worldwide. This process had four distinct elements. The first was increased competition as many institutions established new business schools, re-capitalized more traditional management schools and departments, or sought to raise and extend the profile of their business school. Initiatives include the development of new premises, enhanced program provision, increased international recruitment (with management education becoming a major export in many countries), and/or a higher research profile (Parker, 2018). This led to both winners and losers. Some long established and historically well-regarded business schools battled to cope with much greater competition and arguably lost much of their earlier prominence (e.g., Bradford), while others rapidly gained strong international research reputations when compared to earlier more niche roles (e.g., UCL and LSE). Still more managed to retain their position, but with diluted prominence given the increased level of competition.

What is evident is that shiny new premises may be necessary to meet ever higher student expectations and demand, but this and a relaunch do not ne-cessarily entail headway (c.f. Starkey & Thomas, 2019). Ultimately, some of the most prestigious institutions have been able to leverage their brand identity into securing top status for newly established schools (e.g., Cambridge and Imperial). Many newer rising institutions placed the business school at the heart of their brand and central to their progress (e.g., Maastricht, City University of Hong Kong). However, if the space at the top becomes more crowded, this perforce leaves less room for the squeezed middle and below. Again, although often ne-glected from analyzes of business schools, private for-profit providers made rapid

DOI: 10.4324/9781003095903-3

progress in many national contexts, albeit a progress that has not been without controversy (Pettigrew & Starkey, 2016). However, rarely did they achieve distinction, and, when they have made particularly strong headway toward closing the gap with established universities, this has been due to local market particularities, for example, in Malaysia, where there are strict indigenization policies in play, making it challenging for ethnic minorities to gain university places or jobs in the state institutions. However, even here, it has been private non-for-profits such as INTI, who have made the most progress.

The second element was a focus on much greater internationalization. Internationalization has many elements: outgoing and incoming student mobility; international recruitment; international faculty; offshore programs (by fly in, satellite campus or local partner models); and international collaborative research and knowledge transfer (Hawawini, 2016; Rundshagen, Albers, & Raueiser, 2018). However, in practice, most institutions in the Anglo-Saxon world (but less so elsewhere) battled to entice their students to venture abroad for more than the briefest of study trips; perhaps, this could be taken as a broader reflection of the hubris that surrounded the liberal market model through much of the 1990s and 2000s, and a sense that little could be learned from other contexts, other than the United States.

The third was a much greater focus on research, in order to make progress in rankings, to do well in external evaluation processes such as the UK's Research Excellence Framework, and to meet the requirements of accrediting bodies (e.g., Association to Advance Collegiate Schools of Business [AACSB], European Quality Improvement System [EQUIS]). This has led to a heated transfer market for talented business school academics, and a shortage of skills within specific locations (Hunt, Eaton, & Reinstein, 2009). Invariably, the latter has led to the proliferation of predatory journals, with less than good institutions and scholars conspiring to convince each other that worthwhile research is taking place, that has at least withstood the rigor of peer review (Ferris & Winker, 2017). The transfer market has become truly global, with the most sought-after scholars readily changing institutions and countries (Smith & Urquhart, 2018). On the one hand, while making for greater inequality, the extent to which such individuals are able to leverage up salaries would help mitigate the real decline in academic pay that has taken place in many countries since the early 1970s. On the other hand, a climate of austerity may make it harder for institutions to sustain such pay levels in the future, particularly if post Coronavirus waves of redundancies make job competition harder.

Finally, management education has become a major export industry, again, a phenomenon most pronounced in the Anglo-Saxon world. Indeed, by some accounts, in the United Kingdom, management education has become that country's second largest earner of foreign exchange after money laundering (c.f. Benson, 2020). This does not mean that this development has necessarily been supported or welcomed by those national governments who have benefitted from such windfalls, as will be outlined below. Within institutions, many universities have been able to benefit from handsome revenues from management education, amounting to, in some instances, rates of return of up to eighty percent. Of course, observers might be skeptical of any industry in any area of the economy, and, indeed, of those parent organizations, who base their future prospects on such handsome past rates of return (c.f. Li, 2017). This is not meant to infer that management schools do not provide good value for money (many, if not most reputable schools, make a real difference to future career prospects of students). However, assuming that such rates of return are sustainable without significant reinvestment – and failing to plan for market volatility and increased competition – could be taken as negligence or hubris. Such approaches also stem from a very instrumental approach to learning: the assumption that nothing is of value that cannot be costed, the pursuit of knowledge for knowledge-sake is worthless, and that a focus on maximizing returns results in optimal outcomes for those involved.

The COVID-19 pandemic has greatly reduced international student mobility. Many business schools have compensated with this by allowing international students to study online in their country of origin. At the same time, this makes local universities who can offer at least some aspects of a campus experience more competitive. It is difficult to disentangle the effects of politics (and anti-foreign student rhetoric by politicians) with those of the pandemic. The effects of COVID-19 on international recruitment seems particularly pronounced in the United Kingdom and Australia, where a heavy reliance on overseas students coincided with increasing hostility to immigration. In turn, this has placed some UK and Australian business schools – and their parent institutions – in a parlous financial position. This has been partially compensated for by increased home undergraduate recruitment given a lack of alternatives to study both in terms of the labor market and the prospect of a gap year abroad. At the same time, this has intensified competition between business schools, with clear winners and losers; more prestigious institutions have been able to poach students from less prestigious ones through lowering entrance criteria.

Cyclical and Counter-Cyclical Demand for Management Education

A close evaluation of the experience of business schools suggests that demand has both cyclical and temporal dimensions. In the most general terms, there has been a steady increase in the global growth in the demand for management education. On a positive note, this would reflect the growing complexity and inter-connectedness of the global business ecosystem, and the need for skilled in-dividuals who are capable of navigating its many complexities. However, it might also reflect the rise of more individualistic societal attitudes engendered and nurtured through the hegemony of neo-liberal policies, associated with a greater instrumentalism in terms of key life decisions, and a declining interest in knowledge as something of worth in its own right. The latter possibility places a heavy responsibility on business schools, in combining within their education sought after skills and knowledge with the philosophical insights and wisdom that comes with a well-rounded education in a civilized community (c.f. Starkey & Thomas, 2019). In the following section, we explore changes in demand at Bachelors, MBA, MSc, DBA, and executive education levels.

As the entry point, the rise of bachelor degrees, fluctuations in national demographics notwithstanding, provides many business schools with a stable revenue source for at the minimum three years of a degree cycle. At the same time, it has imparted some challenges further up the system. Most notably, this may help explain the long-term challenges faced by the MBA industry: if more and more graduates have a basic foundation in management, they may have less interest in pursuing an accelerated training in management at a later stage. Again, this means that more and more faculty in business schools have gone through bachelor's programs in management. This means that they have the detailed subject knowledge that academics who have converted from a training in one or other of the foundation disciplines of the social sciences might lack. However, and by the same measure, they may lack the detailed knowledge of the core theories of the foundation fields; this might explain why so often many early and mid-career management scholars confuse theory with concepts (see Wood, Phan, & Wright, 2018).

The MBA industry, as noted, has faced many challenges in recent years. However, a few trends are visible that are likely to continue. Firstly, there has been a general flight to quality (Carton, McMillan, & Overall, 2018). If the value proposition of MBAs persists, it has increasingly been concentrated in a relatively few institutions, and countries (despite progress in many countries, top MBAs remain disproportionately US based). Secondly, coalition MBAs (such as the Trium MBA and the OneMBA) have made rapid progress up the league tables (Slade, 2016). Such programs bring many strengths, most notably the ability to access a wider range of recruitment markets, to expose students to a wider range of teaching styles and knowledge bases, and to undertake problem-orientated learning in different parts of the world. However, global epidemics, such as COVID-19 and the rise of ever more stringent visa regimes in some parts of the world, may undermine this model. There is also the issue of environmental sustainability, and whether carbon mile intensive education is the kind of thing that business schools should support or encourage (the same would be true for short student study trips and fly-in executive education courses). Thirdly, there has been a trend toward more hybrid forms of delivery, given the growing demand for an experience that provides the flexibility of online learning with some exposure to campus life. Finally, although the very top MBA charge quite high fees, sub-premium MBA fee levels have become very squeezed, and many institutions have been forced to discount via "bursaries" or "scholarships." Demand for MBAs tends to be pro-cyclical (as firms wishing to economize may easily cut costs by not sponsoring management to go on MBAs) but with a twist (the start of a downturn often coincides with MBA demand, funded by redundancy payouts and golden goodbyes). MBA enrollment has occurred in different tiers over the years with a gradual decline in overall enrolments and MBA demand dropping in the run up to the 2008 crisis (as organizations became over-extended), and then a redundancy payment-fueled upsurge, prior to a further decline. Again, it is clear that a few top players are capturing an ever-increasing part of the market, with schools ranked below 50 facing decline; although this observations is based on the US data, a similar pattern will be visible with other rankings.

The MSc can be divided into two segments: pre-work-experience management conversion training for those without prior management education; and specialist masters building on prior undergraduate education. However, apart from specialist degrees in areas such as finance that require advanced econometric skills that may be difficult to impart in a year, it could be argued that this dichotomy is something of a false one. Bachelor graduates vary greatly according to language skills (language tests notwithstanding) and indeed, with the broad scale and scope of subject knowledge: any master program necessarily has some conversion element to reconcile very different skills and capabilities. Both types of MSc tend to be anti-cyclical: they become more popular in a downturn. However, given the shrinking pool of "good" jobs in many national economies, most notably the United States and the United Kingdom, there may be structural pressures toward increasing demand in the future: if a proliferation of bachelor graduates makes it harder for employers to filter applicants, possession of a masters may help facilitate shortlisting, even if the actual job needs and skills are far lower.

Rather more fraught has been the executive education industry. This segment is highly pro-cyclical, as, again, discretionary management education is an easily trimmable cost for organizations. Indeed, past downturns in executive education saw an end of the independence of two well-regarded business schools in the United Kingdom, Henley, and Ashridge. However, there may be structural reasons as to why the UK executive education is not as lucrative as it once was: the longer-term downturn in this area coincides with the decline in prestige of the intellectual classes, and the extent to which the value of their inputs is regularly dismissed by media commentators and politicians as worthless (up until the coronavirus pandemic at least) (Percival, 2017). Indeed, in other countries where intellectuals remain in high esteem, such as within the coordinated markets of continental Europe, the demand for executive education remains much better.

Finally, there is doctoral education. The rise of business master degrees holders has been matched by a rise in business and management PhD programs. Many schools maintain PhD programs for prestige purposes and because they represent an important mechanism for attracting and retaining talented faculty. However, it is presently the case that doctoral program capacity greatly exceeds demand, and this has led to many business schools aggressively competing for talented students by means of scholarships and stipends. This does not mean that such programs succeed in this endeavor, and the most talented PhD students remain concentrated at a very small number of elite institutions. The reason for this is quite simple. Academic careers depend on an ability to get published, ideally in highly ranked journals: if faculty seemingly lack this talent, or appear to be not naturally skilled at publishing, then discerning potential PhD students may look elsewhere. Many business schools have battled to grasp this reality, and instead have attempted to ever more closely replicate the very top PhD programs; yet without this crucial element, they may battle to succeed in this purpose.

The DBA industry tends to be fairly bifurcated, with a few top programs and a very large second tier. Again, these programs can be broadly divided between those that place a strong emphasis on subject knowledge and reflective learning, and those that provide a more structured variant on the PhD that employed executives can avail of more easily. It is a basic feature of the human condition that many like the prospect of a doctoral title, and this will always provide a significant component of the demand for DBAs. However, by the same measure, many also lack the perseverance, and many DBA programs battle with throughput, leading to high dropout rates, or heavy staff commitment coupled with lowering standards.

Trends in Internationalization

Key issues and trends in internationalization include the ratios of incoming versus outgoing students, the increased availability of English language programs in non-English speaking countries, the politics of international student recruitment including rising right wing anti-immigrant populists in receiving countries and response by sending countries, and the changing emphasis on offshore campuses and degree programs. As noted above, the relative success of business schools as destinations for incoming and outgoing exchange students is very much a function of nationality (Hawawini, 2016). In particular, the Anglo-Saxon countries have been popular incoming destinations, but the United Kingdom has underperformed in outgoing student traffic, despite the challenges this has posed in meeting EQUIS internationalization standards (Alsharari, 2018). This is despite all the good work of the Erasmus program in making international learning experiences much more affordable. At the same time, increasingly challenging visa regimes and post-coronavirus travel restrictions may make international student exchanges more challenging in future, especially outside the EU zone of internal free movement.

Three other trends are visible in terms of international student mobility. The first is that the rise of English language courses has meant that continental European institutions have significantly increased international enrollments. Perhaps surprisingly, given the relative prestige and league table ranking and competitive fees, they only made limited headway in the UK market (especially, when the United Kingdom was a member of the European Union, making UK students eligible for free fees in some instances). Again, this might reflect parochial attitudes as to the worth of different national institutional orders. Given the increased popularity of the Netherlands as a destination of choice for overseas students, it is evident that such views are not universally shared.

The second is that the Anglo-Saxon nations have over the years recruited massively in China, India, and many other emerging markets (Alsharari, 2018; Hawawini, 2016). In many respects, this represents a great success story, representing the strong performance of national university systems, the desire of overseas students to learn more on Western management, and, indeed, in some instances, a desire for families to have a member with experience of living in the West. The latter would serve as a means of making better informed individual and family emigration decisions and, indeed, to facilitate an individual or family migration process. Even if international student fees are high, for families living in countries with political uncertainty, bolt holes may be priceless. On the one hand, this market has proven quite robust for many years, given the attractiveness of host countries' management education provisions and potential as future migration destinations. On the other hand, it has proved quite a volatile one, given that ever more stringent and capricious visa regimes have deterred many potential students. For example, Pakistan recruitment to English universities never really recovered after the introduction of stringent and humiliating medical checkup processes. Again, xenophobic outbursts – such as the anti-India violence in Australia in 2009, and the hostile atmosphere to migrants in post-Brexit Britain (Cumming, Wood, & Zahra, 2020) – may serve to deter future overseas recruitment.

The capturing of the political commanding heights by right wing populist governments in the United States, Australia, and Britain (Cumming et al., 2020) has not only further inflamed xenophobia, but also soured relations with China, a major sending destination. Indeed, following on a series of attacks by the Australian government in 2020, the Chinese government cautioned that many Chinese families would likely be reluctant to send family members to study in that country in the future (Doherty, 2020). The 2020 coronavirus pandemic has imparted a further layer of general uncertainty, with, at the time of writing, many countries' borders being closed to many or all foreign nationals. It is likely that the world will open on an uneven basis, creating challenges for universities and potential students alike. Finally, traditional sending countries that have invested heavily in their national university systems may take the opportunity presented by these circumstances to embark on a round of formal or informal academic protectionism, encouraging potential students to stay at home for their studies. In this instance, the Chinese government's caution to parents considering sending their offspring to study in Australia might be a harbinger of things to come (Zhang, 2020).

Thirdly, many universities, most notably, a number of British players, established offshore operations, typically in collaboration with local partners (Healey, 2016). Such operations have ranged from full-fledged university campuses, to modest office-based operations, or fly in concentrated teaching at rented premises, independently or with a local, typical for profit, partner. It is thus difficult to reach general conclusions as to their relative success and potential. However, three factors are worth considering. The first is that it could be argued that, at least in some instances, traditional university administrators have proven ineffective in bargaining with skilled negotiators from overseas private for-profit providers, leading to all too many one-sided deals that are hard to exit from for reasons of law or face. Or, to put it simply, not many universities have made much money or added to their prestige, through partnerships with private for profits aboard. The second is that regulatory environments may prove challenging; most notably overseas universities have often battled to repatriate monies accrued from ventures in China. The third is that it is often challenging to staff such degrees, leading to fly in faculty, either from the parent institution or itinerant moonlighting academics. This may indeed be nice work for those who can get it, but it may detract from their contribution to their home institution. Given these problems, after a proliferation of such programs in the early 2000s, many have closed, and institutions seem a lot more cautious in setting up new operations overseas.

Research, Publications, Journal Rankings, and the Business School

The relative shortage of business school academics capable of getting published in top journals has created a "global premium league" of highly paid and mobile academics. On the one hand, the uneven opening of the world following on the coronavirus pandemic, visa regimes and university financial issues may stem the flow of this market. Also, global warming has meant that many hitherto highly attractive destinations (e.g., Australia) may be much less so in the future. On the other hand, there remains a considerable gap between the demand and supply of highly productive business school academics, and universities have to contend with this reality if they wish to make progress in league tables, and sustain status and esteem (c.f. Jensen & Wang, 2018).

Increasingly, many business schools worldwide are prioritizing staff publications in international journals. This reflects a desire to move up league tables, demonstrate credibility, and provide teaching that transcends the applied and textbook model often followed by private for-profit colleges. This has led to great increases – and rejection rates – within top journals. At the same time, most schools and authors remain disappointed; this reflects a disjuncture between will and capacity, the inherent human instinct to discount bad news, and the real costs associated with building a research culture.

There has also been a proliferation of journal ranking lists, although only a few have received a degree of prominence. Such lists can roughly be divided into whether they are single school-based or not, and/or whether they seek only to identify a few top journals or grade many. School-based lists have the advantages in speaking to local institutional needs and priorities. However, with a few exceptions, such lists tend to combine sound choices with shameless self-dealing, as senior professors seek to bid up their own work. General lists tend to have a much wider base of consultation, diluting any self-dealing tendencies. However, in turn, they face challenges of mitigating inflationary pressures versus recognizing top journals in all areas. There also may discourage research in top but non-core business and management journals, for example, in the sciences (albeit that the Chartered ABS Guide does capture a wide range of social science journals). Again, constituents may have different views on rigor and relative exclusivity, especially if they battle themselves to reach the very top journals; some may hold that it is only an ability to reach journals of a basic quality standard that matters, and others that publications only in really top journals matter. Elite lists – focusing on selecting a few top journals – have the advantages of simplicity. At the same time, the FT List is based on surveys of AACSB- and EQUIS-accredited schools; the considerable variations in the relative research capabilities of the former may again make inclusion, at times, not removed from controversy. As there is only so much space in the very top journals (however defined), this means that such lists are largely irrelevant to most business schools and scholars. It is also worth noting that there are often quite big disparities between the research ambitions of many business schools and their actual capacity: bouts of wishful thinking, and the disruption that goes with it are often followed by renewed periods of bluffing that sub-optimal research is good after all.

There are two other effects of journal ranking lists. The first is that the best have leveled the playing field between different disciplinary areas. In the United Kingdom, there were historically some business schools dominated by psychologists, and others by sociologists and economists, who too often held each other's work with barely concealed contempt. In turn, this led to lop-sided hiring decisions, and great disparities between teaching needs and research capacity. As business schools battle to maintain and develop their research, ranking lists have enticed them to consider candidates from a wider range of backgrounds than might hitherto have not been the case. The second is that while journal ranking lists have contributed to challenge traditional patronage-based models (as publications in highly ranked journals represent objective currency on the job market), in some instances, they have contributed to an anti-intellectual instrumentalism, whereby the act of getting published in a prestigious journal becomes more important than the idea itself. In turn, this may lead to a proliferation of papers that are well researched and crafted but intellectually thin (Berger, 2002).

A major disrupter is that the traditional journal model is breaking down. Traditionally, publishers have made money out of journals for free or nearly free academic labor in writing, reviewing and editing journals, as well as levying handsome subscription charges from the institutions where said academics work. There have been two disrupters. The first is the "gold" (for publishers at least) open access movement, whereby publishers get paid an additional sum by individuals, institutions and/or block payments by national funding bodies in return for free access (Beall, 2013). Obviating journal subscription charges depend on all nations following suit, and it is worth reflecting that the gold open access movement has only made limited headway in North America. In any event, Elsevier and others have sought to hold the line around maintaining journal subscription charges at the same rate, even for institutions paying for open access (Barker & Nilsson, 2020). This may mean that the journal ecosystem fragments on regional lines (Beall, 2013).

The second is that publishers have traditionally adopted a cable TV model, whereby universities pay for block subscriptions of an entire stable of journals, even if most are of little interest; in turn, this makes for quite high de factor pricing for journals (Green, 2017). An unforeseen recent (March 2019) development was when Florida State University declined to renew their block subscription for Elsevier, instead funding faculty members' individual downloads of papers; in doing so, they reduced costs for Elsevier subscriptions from two million dollars to $20,000 for pay per view downloads by individual faculty (Barker & Nilsson, 2020). Should other universities join this mutiny, it is likely that undownloaded, and presumably unloved, journals may be jettisoned, reducing the amount of reputable (in terms of basic scholarly standards) journal space. Finally, the author pays model may further blur the boundaries between regular and predatory journals, and make it harder to robustly categorize the latter, making for further confusion among ill-informed scholars (Beall, 2013). All this may have implications for many areas of enquiry, but may be particularly pronounced for business schools, given the strong emphasis on peer-reviewed articles in a limited number of prestigious journals (as adverse to other outputs, such as books, or indeed, the production of artworks, etc.), because they are more likely to have the financial wherewithal to fund submission charges, and because of the fact that business schools typically monitor faculty research performance more closely in return for superior rates of pay.

Online Education

The ready availability of online learning platforms, and new technology enabling a greater degree of interactive content, led to many business schools venturing into the online market (Andrade, Miller, Kunz, & Ratliff, 2019). However, it soon became apparent that many or most students greatly prize a university-based learning experience and wish for some experience of belonging to a campus-based community, even if they are not in a position to attend face-to-face lectures on a regular basis. Again, if much of the content of a business school's online portfolio is provided by third-party providers, issues of value for money emerge. As an aligned point, the research and institutional culture, and the research-informed basis of teaching, may become less visible. Both seemed to suggest that quality online education would, in almost all cases, evolve to a hybrid face to face/online model. The coronavirus epidemic accelerated the move toward online technologies; at the time of writing, much of large class learning will for the foreseeable future remain online, with students gaining the face-to-face campus experience through taking optional courses/modules with smaller class sizes and/or small group seminars and tutorials. This may lead to a further bifurcation of learning, with senior research active scholars becoming even more removed from the classroom, and with temporary teachers doing the bulk of classroom-based activity.

However, this also leads to a much more serious problem. Part of the high profit rate of many business and management schools is due to relatively low contact hours, with students receiving additional value for money through building networks for life with their peers. Online learning makes it much easier for students – and parents – to compare what is provided between subjects, and, indeed, between institutions. Already this has led to pressures to up the contact hour game (whether by face to face or synchronous learning) and increases in workloads (Brammer & Clark, 2020). In turn, the latter may undermine the broad research base, even if a few, typically late middle-aged male scholars, are able to benefit from homeworking. Increasing contact time on a sustainable basis will necessarily necessitate more faculties, and, in turn, reduce the scope for quite such generous cross-subsidization of other fields.

Business Education, Elites, and Politics

An influential strand of thinking on elites highlights the extent to which the intellectual classes get marginalized in times of oligarchic excess (Priestland, 2013). Indeed, within the United States, Australia, and the United Kingdom, all countries where the populist right has attained the upper hand, along with countries such as Orban's Hungary, the intellectual classes have been subject to much vilification (Cumming et al., 2020). This has meant that requests for university bailouts in Australia, the United Kingdom, and the United States in the aftermath of the 2020 coronavirus epidemic have been received coldly by their governments. At the same time, generous corporate bailouts with no strings attached have enriched private equity and hedge funds in the United Kingdom and the United States (Farand, 2020). What assistance has been given to universities has been meager, with strings attached, and suggestions that some providers should fail (Morgan, 2020). While the great success of the universities in providing skills, employment, and as drivers of urban regeneration might suggest that a failure to provide state support in times of unexpected crisis might be considered negligence. Yet, at the very least, there is little doubt that many right-wing politicians would view the closure of universities with outright glee.

Particularly in the line of fire have been social scientists, who are seen as having dangerously progressive world views (Sayer, 2009); business schools are cast in this category, as distinct from the "useful" STEM subjects. Indeed, while management education providers frequently face calls to be more relevant, in the United Kingdom and Australia, politicians and commentators routinely dismiss out of hand that anything other than the STEM subjects can ever be relevant. Again, it is one of the broader contradictions of neo-liberalism that lip service to market supremacy is soon forgotten when other concerns come into play. Demand for management education is much greater than many STEM subjects, as students are well aware that the former provides better job prospects; however, the former is seen as much less worthy as it is both a social science, and typically associated with mass education. In addition to this, much of the hostility reflects the fact that the top business schools have developed a highly successful business model on a non-profit bases; the record of private for-profit providers has been much more patchy. As such, this provides a visible reminder of the limits of private for-profit actors within key spheres of social and economic life. Quite simply, non-for-profit business schools generally do much better than the for profits. Finally, from the point of view of the oligarchic elites, a thinning of the ranks of universities would reduce competition between their own offspring and other degree holders, as the former are much more likely to find their way into elite institutions (as numerous scandals involving philanthropic donations in the United States will evidence). Hostility to universities and their business schools at least in part reflects the extent to which they provide opportunities for upward mobility. As such, an antipathy to universities represents an effective admission that inherited wealth poorly coincides with talent, and, indeed, in the case of some obvious examples, even basic intelligence.

Conclusion

Within many national contexts, the business school sector represents a great success story. This has been marked by exponential growth in student numbers, in infrastructure and capacity, and research quality. At the same time, the sector has had to contend with many challenges, ranging from volatility in the global student market, to shortages of talent in key areas, to erratic government policies. Again, many universities have become heavily reliant on the revenue from business schools, but this has not always coincided with adequate reinvestment for sustaining them. The coronavirus epidemic has highlighted the limited financial reserves of many universities, and their over-reliance on continued growth, and poor contingency planning for unexpected downturns or shocks. However, while many universities seem capable of regularly generating seemingly terminal financial crises, they seem also extraordinarily adept at navigating them.

Clearly the business school ecosystem is facing serious challenges, assailed by both critics of conventional management (Parker, 2018), and those who deny the broader social good of universities per se. Yet, in the case of the former, a Manichean view of management and organizations denies that in specific times and places, there are broad islands of competence that leave stakeholders better rather than worse off, and, in most objective measures, a large number of business schools and management departments have been very successful. A common response to critics from the right has been to make desperate attempts to justify immediate impact on business activities. However, it is worth re-flecting that this is not what business schools and universities were set up to do. The best business schools and management departments are about providing education in business and management, informed by research of the same; in turn, the latter may enrich wider debates and broader understanding of the world today. It could be argued that there is a need for a greater confidence in the many successes attained in these areas, rather than diluting the message of them through attempting to demonstrate something which business schools were generally not set up to do.

This chapter has sought to explore the many challenges facing business schools, strategies for coping, and likely future challenges. Most business schools claim in their missions to be getting better, and the word excellence litters business school promotional materials. Yet, many have indeed raised their games, resulting in more and better research, enhanced recruitment and a "can do" approach to problems that has helped facilitate a relatively smooth move to online learning. At the same time, there are a number of challenges. Firstly, different types of program (Bachelors, MBA, MSc, executive educa-tion) do better at different times; this may help offset risk, but as each is associated with different fee models and rates of return, a downturn in one may have much more serious consequences than a downturn in others. Secondly, although many business schools have made significant progress in developing their research, the entire journal ecosystem is changing, and how business schools respond will have far reaching implications for research budgets. Thirdly, the previous model of internationalization is increasingly under question, given political barriers to student mobility, the effects of the COVID-19 pandemic, and in the case of shorter-term study abroad and fly in program provision, the disproportionate environmental costs. Business schools have been remarkably adept at dealing with a wide range of challenges historically, most notably in the dramatic upscaling of teaching and research, and in weathering downturns in the world economy; at the same time, they face a host of new challenges given structural and far-reaching changes in the global ecosystem.

References

Alsharari, N. M. 2018. Internationalization of the higher education system: An interpretive analysis. *International Journal of Educational Management*. https://www.emerald.com/insight/content/doi/10.1108/IJEM-04-2017-0082/full/html

Andrade, M. S., Miller, R. M., Kunz, M. B., & Ratliff, J. M. 2019. Online learning in schools of business: The impact of strategy on course enrollments. *Journal of Higher Education Theory and Practice*, 19(5). 10.33423/jhetp.v19i5.2280

Barker, A., & Nilsson P., 2020. Mutinous librarians help drive change at Elsevier. *Financial Times*, February 11, 2020. https://www.ft.com/content/c846c756-49ac-11ea-aee2-9ddbdc86190d

Beall, J. 2013. Predatory publishing is just one of the consequences of gold open access. *Learned Publishing*, 26(2): 79–84.

Benson, K. 2020. *Lawyers and the proceeds of crime: The facilitation of money laundering and its control*. Abingdon: Routledge.

Berger, P. L. 2002. Whatever happened to sociology? (Opinion). *First Things: A Monthly Journal of Religion and Public Life*, 10: 27–30.

Brammer, S., & Clark, T. 2020. COVID-19 and management education: Reflections on challenges, opportunities, and potential futures. *British Journal of Management*, 31(3): 453–456.

Carton, G., McMillan, C., & Overall, J. 2018. Strategic capacities in US universities – the role of business schools as institutional builders. *Problems and Perspectives in Management*, 16(1): 186–198.

Cumming, D. J., Wood, G., & Zahra, S. A. 2020. Human resource management practices in the context of rising right-wing populism. *Human Resource Management Journal*. https://onlinelibrary.wiley.com/doi/abs/10.1111/1748-8583.12269

Doherty, B. 2020. China and Australia: How a war of words over coronavirus turned to threats of a trade war. *Guardian*, May 2, 2020. https://www.theguardian.com/australia-news/2020/may/03/china-and-australia-how-a-war-of-words-over-coronavirus-turned-to-threats-of-a-trade-war

Farand, C. 2020. Coronavirus: Which governments are bailing out the big polluters? *Climate Home News*. https://www.climatechangenews.com/2020/04/20/coronavirus-governments-bail-airlines-oil-gas/

Ferris, L. E., & Winker, M. A. 2017. Ethical issues in publishing in predatory journals. *Biochemia Medica: Biochemia Medica*, 27(2): 279–284.

Green, T. 2017. We've failed: Pirate black open access is trumping green and gold and we must change our approach. *Learned Publishing*, 30(4): 325–329.

Hawawini, G. 2016. *The internationalization of higher education and business schools: A critical review*. Cham: Springer.

Healey, N. M. 2016. The challenges of leading an international branch campus: The "lived experience" of in-country senior managers. *Journal of Studies in International Education*, 20(1): 61–78.

Hunt, S. C., Eaton, T. V., & Reinstein, A. 2009. Accounting faculty job search in a seller's market. *Issues in Accounting Education*, 24(2): 157–185.

Jensen, M., & Wang, P. 2018. Not in the same boat: How status inconsistency affects research performance in business schools. *Academy of Management Journal*, 61(3): 1021–1049.

Li, M. 2017. Profit, accumulation, and crisis: Long-term movement of the profit rate in China, Japan, and the United States. *The Chinese Economy*, 50(6): 381–404.

Morgan, J. 2020. Ministers announce UK sector support but no bailout. *Times Higher Education Supplement*, May 4, 2020. https://www.timeshighereducation.com/ministers-announce-uk-sector-support-measures-no-bailout

Parker, M. 2018. *Shut down the business school.* Chicago: University of Chicago Press Economics Books.

Percival, J. 2017. The historical and philosophical foundations of conservative educational policy. *FORUM: For Promoting 3–19 Comprehensive Education,* 59(2): 273–280.

Pettigrew, A., & Starkey, K. 2016. From the guest editors: The legitimacy and impact of business schools – key issues and a research agenda. *Academy of Management Learning and Education,* 15: 649–664.

Priestland, D. 2013. *Merchant, soldier, sage: A new history of power.* Harmondsworth: Penguin.

Rundshagen, V. M., Albers, S., & Raueiser, M. 2018. Business school internationalization narratives: An interplay of myth and realpolitik. *Academy of Management Proceedings,* 2018(1): 15012.

Sayer, A. 2009. Who's afraid of critical social science? *Current Sociology,* 57(6): 767–786.

Slade, C. 2016. Small, regional and global: Bath spa university. In L. Schultz and M. Vickzko (Eds.), *Assembling and governing the higher education institution*: 349–360. London: Palgrave Macmillan.

Smith, S. J., & Urquhart, V. 2018. Accounting and finance in UK universities: Academic labour, shortages and strategies. *The British Accounting Review,* 50(6): 588–601.

Starkey, K., & Thomas, H. 2019. The future of business schools: Shut them down or broaden our horizons? *Global Focus: The EFMD Business Magazine,* 13(2): 4–49.

Wood, G., Phan, P. H., & Wright, M. 2018. The problems with theory and new challenges in theorizing. *Academy of Management Perspectives,* 32(4): 405–411.

Zhang, M. 2020. Students in China heed their government's warning against studying in Australia. *The Conversation,* July 5. https://theconversation.com/students-in-china-heed-their-governments-warnings-against-studying-in-australia-141871

3

MANAGEMENT EDUCATION AND BUSINESS SCHOOL STRATEGIC POSITIONING: EXPLORING AND EXPLOITING HISTORY FOR COMPETITIVE ADVANTAGE

Paul Hibbert and William M. Foster

Introduction

There is a growing awareness that business schools face, and will continue to face, challenges that will impact how management education is delivered. Although the demand for business education is high, so too is the competition among business schools for limited resources. We encourage institutions centrally involved in management education to specifically focus on exploiting their histories during difficult times by develop new narratives that provide alternative options for an uncertain future. In so doing, this will also make new resources available for business schools to engage in speculative exploration of new opportunities.

We define business school education as the formal, institutionally recognized degree programs (e.g., undergraduate business, MBAs, specialist masters, PhDs, and DBAs) that are offered by a business schools or another similar institution (i.e., liberal art school, school of education). This definition is intended to capture the breadth of demand for business education and to demonstrate the wide appeal that has led business schools to be seen as the "cash cows" of their universities. As such, there is continued pressure on these schools and their administrative teams to find new ways to capture and secure key resources, while managing finances to continue to provide a net positive contribution to the host institution. This means that business schools are continually looking for ways to innovate and provide new offerings such that they can retain the students they have and to entice the students who have shown an interest. The typical approach is to tout the virtues of the school by, for example lauding its facilities such as new, and often named, business schools buildings, promoting its world-recognized professors and instructors and emphasizing its learning opportunities in the form of different types such as experiential and blended approaches. In all, these typical

DOI: 10.4324/9781003095903-4

paths toward resource acquisition have been heavily reliant upon the *tangible* resources that these organizations control and can leverage.

Nevertheless, this approach to differentiation is fraught with problems because there are only a limited number of possible ways that business schools can demonstrate their uniqueness and value. That is, when looked at closely there is little that truly distinguishes the tangible assets of business schools from each other. Course offerings vary little, professorial credentials are similar and the new facilities all tend to conform to similar guidelines and architectural standards. From a strategic perspective the question can be asked: *how can business schools demonstrate that they are significantly different from others?* Toward that end, we propose that business schools embrace and leverage the *intangible* assets that they have at their disposal.

Currently, business schools compete with each other through branding. In other words, they brand themselves and communicate this brand image to key stakeholder such as alumni, student, recruiters, donors, employers and staff. But, once again, these messages are relatively homogenous and tout similar experiences and opportunities. In contrast, we argue that business schools develop their strategic advantage by looking backward to move forward in their strategic thinking. That is, we humbly suggest that business schools can more successfully differentiate, and thus enhance their strategic opportunities, by exploring the unique, intangible resources located in history and tradition.

To be more precise we advocate for a dynamic capabilities approach (Teece, Pisano, & Shuen, 1997) to the strategic understanding of history and tradition in business schools. The appropriation and re-interpretation of history and tradition is a unique skill that allows business schools to develop both externally and internally oriented narratives (Foster, Coraiola, Suddaby, Kroezen, & Chandler, 2017). In so doing, business schools can strategically provide focal possibilities for enhancing, and possibly delimiting, the credible potential for appropriation and re-interpretation of history and tradition.

We make two contributions with our discussion of the uses of the past and a dynamic capabilities approach to history and tradition as applied to business schools. First, we demonstrate how the past, and the strategic use of history and tradition, can help business schools and faculties create strong positions within the crowded, global competitive market for resources. Second, we outline different strategic historical narratives that address the interests of key stakeholders and the strategic needs of the organization. Both contributions highlight *how a dynamic capabilities approach to the use of history and tradition can be the source of a strong and distinct competitive advantage* for business schools.

In this chapter, we outline our argument by first discussing the constraints on business schools as they seek to adapt in the face of challenges and go on to consider how dynamic capabilities can support their development. Next, we discuss the uses of the past literature and explore how this approach can enhance the strategic opportunities of business schools as they explore the different ways to innovate to secure and expand their resources. We then present a typology of four different patterns of appropriation of strategic historical narratives that help explain how schools of business can exploit and leverage their past to address the concerns of key internal and external stakeholders. We illustrate this typology with examples of business schools that show how these patterns of appropriation are already evolving. Lastly, we discuss the implications of our approach and speculate on how a focus on history and tradition can help enhance the strategic value of the business school.

Current Constraints on Business Schools

Business schools are uniquely complex organizations for a number of reasons. First, they usually operate within significantly larger and usually much older host institutions. However, the relationship is complex, since many of their hosts are dependent on these younger, more profitable schools for financial stability. Business schools generally make a positive contribution to university or college finances, subsidizing both older disciplines and cutting-edge science.

Second, in addition to financial expectations, business schools have significantly more demands from internal and external constituents than most other faculties or schools. Schools of business may also need to satisfy stakeholders from business, accreditation agencies and government while meeting the employability expectations of their students. This pattern of constraints has evolved to be a global structure, over relatively long periods of time (Abreu-Pederzini & Suárez-Barraza, 2020).

For example, the most ubiquitous of the accreditation agencies, The Association to Advance Collegiate Schools of Business (AACSB), has been in operation since 1916 and has grown from a US association to a global organization. Similarly, The European Foundation for Management Development's influence – through its Quality Improvement System (EQUIS) has grown to worldwide importance since the foundation was established in 1976. In addition, program specific accreditations also exist, most prominently that provided by The Association of MBAs (AMBA) since 1967. The influence of these important agencies, stretching back over many decades, has tended to establish core standards, expectations, and constraints about the training and qualifications of academic staff, the teaching processes, and content of curricula and the basis on which degree awards are made (Julian & Ofori-Dankwa, 2006, see also Hommell and Mijnhardt and Bryant et al., in this volume.)

Lastly, governmental influences and constraints on higher education – taking in all disciplines, not just Business and Management Studies – are too complex to summarize effectively in this chapter. What we note is: the increasing commonality of quality assessment schemes for research (and latterly teaching, as exemplified by the UK's Teaching Excellence Framework); in a related vein, the increasingly interventionist stances in relation to the provision of state funding to deliver higher education; and a shift to marketization and (with exceptions) an increased expectation of students to pay more of the costs of tuition directly, even in state-funded systems (Vos & Page, 2020). The latter shift has increased student expectations for good employment prospects at the end of their degree.

These long-term developments and shifts, along with the historical actions of key stakeholders, influential agencies, and the rise of science as the perceived pinnacle of knowledge (McLaren, 2019), have placed business schools in increasingly constrained circumstances in relation to the possibility of dynamic change and resource acquisition. Accreditation tends to drive mimetic isomorphism (DiMaggio & Powell, 1983) in that organizations tend to resemble each other in presentation and operation to gain legitimacy. The result is that research and teaching are constrained and staid. Narrow metric-oriented (and short-term) assessments of research quality and employability outcomes from teaching make radical innovation appear too risky. In other words, the current environment in which business schools operate is demanding, yet the strategic responses available to these schools are constrained by risk and the desire to not be too different from other, legitimate competitors (Deephouse, 1999).

Dynamic Capabilities Approach to Business Schools

However, within this constrained context the possibility of making innovative strategic decisions in business schools is still possible. One potential way to approach the strategic challenges facing business schools is through dynamic capabilities (Helfat & Peteraf, 2015; Teece et al., 1997; Vogel & Güttel, 2013). *Dynamic capabilities* describe an organization's latent abilities to renew, augment and adapt its core competence over time (Teece et al., 1997). This adaptability is achieved through balancing *exploration* to develop new knowledge which may *potentially* be useful in the future (Pandza & Thorpe, 2009; Volberda & Lewin, 2003) with the exploitation of acquired knowledge through integration in current operations (March, 1991). In this way, there is an apparent augmentation of business as usual that still meets with external constraints, while new possibilities are developed with an eye to future use, even if the appropriate circumstances are not yet clear. An "accidental example" of this is provided by Massive Open Online Courses (MOOCs) which were initially touted as likely to transform higher education in a rapid process of transformation (Kizilcec et al., 2020) but did not deliver on this promise. However, multiple explorations of online learning across the globe, triggered by the hype, proved to be of great utility in helping institutions adapt to the COVID-19 crisis (Lund Dean & Forray, 2020), even if they did not function as a sustainable strategy (see also Lefevre and Caporarello chapter in this volume).

An organization's ability to identify and leverage dynamic capabilities can lead to situations where change can be strategically managed and leveraged, as is evident in how business schools responded to the shift to online learning because of the COVID-19 pandemic. The result is that organizations, such as business schools, through the identification and exploitation of dynamic capabilities are better able to continue to acquire resources and expand their resource base in the face of unexpected and sudden changes to the organization and/or its environment.

Although dynamic capabilities have the potential to facilitate and enhance resource acquisition, the primary concern for these organizations is the development and use of the capabilities that are most useful for their focal purpose. There is research, however, that suggests that organizations can develop and leverage dynamic capabilities from other elements of the organization. For example, Harsch and Festing (2020) argue that dynamic talent management is an organizational dynamic capability. Similarly, Helfat and Peteraf (2015) introduce the idea of "managerial cognitive capability" and argue that this capability is the underlying component that activates the dynamic managerial capabilities of sensing, seizing, and reconfiguring. The recognition that dynamic capabilities are housed in different locations within organizations and within the different cognitive capacities of managers suggests that that dynamic capabilities are more than just organizational routines. That is, dynamic capabilities can be understood as the processes involved with evaluating and adjusting to change.

With this understanding of dynamic capabilities, organizations such as business schools are poised to further develop new foundations from which to build a long-term competitive advantage. As we argue below, one such capability is the ability to recognize and use an organization's history and tradition for strategic gain in the face of changing internal and external environments.

The Past, History, and Tradition: Interpretation and Strategic Use

It has been long recognized that the past and history are different. The past is an accumulation of all events that have previously occurred. In an organizational context, this includes, but is not limited to, all the decisions, actions, people, documents, and engagements that happened prior to the present. For example, when considering business schools, the past is comprised of former Deans and Associate Deans, their decisions about courses, who they hired and fired and the various actions that have led to the current state of the school.

History, while related to the past, is separate and distinct. It is the deliberate narrative construction of what occurred in the past. That is, the stories that we tell about the past, that are written down and recorded for posterity, are history.[1] The distinction between history and the past has implications for how these constructs are identified and understood. As Lowenthal (1985) notes, history is both more than and, at the same time, less than the past. History is less than the past because, when written, history is limited in its scope. And although broader than memory (Nora, 1989), it still does not encompass the same breadth of experiences as does the past nor can it capture all the events that occurred previously. Nevertheless, history is also more than the past because the function of history is not only to communicate about the past but to convince others as to the veracity and importance of events that have occurred because "unless history displays conviction, interest, and involvement, it will not be understood or attended to" (Lowenthal, 1985: 218).

This insight has had significant impact on the organizational history and strategic management literature. Early discussions of history in organizations equated history with the past. That is, history was thought of as an indelible aspect of the organization. The events of the past "locked-in" organizations into a specific path that was either strategically advantageous or limiting. An organization's history was a strength or a burden depending, for all intents and purposes, on a matter of chance.

The burden of history, however, was soon recognized to be a limiting view of the potential for managers to identify and construct histories that could strategically advantage the organization. In contrast, Suddaby, Foster, and Quinn-Trank (2010) forwarded the construct of rhetorical history, defined as "the strategic use of the past as a persuasive strategy to manage key stakeholders" (p. 157). For them, history is not something that happens to organizations; history is a strategic resource that can be identified, built, leveraged and exploited like any other intangible, symbolic resource. The implication is that history, because it is a narrative, can be written in a way that allows organizations to strategically achieve their goals.

The re-interpretation of history, however, does not mean that "anything goes" (Cummings & Bridgman, 2011). The scope of the stories that managers tell is wide but not unlimited. The same holds true for the veracity and accuracy of historical narratives. For example, some organizations have almost wholly fabricated histories that they leverage to sell their products or construct a public image. Hendrick's gin is one such organization (Vanderbilt, 2019). The company's invented history has proven to be quite helpful in selling the brand by fabricating a past that reinforces the supposed distinctiveness of the product. Of note, Hendrick has used this technique as a marketing tool to convey authenticity to a broad audience. The result is that despite its relative newness in the market for gin, the product is thought of as a long-standing brand with a distinct and unique past. Other organizations have not been as capable of managing their historical narratives. For example, many German companies (e.g., Bertelsmann, Mercedes Benz and Bayer) have all been publicly shamed for their connections to the Nazi government (Booth, Clark, Delahaye, Procter, & Rowlinson, 2007). In addition, contemporary organizations have also been held to account for fabricating the organization's past. One example is the retailer Hollister whose invented company history (Brown, MacLaren, Ponsonby-McCabe, Stevens, & Wijland, 2017) is so fiercely guarded that the company has enacted lawsuits to protect its supposed past. And, lastly, some companies have found historical narratives so compelling that they have purchased the history of other organizations. The lifestyle company Shinola purchased the name, and thus the past, from Shinola shoeshine, to invoke the heritage feel of the company to provide an air of authenticity to their products (Danziger, 2017). The above examples demonstrate that history is flexible and malleable, but it can also be a cruel taskmaster. In some instances, history can be used effectively to market the organization and present an image that reinforces a key aspect of brand and organizational identity. On the other hand, the stories told about the organization's past, if they are not seriously vetted and carefully controlled, can do significant damage to the image and the brand of these organizations.

It is with the aforementioned caveat in mind that we focus on the pliability of historical narratives and why historical narratives are used strategically. In one such discussion, Foster and colleagues (2017) argue that as strategic resources, historical narratives can be constructed with particular outcomes in mind. In particular, these authors indicate that managers can strategically develop historical narratives depending on the audiences that they wish to reach (internal or external stakeholders) and the form of identification they want to elicit from their stakeholders (similarity or difference). The argument Foster and colleagues forward is that when managers target particular outcomes such as legitimacy, authenticity, identity, and culture, they need to tailor their narratives to achieve these goals. This helps explain why some historical narratives are more effective and persuasive that others.

A similar argument can be made for organizational traditions and how they are invented and re-interpreted. Tradition is not simply a common-sense term; instead, following Hibbert and Huxham (2010), tradition is constituted in the relationship of symbolic *content,* interpretive *processes* that preserve (and change) this content, and the *authority* that develops over time, that partially constrains the rate or limits of (re)interpretation (Friedrich, 1972).

History, understood as the content of tradition, needs to be understood in a diachronic sense. That is, it does not simply include some preserved artifact, text or other symbolic resource, but rather it also includes the pattern of interpretations built up around the "foundational elements," that give it a richer potential scope of meaning (Brown, 1999; Shils, 1981). The longer the chain of interpretations of the/any tradition, and with it the patina that accumulates upon it/ them, the richer the resources and the accumulated wisdom of the/a tradition become (Pelikan, 1984).

The second element of tradition is the processual; it is through interpretation and reinterpretation that the resources of the tradition accumulate (Boyer, 1990; Thompson, 1990). Eventually it may be difficult to distinguish "primary content" from "interpretation" within a tradition, as the latter may obscure the tradition's origins, or assume a significance of its own (Dobel, 2001; Friedrich, 1972; Hobsbawm & Ranger, 1983). However, coherence with this chain of interpretations becomes a central aspect of the emergent authority of the tradition (Shils, 1981), and the past is perceived to support only a certain range of futures.

The question that arises is: why is the constraint of tradition's authority accepted at all? Giddens (1984, 1994) saw the role of tradition being undermined by the progress of modernity, but others have pointed toward its continued endurance and relevance in situations that are not initially perceived as "traditional" (Dobel, 2001; Shils, 1981) because it has a role in providing continuity of meaning (Boyer, 1990; West Turner, 1997). For managers to approach history and tradition as resources they need to recognize the distinction, highlighted earlier, between the past and history. This creates difficulty for some managers because they remain stubbornly connected to the idea that history is fact and this impacts their perception of how they see not just the past, but also the future (Suddaby & Foster, 2017). Moreover, managerial perceptions of the past will significantly impact not just how history is constructed and understood, but also how change and strategic decisions can and will be made. This recognition can be extended to include how managerial cognitive capabilities impact the development and use of dynamic capabilities when managing change. For example, for long-established organizations and even in the context of unexpected and disruptive events, dynamism can be built on tradition through appropriating and re-interpreting historic knowledge (Cummings & Bridgman, 2011; De Massis, Frattini, Kotlar, Messeni Petruzzelli, & Wright, 2016). Further, Suddaby, Coraiola, Harvey, and Foster (2020) describe how managing history can be an integral component of developing dynamic capabilities. Their specific argument is that managerial perceptions of the past impact the different capacity of managers to control the interpretation of history and tradition, in the present for the future. This critical and crucial skill is essential for organizations to successfully navigate the changes that occur because of disruptive technologies. The significance of Suddaby and colleagues' (2020) argument is that there are specific micro-foundational approaches that are enhanced, depending on the organization's temporal orientation. When these insights are combined with previous discussions of how history can be used to achieve different organizational outcomes, it becomes more evident that the ability to leverage history and tradition to develop a competitive advantage depends significantly on the temporal orientation of management and the historical narratives that they construct.

Thus, our concern is to pay particular attention to business schools and to take a contextual focus on the question of "...how the past might provide organisations with a strategic advantage because of the way historical narratives are appropriated, mobilised and used, in the present [...that is...] how history is used as a strategic resource" (Foster et al., 2017: 1176).

The Appropriation of History and Tradition within Business Schools

The histories available for appropriation by business schools include internally focused and externally focused narratives. Internally focused narratives draw upon internal organizational characteristics to sustain, enhance and develop narratives that emphasize a strong culture and/or a unique identity (Foster et al., 2017). Internally focused historical narratives of this sort may focus on the nature and longevity of the host institution, the establishment of key methods or bodies of work, or growth in scope, scale, or influence. Externally focused historical narratives are built upon long-established indicators of authenticity and legitimacy that have developed over decades. For example, external sources of regulation, formal accreditation, and (positions in) specialist rankings; but, as we have alluded to earlier, these can often limit distinctiveness (especially in relation to curricula) and do not always favor dynamism.

Internally focused narratives may offer better support for distinctiveness, in a number of ways. Doing so requires that these narratives mobilize what has already been developed over time, and three examples help to illustrate this. First, business schools may draw on the history of their host institution as a source of distinctiveness. Thus, Said Business School, at the University of Oxford, markets its principal qualification as the "Oxford MBA." Other histories highlight how particular pedagogic approaches have become synonymous with certain schools, most notably in relation to the Harvard Case Method. A third alternative is to weave implications of scale, scope and influence into the history of a School and/or its principal degree; thus, many schools offer a "Global MBA" – and there is hardly an MBA to be found that does not mention the word "global" or "international" as part of their story. Of these examples, historical narratives that convincingly mobilize the heritage value of the School's host institution, or develop a story of growth and global significance through scale and reach offer possibilities for crafting a strategic position, albeit an increasingly generic one.

The challenge is the potential to become myopic when developing and deploying internally focused historical narratives because they do not offer clear possibilities for resourcing dynamic change. A more prudent approach is one that allows for the development of historical narratives that exploit opportunities for both the development of distinctiveness *and* dynamic change. To do so, business schools have to look beyond their borders to external sources of legitimacy and authenticity. For example, innovative faculty members at the University of Queensland Business School (UQBS) have been engaged in the development of experiential education for many years. UQBS is able to point to specific historical incidents to build on this approach, such as a faculty member assigning her students to practical support projects in the School's home city, Brisbane, after devastating floods (Wright, Nichols, McKechnie, & McCarthy, 2013; Wright, Hibbert, Strong, & Edwards, 2018). When the School's MBA program was revised in 2013 it was positioned, externally, as "The MBA for Experiences," when every other Australian MBA was trading on narratives that wove together external legitimacy (multiple accreditations and/or stories underlining the identity of their host institution, UQBS chose to emphasize their culture and the legitimacy of their approach. In so doing, the distinctive pedagogic culture at UQBS supported a different, externally legitimated historical narrative that informed the School's MBA program which helped it become the highest ranked MBA in Australia at that time. In other words, it was the combination of the different historical narratives that, in tandem, allows business schools to move beyond the exploration of their past toward the exploitation of their history. Bringing these possibilities together leads to four possible outcomes, as indicated in Figure 3.1.

We take the view that in difficult times (and writing in mid-2020 at the height of the COVID-19 crisis, we have seen none more challenging) organizations have to look to their areas of knowledge developed through past exploration and see how they may be shifted into exploitation to gain traction on a new way ahead. Business schools will therefore seek to prioritize the internal narrative focus on identity or culture that is most open to exploitation, provided it fits within an overall sense of the externally focused narratives they craft based on their history and standing (Foster et al., 2017; Petriglieri & Petriglieri, 2010). In times of constrained resources and heightened competition, moves to develop significantly expanded scope and scale would seem to be very risky. However, focusing on narratives that emphasize robust high standing or prioritizing pedagogic narratives to develop distinctiveness are both possibilities. At the same time, business schools will need to pay attention to the constraints of external narratives, such as accreditation and stakeholder interpretations of the history of the

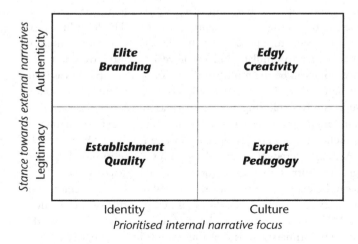

FIGURE 3.1   The appropriation and exploitation of internal and external narratives

school and the field (Abreu-Pederzini & Suárez-Barraza, 2020; Julian & Ofori-Dankwa, 2006). Schools will either seek to weave these external narratives tightly into their history to underpin the legitimacy of their future positioning, or strive to be (somewhat more) independent of them by expressing their authenticity, and representing the external narratives as ladders climbed long ago that are now of less importance.

Strategic Positions to Explore and Exploit History in Business Schools

The mobilization of historical narratives to support new futures for business schools can be illustrated through examples where these patterns of appropriation and exploitation are already evolving, since practically every business school makes some explicit or implicit allusion to key events and achievements from their (more or less recent) past. These examples of historical narratives authored in the present (at the time of writing), may help schools of the future to consider how to strategically reinterpret their tradition and historical narratives to emphasize new possibilities. However, different schools will be able to leverage past exploratory knowledge creation, deliberately associated with historic events and traditions, to support some strategic positions with more success than others. We discuss each of the four strategies in turn.

Elite Branding

Business schools whose historic narratives support *an elite branding* position are likely to remain few. Such schools have developed, over time, a strong "identity angle" to their history; it may include links to pedagogy but while this may have become closely associated with the tradition of the school (e.g., Harvard Case Method), others may also be using similar approaches now. The long history of development and use of a signature pedagogy is usually the distinctive element in such cases, which is harder to emulate and mobilize in a distinctive narrative. However, longevity alone can be the foundation for distinctive narratives as is the case with, for example, Wharton (1881) and Copenhagen Business School (1917). Schools successfully exploiting their history as an identity narrative, to support an elite branding position, have enough connection to external narratives to support their authenticity, but do not "lean" on these resources. For example, Harvard only has AACSB accreditation and does not even mention it anywhere on the MBA page, in contrast to the 90 (or so) schools that trumpet "triple accreditation." As can be expected, this is a strategy few schools can deploy. The use of these historical narratives requires a distinguished past that is unchallenged and unquestioned. Thus, there is some risk for business schools that choose this positioning strategy. The primary risk is that the school doesn't possess the material resources to support their historical narrative. Although this might not be discovered, if the reputation of the business school is deemed to be fraudulent or fabricated, the authenticity of the school is tarnished. The moment the veneer of authenticity erodes, so too does the effectiveness of the strategy. This is why this strategy is so rarely seen or implemented. Nevertheless, the risk involved with implementing this strategy is also why it produces significant benefits and long-term advantages to these schools.

Establishment Quality

Schools that strategically mobilize historical narratives toward identity, but also connect to the legitimacy offered by external narratives, have crafted stories of *establishment quality*. Their histories can include some distinctiveness as individual institutions, but the strategic strength of these organizations is the association they have through membership in select institutional groups (e.g., the UK's Russell Group, Australia's Group of Eight, World University Rankings) that confer status, and multiple accreditations and rankings achievements of recent years. Sometimes these are the bulk of the story and there is little about the educational tradition of the school. For example, The UK's Leeds MBA web-page[2] features three accreditations and four rankings achievements. Yet, the only mention of their educational offerings is "a top-quality learning and development experience." This affectation is as close to *establishment quality* so as to make no difference. Similar narratives are offered by other Russell Group and Group of Eight business schools; their mobilized histories connect identity with rankings and accreditation achievements that have come to signal legitimacy (accreditation has come to be, for most MBA students, a baseline expectation). The *establishment quality* strategy does not present the same risk as does the *elite branding* strategy. The legitimacy conferred by the historical narratives that are appropriated by association are highly effective strategic markers of success. However, this strategic approach offers business schools less leeway to develop unique historical narratives that may provide significant points of differentiation amongst their competitors. Moreover, sharing historical narratives is not risk free. The legitimacy of the group can also be damaged by the actions of other members of the group which, again, limits strategic decision-making.

Expert Pedagogy

Those schools who can underpin confidence in new teaching modes with a narrative of *expert pedagogy*, linked to exploratory education research over many years, may stand out. This can be seen in the schools that have already moved pedagogic expertise from historical exploration into exploitation. The University of Queensland Business School, discussed earlier, has been badly affected by the COVID-19 pandemic and a switch to online education, but in earlier years had provided an example of mobilizing the story of pedagogic expertise embedded in the culture of the school, while still retaining all the external legitimacy signals (rankings, accreditation achievements) in its overall narrative. Similarly, Babson College has developed a distinctive position in relation to entrepreneurship education. In addition, there may be unexploited historic developments in expertise and innovative pedagogy that can be mobilized in other business school narratives, although these might be hard to find behind the marks of external legitimacy and research rhetoric. A strategic approach based on innovative pedagogy could be layered on the external signals of legitimacy used by business schools. Distinctiveness is developed by weaving an innovative teaching initiative approach developed over time into historical narratives. Although these programs can be imitated, mimesis does not guarantee strategic success for other schools because of the distinct historical roots of the program located in the school's culture.

Edgy Creativity

The future also presents opportunities for those business schools that have developed a historical narrative about a distinctive culture for some time, while weaving external narratives into their story without undermining their uniqueness. Such schools have mobilized narrative elements that shape an authentic, *edgy creativity* position. This may be as effective in supporting a standout position as elite branding. A good example of a school that has already developed this story is Karlshochschule ("Karls"), and in particular its management master's program.[3] Karls is a German *Fachhochschule*, a small technical university (less than 1000 students), in this case specializing in management. While it is usually amongst the highest rated *Fachhochschulen,* it is important to note that this class of technical university, closely associated with industry and associated with vocational outcomes, has historically been regarded as a second tier in Germany. Their narrative focuses on their creative, humanist-oriented pedagogy and under the surface also weaves in interdisciplinary approaches, faculty with industry experience (a requirement for all *Fachhochschulen*) and often atypical (in comparison with conventional business school faculty) research interests. The overall impression of their narrative position is of a school with a consistently different and irreverent approach. Some quotations from their Master's program website give an idea of this difference:

> What good would all your management tools be if you were a tool at managing?

> ...you will creatively build bridges between research and practice. To do so, you and your peers will moisturize the apparently dry ink on paper in various projects. Look! Oh, what beautiful new images the blurring lines create!

Karlshochschule is also an example of how a tradition of *edgy creativity* can be developed relatively quickly (the institution has only existed since 2004) based on a clear commitment to a unique teaching and learning culture – that still gathers external recognition. However, not all experiments of this kind are enduring. For example, Leicester University was once positioned as the home of Critical Management Studies, but the university decided to eliminate that field of scholarship (making staff redundant in the process, on the basis of their research focus) and its business school now presents a generic historic narrative signaling establishment respectability through longevity, global positioning and accreditation.

Conclusions and Implications for Business School Strategic Positioning

Our chapter has outlined a distinct strategic approach to business schools and how they are positioned in the field. The goal of our discussion has been to explain that current business school strategies that emphasize marketing and branding are limited. Because these approaches are focused on exploitation, there is little in these current communications that truly distinguishes them from each other. The result is that business schools, despite their claims to the contrary, are usually quite homogenous. This causes problems for business schools because of the increased competition for resources. Students are become ever more discerning in their educational choices with reputation and accreditation serving as proxies for quality. Similarly, as executive education becomes ever more lucrative, business schools are looking for ways to demonstrate that their programs are significantly different than the competition.

In response, our argument is focused on how to best articulate the distinctive aspects of business schools such that imitation can be limited. The construction of an historical narrative is one way to do this; it has proven to be useful for organizations in other industries and it has the same value for business schools. The typology of positioning strategies demonstrates how business schools can move beyond regurgitating the same marketing ideas as their rivals and can move toward exploiting their valuable and inimitable resources. Our four positioning strategies (Elite Branding, Establishment Quality, Expert Pedagogy, and Edgy Creativity) offer different approaches to developing and mobilizing historical narratives that can help business schools evaluate and change their current position within the industry. Of note, not all positioning strategies are open to all business schools. As we discussed previously, Elite Branding is risky for those schools that lack the long-storied tradition of Harvard Business School or Wharton. Nevertheless, most of the strategies we present are available to most business schools. The challenge is finding the internally focused and externally focused historical narratives that support and reinforce the goals of the business school, and to plant the seeds for the development of new narratives.

The four strategic positions described above are "ideal types" explaining how business schools may exploit internal and external narrative elements. Nevertheless, there is always the possibility for the creation of hybrid historical narratives and movement between the strategies. For example, an institution known for edgy creativity might eventually be able to tell a story of elite branding or establishment quality, as with Leicester; as the culture keeps developing and if external recognition markers can be consistently added, this mix inevitably supports an identity narrative too. The patina of the tradition (Shils, 1981) grows and adds a meaning of its own. This does not indicate that there are defined development trajectories for business schools. Instead, what this suggests is that business schools can build upon previous historical narratives to create new and different stories. This can apply whether or not the history articulated bears scrutiny in relation to a "factual" and distant past (Nora, 1989), given that all tradition is more-or-less invented (Hobsbawm & Ranger, 1983) through creative interpretation and re-interpretation.

To some extent all of the examples we have cited – like every historical narrative – were constructed with certain stakeholders in mind. However, the use of history is also generally implicit and is not necessarily a sign of deliberate exploitation. Mimetic bricolage is also evident. Nevertheless, we argue that schools whose traditions (e.g., of expert or creative pedagogy) are active, or can be reimagined, will have opportunities to develop a more explicit historical narrative into which their (desired?) stakeholders are clearly written.

There are good reasons to think that business schools may want to take a more deliberate and distinctive approach, when they can. Turbulent times create possibilities for change; at the time of writing, we saw the potential and motive for more business schools to exploit internal cultural narratives around teaching (that hitherto played second fiddle to research stories), and so craft expert or edgy narratives that they can then inhabit. However, turbulence also creates a desire for safety, in which traditionalism can be a place to hide (Hibbert & Huxham, 2010; Pelikan, 1984); this is a strong impetus for main-stream "*establishment quality*" institutions to articulate an unchanging historical narrative. Nevertheless, we take the view that histories need to be rewritten and articulated afresh to engage with stakeholders over time, within certain bounds (Cummings & Bridgman, 2011; Suddaby et al., 2010).

In addition, all institutions will need to consider how their traditions can be reinterpreted and articulated through times of dramatic change, if they are to remain salient and persuasive to those they are seeking to reach. For example, both elite branding and establishment quality narratives may also weave the locale into the story; for example, Harvard lauds its "vibrant residential campus"[4] and Leeds states that it draws "…on the strengths of this vibrant city…." We speculate that, following a period in which the physical and artifactual elements of in-stitutions' historic identity are inaccessible due to COVID-19 crisis conditions, *establishment quality* and *elite branding* status narratives will persist, but will be challenged by, or integrated with, other possible histories which incorporate cultural distinctives, especially exploratory knowledge developments that can be used to offer a new interpretation of the educational experience.

A current example of this is offered by Harvard; it certainly highlights the importance of the Case Method in its history[5]... but also makes it clear that it is still investing in pedagogy and that there is expertise to support delivery in multiple ways. Their website mentions *"...case method courses, FIELD projects, tech simulations, introspective exercises, and more...."* While it is unlikely that Harvard will *radically* reinterpret its history, in dynamic capability terms the mobilization of historical elements to do so are already being explored. If in the future continued shifts in the learning environment make the traditional case method feel simply like the past (rather than cherished history), the school would have other approaches to move to exploitation in its stead, while sheltered by its elite status.

Similarly, we do not think that online and technology-led learning in and of itself will offer distinctiveness, despite – at the time of writing – an intense global focus on this mode of teaching. Technology will not make a strategic difference in the business school of the future; it will simply be another baseline expectation for students. Instead, we think that the current shock to the system provides an opportunity for business schools that have *always* strongly cared about teaching to exploit this in their histories, and reinterpret their traditional teaching-oriented research and scholarship to give it a more central place in their narrative (see also Leferve and Caporapello and Fukami et al., chapters in this volume).

Lastly, for faculty, a period of turbulence in which teaching and learning are now more clearly recognized as mission-critical presents challenges and opportunities. A career is also a historical narrative and faculty will need to think how they anchor and develop their narratives through this turbulence. We believe that research and scholarship will continue to be the most highlighted features of most individual narratives, but the Scholarship of Discovery *focused on education theory* and the Scholarship of Teaching and Learning (Boyer, 2016) could now be more important elements in all of our narratives, if we wish them to be. We think that is no bad thing.

Notes

1 There is also a difference between history and memory. History is primarily considered narratives about the past that are recorded and stored. Memory is also a narrative about the past; however, the distinction is that memory tends to be more locally based and is rarely written or recorded.
2 This is available at https://business.leeds.ac.uk/leeds-mba
3 Details of the program are available at https://karlshochschule.de/en/master/masters-program/management-ma/
4 Details and context are available at https://www.hbs.edu/mba/Pages/default.aspx
5 Although you have to scroll a long way down their MBA webpage before you find the first mention of it, as detailed at https://www.hbs.edu/mba/Pages/default.aspx

References

Abreu-Pederzini, G., & Suárez-Barraza, M. 2020. Just let us be: Domination, the post-colonial condition, and the global field of business schools. *Academy of Management Learning & Education*, 19(1): 40–58.

Booth, C., Clark, P., Delahaye, A., Procter, S., & Rowlinson, M. 2007. Accounting for the dark side of corporate history: Organizational culture perspectives and the Bertelsmann case. *Critical Perspectives on Accounting*, 18(6): 625–644.

Boyer, E. 2016. *Scholarship reconsidered: The priorities of the professoriate (expanded edition)*. San Francisco: Jossey Bass.

Boyer, P. 1990. *Tradition as truth and communication*. Cambridge: Cambridge University Press.

Brown, D. 1999. *Tradition and imagination*. Oxford: Oxford University Press.

Brown, S., MacLaren, P., Ponsonby-McCabe, S., Stevens, L., & Wijland, R. 2017. Is Sweaty Betty a hollister follower? Parsing the poetics of branding. *Advances in Consumer Research*, 45: 397–400.

Cummings, S., & Bridgman, T. 2011. The relevant past: Why the history of management should be critical for our future. *Academy of Management Learning & Education*, 10(1): 77–93.

Danziger, P. 2017. What makes a brand luxury and why Shinola earns the title. *Forbes online*, https://www.forbes.com/sites/pamdanziger/2017/05/07/what-makes-a-brand-luxury-why-shinola-earns-the-title/?sh=3f67ef5c6976

Deephouse, D. L. 1999. To be different, or to be the same? It's a question (and theory) of strategic balance. *Strategic Management Journal*, 20: 147–166.

De Massis, A., Kotlar, J., Frattini F., Messeni Petruzzelli, A., & Wright, M. 2016. Innovation through tradition: Lessons from innovative family businesses and directions for future research. *Academy of Management Perspectives*, 30(1): 93–116.

DiMaggio, P., & Powell, W. W. 1983. The iron cage revisited: Institutional isomorphism and collective rationality in organizational fields. *American Sociological Review*, 48: 147–160.

Dobel, J. 2001. Paradigms, traditions and keeping the faith. *Public Administration Review*, 61: 166–171.

Foster, W. M., Coraiola, D. M., Suddaby, R., Kroezen, J., & Chandler, D. 2017. The strategic use of historical narratives: A theoretical framework. *Business History*, 59(8): 1176–1200.

Friedrich, C. 1972. *Tradition and authority*. London: Pall Mall Press.

Giddens, A. 1984. *The constitution of society*. Cambridge: Polity.

Giddens, A. 1994. Living in a post-traditional society. In U. Beck, A. Giddens, & S. Lash (Eds.), *Reflexive modernization*: 56–109. Cambridge: Polity Press.

Harsch, K., & Festing, M. 2020. Dynamic talent management capabilities and organizational agility—A qualitative exploration. *Human Resource Management*, 59(1): 43–61.

Helfat, C. E., & Peteraf, M. A. 2015. Managerial cognitive capabilities and the microfoundations of dynamic capabilities. *Strategic Management Journal*, 36(6): 831–850.

Hibbert, P., & Huxham, C. 2010. The past in play: Tradition in the structures of collaboration. *Organization Studies*, 31(5): 525–554.

Hobsbawm, E. J., & Ranger, T. O. (1983). *The invention of tradition*. Cambridge: Cambridge University Press.

Illia, L., & Zamparini, A. 2016. Legitimate distinctiveness, historical bricolage, and the fortune of the commons. *Journal of Management Inquiry*, 25: 397–414.

Julian, S., & Ofori-Dankwa, J. 2006. Is accreditation good for the strategic decision making of traditional business schools? *Academy of Management Learning & Education*, 5(2): 225–233.

Kizilcec, R. F., Reich, J., Yeomans, M., Dann, C., Brunskill, E., Lopez, G., Turkay, S., Williams, J. J., & Tingley, D. 2020. Scaling up behavioral science interventions in online education. *Proceedings of the National Academy of Sciences*, 117(26): 14900–14905.

Lowenthal, D. 1985. *The past is a foreign country*. Cambridge: Cambridge University Press.

Lund Dean, K., & Forray, J. M. 2020. A silver linings playbook, COVID-19 edition. *Journal of Management Education*, 44(4): 399–405.

March, J. 1991. Exploration and exploitation in organizational learning. *Organization Science*, 2(1): 71–87.

McLaren, P. G. 2019. Stop blaming Gordon and Howell: Unpacking the complex history behind the research-based model of education. *Academy of Management Learning & Education*, 18: 43–58.

Nora, P. 1989. Between memory and history: Les lieux de mémoire. *Representations*, 26: 7–25.

Pandza, K., & Thorpe, R. 2009. Creative search and strategic sense-making: Missing dimensions in the concept of dynamic capabilities. *British Journal of Management*, 20(1): 118–131.

Pelikan, J. 1984. *The vindication of tradition*. New Haven: Yale University Press.

Petriglieri, G., & Petriglieri, J. 2010. Identity workspaces: The case of business schools. *Academy of Management Learning & Education*, 9(1): 44–60.

Shils, E. 1981. *Tradition*. Chicago: University of Chicago Press.

Suddaby, R., Coraiola, D., Harvey, C., & Foster, W. 2020. History and the microfoundations of dynamic capabilities. *Strategic Management Journal*, 41(3): 530–556.

Suddaby, R., & Foster, W. M. 2017. History and organizational change. *Journal of Management*, 43(1): 19–38.

Suddaby, R., Foster, W. M., & Quinn Trank, C. 2010. Rhetorical history as a source of competitive advantage. In A. C. B. Joel & J. Lampel (Eds.), *The globalization of strategy research (advances in strategic management)*, vol. 27: 147–173. Bingley: Emerald Group Publishing Limited.

Teece, D. J., Pisano, G., & Shuen, A. 1997. Dynamic capabilities and strategic management. *Strategic Management Journal*, 18: 509–533.

Thompson, J. B. 1990. *Ideology and modern culture: Critical social theory in the era of mass communication*. Cambridge: Polity Press.

Vanderbilt, T. 2019. Why a gin maker invented its own history. *1843 Magazine*, October/November. https://www.1843magazine.com/design/brand-illusions/why-a-gin-maker-invented-its-own-histor

Vogel, R., & Güttel, W. 2013. The dynamic capability view in strategic management: A bibliometric review. *International Journal of Management Reviews*, 15(4): 426–446.

Volberda, H., & Lewin, A. 2003. Co-evolutionary dynamics within and between firms: From evolution to co-evolution. *Journal of Management Studies*, 40(8): 2111–2136.

Vos, L., & Page, S. 2020. Marketization, performative environments, and the impact of organizational climate on teaching practice in business schools. *Academy of Management Learning & Education*, 19(1): 59–80.

West Turner, J. 1997. Continuity and constraint: Reconstructing the concept of tradition from a pacific perspective. *The Contemporary Pacific*, 9: 345–381.

Wright, A., Nichols, E., McKechnie, M., & McCarthy, S. 2013. Combining crisis management and evidence-based management: The Queensland floods as a teachable moment. *Journal of Management Education*, 37(1): 135–160.

Wright, A., Hibbert, P., Strong, R., & Edwards, M. 2018. Exposing practical, psychological, and pedagogical shadow sides of experiential learning. *Journal of Management Education*, 42(6): 761–771.

4

MANAGEMENT EDUCATION AND DIGITAL TECHNOLOGY: CHOICES FOR STRATEGY AND INNOVATION

David Lefevre and Leonardo Caporarello

Introduction

In an atrium at Harvard Business School, the original MBA curriculum from 1908 sits on display in a glass cabinet upon a pedestal. What will be striking to many involved in management education (ME) is not the import of this document but how little the structure of the core MBA curriculum taught across our sector has changed since this original template. Harvard Business School adopted the case-study method as the primary method of instruction in 1924 and the horseshoe-shaped classroom layout specifically designed to facilitate case-method teaching in 1953 (Harvard Business School, 2020). Thus, the template for the teaching method most associated with the modern business school, together with its associated business model based on enrolment fees, was set nearly 70 years ago. In this chapter we consider the extent to which the present acceleration in the adoption of educational technology (EdTech) will result in the emergence of new, technology driven models for ME.

Prior to the disruption caused by COVID-19, digital technologies had less impact on ME compared to other service sectors such as banking and tourism and the evolution of digital products was evolutionary rather than revolutionary. Digital education was gaining purchase, for example an emerging and growing market for online degree programs had been established. In 2010, online MBAs were offered at 90 Association to Advance Collegiate Schools of Business (AACSB)-accredited business schools (Poets & Quants, 2010). By 2019, this figure had grown substantially, with 33% of 710 AACSB accredited business schools offering an online MBA program, and 26.5% of 645 business schools offering a specialist online master's program (AACSB, 2020). In addition, the provision of free or low-cost open courses via MOOC platforms such as Coursera and EdX had become

DOI: 10.4324/9781003095903-5

common, commercial vendors such as Emeritus and GetSmarter were actively creating a market for online open executive education courses and, as will be explored later in this chapter, some schools such as Harvard Business School and Wharton Business School had begun to experiment with innovative EdTech-driven business models. However, the core provision of established business schools within the management education sector had remained largely untouched by technology, prompting commentators to remark that "(even as) the world of business has been changing dramatically, the world inside the business school continues in the same manner and tradition as it has for decades" (Peters, Smith, & Thomas, 2018: 4).

The COVID-19 pandemic emerging in early 2020 changed this situation dramatically. In response to a global crisis involving severe travel restrictions and limitations to in-person teaching, EdTech moved center stage to enable business schools to continue delivering their educational programs. The sudden move to an online provision of ME resulted in an unprecedented period of innovation in which staff was rapidly required to acquire the knowledge and skills necessary to teach and administer their programs online, sometimes in a matter of days. Program components such as classes, tutorials, assessments, events, careers support, clubs, and even graduation ceremonies all rapidly moved online. Govindarajan and Srivastava (2020) considered this to be a pivotal moment for higher education as a whole, drawing parallels between the COVID-19 pandemic and previous unexpected events such as World War II and the Y2K problem, both of which resulted in fundamental and enduring shifts within society and business. It remains to be seen which, and to what extent, the new online educational, administrative, and marketing practices will persist, but a reasonable expectation is that at least some of these processes will endure and that most programs will include enhanced roles for EdTech post pandemic.

In this chapter, we seek to look beyond the immediate disruption and consider the more enduring challenges and opportunities presented by the rise of EdTech. While exploring the likely future of an evolving, technology-enhanced ME sector, this chapter also outlines a road-map for those business schools looking to successfully advance engagement with EdTech.

The Evolving Educational Technology Landscape

A recent survey of 358 business school leaders conducted by the Association of MBAs (Dawes, 2020) found that the majority believed their school was "using new technology to deliver teaching and learning well" (66%) and agreed with the statement that their business school was "well prepared to embrace the oppor-tunities of the fourth industrial revolution" (63%). This optimism is reassuring, however vigilance is required as the ME sector is likely just navigating the foothills of technology adoption ahead of the main ascent.

To form an effective technology strategy, business school leaders need to keep abreast of EdTech developments and their strategic implications. At any given time, there will be a range of emerging technologies whose proponents claim will be transformational. In the early 2000s, virtual worlds, open educational resources and personal learning environments were such examples. At present, technologies such as blockchain, virtual classrooms, artificial intelligence (AI) tutors, and learning analytics have advocates. A 2018 report from the AACSB lists augmented and virtual reality (AR, VR) as technologies with the "potential to transform business and business education" (AACSB, 2018). History tells us that the majority of these new technologies will impact only certain niches within the student experience, if at all. A critical task for business school leaders is to interrogate the nature of new technologies and identify those with the potential to make a significant impact on the operations of the school.

Within this milieu of a continually evolving technology landscape there is one predominant category of influential technologies of which leaders should be cognizant, those relating to Web 2.0.

Web 2.0 and the Innovation Life Cycles in Management Education

While many technology trends in higher education have proven to be of fleeting or peripheral importance, the migration of education provision to online format has been slowly but steadily unfolding for decades. Boosted by the emergence of Web 2.0 and related technological innovations such as online video (e.g., YouTube) and video-conferencing (e.g., Macromedia Breeze Live), 2005 represents a pivotal step change in the development of digital education. Online educational practices that combine interactive learning materials, video lectures, asynchronous communication tools, and video conferencing were in use (e.g., at Imperial College Business School) in 2006. Such Web 2.0-based online education offers two powerful affordances. The first relates to flexibility regarding when and where courses are taught or studied, while the second encompasses cost reduction and profit opportunities. These two affordances will continue to drive adoption and provision of online education beyond the disruption caused by the pandemic.

The impact of the Web 2.0 technologies can be considered with reference to the Innovation Life Cycle model (Abernathy & Utterback, 1978) which relates innovation to the development stage of product/service process technology and an entity's competitive and growth strategy. The model describes an initial "fluid" phase characterized by product or service innovation, while the focus in the second "transitional" phase is on experimentation around new product and service offers until these coalesce into a dominant design. Following this, the opportunities for innovation shift in the subsequent "specific" phase toward process innovation such as operational improvements and cost savings.

The application of Web 2.0 technologies to education instigated a cycle that has been considerably accelerated by COVID-19, and this model highlights that a small number of dominant designs for digital ME will emerge from the continual exploration of ways in which the Web 2.0 technologies can be deployed. Additionally, decentralized process innovation will improve the manner in which these approaches can be deployed to deliver and support online ME.

Beyond this current innovation life cycle, technological development will lead to new innovation life cycles that will shape and change ME. The World Wide Web itself is on the verge of a further transformation as technologies relating to the "semantic web," AI, the "Internet of Things," and brain-machine interfaces (BMIs) are applied. While some of these technologies (e.g., VR) will result in incremental change, others such as AI have the potential to disrupt ME (see also Rivers & Holland, this volume).

A necessary initial step and enabler of these related technologies will be the digitalization of education. As increasing components of the educational process including student experience become digitalized, the resulting data footprint can be considered a "digital education system" (see Figure 4.1) with measured inputs (student profiles), interactions (e.g., learning events) and outputs (e.g., changes in student profiles, grades, and career outcomes).

This digital education system resembles a classic "control system" whose inputs are within a school's gift to adjust and whose elements are increasingly analyzable through data analysis and mathematical modeling. Identified data patterns provide insights into the workings of the educational system (Peach, Yaliraki, Lefevre, & Barahona, 2019). For example, schools will be able to identify which profiles of students benefit most from different program

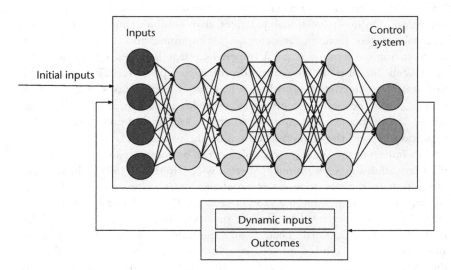

FIGURE 4.1 The digital education system

components and which components best enable students to achieve their career ambitions. Such patterns can be used for evidence-based decisions with regard to strategy, recruitment, resourcing, and educational design. Personalized learning journeys (see Fukami et al., this volume; Rivers & Holland, this volume) become more possible, providing students with the curricula that will enable them to achieve their personal objectives. Impact measurement can become more sophisticated and educational design more precise. Such "Precision Education," enabled by digitization, data analysis, and machine learning, may lead to ever more sophisticated educational AI increasingly capable of performing educational functions and enabling human tutors to teach more students (Rivers & Holland, this volume). Significant steps in this direction have already been taken. Ashok Goel implemented an AI Tutor on a module within an online MSc computer science program at Georgia Tech and students reported they were unaware that responses had been generated by an AI rather than their human tutor (Maderer, 2016). Ultimately, the emergence of AI capable of performing such educational tasks represents a transformative development for ME, with the prospect of schools that master its deployment able to deliver high quality education at scale and at low cost. This attractive promise will attract much attention and investment, and success in this endeavor depends in large part on business schools ensuring that sufficient internal knowledge and capability about technology, education, and their combination is secured in order to engage with such developments in an informed and effective manner.

Implications for Business School Strategy

COVID-19 has certainly crystallized the importance of EdTech as a component of business continuity planning. However, which strategies should be pursued to secure value from EdTech beyond its role as the digital equivalent of an emergency campus? This question is more difficult to answer than might be thought, and embracing EdTech cannot be considered a strategy within itself. As Michael Porter commented in a discussion on this topic, "I think the big risk in any new technology is to believe the technology is the strategy. Just because 200,000 people sign up doesn't mean it's a good idea." (Useem, 2014). Technology adoption should be conducted to enable or support a broader business strategy, and generalization quickly becomes misleading as different business schools work to different missions with regard to the volume of enrolments, the target student audience, the program portfolio, faculty profiles, pedagogic methods, and societal commitment (see Hibbert & Forster, this volume). Developing a portfolio of online courses in order to increase enrolments or to lower fees may support the mission of some schools but be counterstrategy for others.

Sometimes EdTech is simply an enabler of existing strategy. This occurs when consideration of the affordances of technology leads to the solution of an existing strategic challenge. The University of the Highlands and Islands is a university spread across multiple campuses in northern Scotland with a mission to have a transformational impact on the prospects of this sparsely populated area of 300,000 people (University of the Highlands and Islands, 2021). The flexibility afforded by EdTech enables the university to reach out to this population as opposed to requiring students to attend a physical campus and thus enables the university to further its mission. Conversely, Pace University is a private school based in New York City, a densely populated area. The business school has approximately 3,000 undergraduates and a strategy to grow these enrolments but has been constrained by the limitations of its available physical space and the rising costs of real estate in Manhattan. The creation of online programs has allowed Pace University to continue its growth (Peters et al., 2018: 126). Such examples show how EdTech can support strategy in very different circumstances and in different ways.

Such a problem-solving role can have a domino effect and lead to further opportunities. Those running the Weekend Executive MBA at Duke University's Fuqua School of Business found that a significant proportion of students on the program were not always able to travel to Durham from the wider North Carolina, DC and Virginia area in order to attend class. To address this, they implemented a hybrid class format which enabled such students to attend a class remotely in an equivalent manner to being physically present. This resulted in a new flexible model of education in which students are able to choose between online and campus-based models on a class-by-class basis.

Educational Technology as a Determinant of Strategy: The Digitally Enhanced Education Portfolio

A more pro-active approach to incorporating digital education into strategy is through consideration of the notion of a digitally enhanced education portfolio. This framework considers four different modes by which digital education can be introduced into traditional education portfolio. These being terms "enhance," "migrate," "change," and "disrupt" (Figure 4.2).

Enhance

This refers to the incorporation of EdTech into existing programs within a portfolio with the aim of enhancing the existing design. For example, online synchronous activities focused on knowledge transfer can be added to free up class time to focus on more interactive activities, the so called "flipped classroom" approach. From an implementation perspective, this approach is a low-risk activity as failure can mean simply reverting to the prior format. However, a significant drawback is that this category of activity tends to increase a school's cost base while having only an indirect impact on revenue.

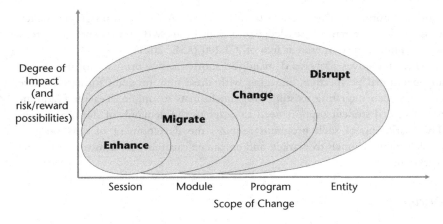

FIGURE 4.2   The digitally enhanced education portfolio – modes of activity

Migrate

This refers to the migration of existing campus-based programs in the portfolio to online or blended format. Or alternatively, it creates new online programs that offer an existing qualification such as a master's degree. The Imperial College Business School, Boston University's Questrom School of Business, and the University of Illinois all created online MBA programs having previously delivered campus-based equivalents. Such an approach offers significant pragmatic advantages. The concept of an online master's degree is more straightforward for an organization to grasp conceptually than a more innovative project such as a stackable portfolio of micro-credentials. From an operational perspective, such initiatives require a reworking rather than a rebuilding of existing business processes as much expertise remains applicable. However the weakness of this approach is that it represents a supply side strategy and a school may lose share to more market orientated competitors.

Change

This refers to the application of online delivery models to different, invariably shorter, program formats. Reducing the study hours on a program usually necessitates a change to the qualification awarded and this category of activity is leading to the emergence of so-called "alternative qualifications." Much activity in this category is being driven by disruptive third-party providers working in partnership with established business schools. One such provider, Singapore-based Emeritus, partners with business schools such as MIT Sloan, Columbia Business School, and the Tuck School of Business at Dartmouth to offer "globally oriented" management certificates comprising 8–12 weeks of part-time study for a fee of around £1,500. The London School of Economics has partnered with another commercial partner, 2U, to offer its "MBA Essentials program," which aims to distil the target knowledge and skills of an MBA programs into a ten-week online course offered at fees of £3,200 (LSE, 2021).

These initiatives address a demand for, shorter online program formats. From an operational perspective, engaging with these new program formats is more complex than migrating existing program formats to online. Teaching, administration, and student support need to adapt to the demands of shorter courses. The marketing of such programs requires the development of new business models, new channels to market, and enhanced capability in areas such as digital marketing.

Disrupt

This refers to the development of an educational offer that is supported by a different business model to the traditional portfolio. One example is the free-mium model, in which components of a product or service are offered for free in order to entice customers to pay for more premium features. The Imperial College Business School now offers the preparation courses for its MBA suite for free via the EdX MOOC platform with the aim that some of these students will progress their studies into a fee-paying program. While not offering free courses, MIT adopts a form of the freemium model by offering low-cost, online "MicroMaster" programs, in MOOC format via the EdX platform. Students successfully completing a MicroMaster's program obtain credit, usually equivalent to a semester, toward a traditional full-fee campus-based program should they attain admission (MIT, 2021).

A further example of experimentation with new business models is that of Wharton Business School, which currently offers more than 50 online modules via the Coursera MOOC platform. Since its launch in 2012, this program has awarded 200,000 certificates to more than 100,000 learners (Wharton School, 2020). These courses operate on a mass instruction model with very little interaction between tutors and individual students. Assessment is computer based. As such, the marginal costs of teaching one additional student are low and this has enabled experimentation with a number of low fee business models. These courses were originally offered on a freemium basis. Students could enroll for free but were required to pay a small fee of around $50 to receive a certificate. More recently Coursera are favoring a subscription model in which students, or their employer, pay a monthly fee of around $75 to receive access to multiple courses.

A further case study is that of Harvard Business School Online, which os-tensibly operates according to a traditional fee-paying model. After gaining entrance via a selection procedure, students pay approximately $1,600 to study an online module which features a cohort model and has fixed start and end dates. However, as per the low-fee models described above, the delivery is almost entirely driven by computers and administration staff. Enrolments grew from 3,471 in 2015 to 19,304 in 2019, far exceeding the number of students who studied on the HBS campus (Harvard Business School, 2019). The flagship offer is a pre-MBA program branded "CORe" (Credential of Readiness), which has now been adopted for use by other schools, including Boise State University which awards credits to students who complete the program (Lederman, 2017).

At present, such experimentation with new business models remains a niche endeavor and the extent to which such experiments will prove disruptive to the sector remains unclear.

Strategy into Practice: The Hybrid School

This chapter concludes with a consideration of how business schools will need to adapt in order to successfully enact a strategy that fully embraces EdTech. A theme running throughout this chapter is that the external landscape is in a state of flux, responses to this environment require change and this necessarily involves risk. Initiatives are not always successful and the history of EdTech adoption is not simply a list of successes. In 2013, a Georgia Tech course on how to create online courses had to be canceled, reportedly due to technology failure (Strauss, 2013). Technology-enhanced learning initiatives have also met with resistance from both students and faculty. In 2018, the University of Central Florida's College of Business moved its campus-based provision to a blended learning format, which replaced some in-person class time with instructional videos and online textbook learning. Students protested strongly citing the additional costs for digital learning and a desire for a "proper education" as reasons for their protest (Lieberman, 2018).

These initiatives failed post-implementation, although failure can, of course, occur at earlier stages as well. Initiatives start with embryonic ideas and these are intrinsically delicate objects. Jonathan Ive, Chancellor of the Royal College of Art and former Chief Design Officer of Apple Inc, points to the fragility of new ideas, stating these to be "so easily missed, so easily compromised, so easily just squished" (Ive, 2011) and the design of business schools contains structures adept at such squishing. For example, common administrative procedures such as ROI and KPI calculations, designed to mitigate risk and ensure fit with strategy, can be brought to bear at too early a stage, while ideas are still forming. And the critical appraisal of the committee structures commonly adopted for much decision-making does not always act to nurture early-stage ideas. As Sir Barnett Cocks, a former Clerk of the UK House of Commons, is reputed to have put it, "a committee is a cul-de-sac down which ideas are lured and then quietly strangled." A further structural issue is that engaging faculty in new teaching initiatives will be challenging within an incentive framework that prioritizes research.

Consideration of the implementation of new ideas moves our discussion into the realm of innovation studies, a recurring theme being that different administration structures are required to those supporting mainstream business strategy because of the need to comprehensively accommodate uncertainty (Dodgson, Gann, & Salter 2008: 95). Schools thus need to distinguish between decision-making processes relating to business-as-usual activity and those to support innovation. Here we envisage the successful, mature model as a hybrid school in which EdTech has permeated across its operations and in which all key business functions have the expertise to engage with both digital and analogue education across a spectrum of formats from the primarily campus-based to the purely online.

We now refer to a simple model of innovation in order to frame the various requirements for progress toward the hybrid school model. A simple conceptual definition of innovation is the process of turning ideas into reality and capturing value from them, and an innovation strategy can be considered to encompass four stages of search, select, implement and capture (Tidd & Bessant, 2018). Here, we refer to this process as the SSIC model. Searching involves scanning the internal and external environment for signals of potential threats and opportunities together with an exploration of possible responses. Selecting refers to deciding which potential projects should be pursued. Implementing involves translating such ideas into the launch of new products and services. Finally, capture refers to ensuring that an organization secures value from such initiatives, both financially and through learning gains.

Progression to becoming a hybrid school can be considered in terms of successfully implementing a series of initiatives, each of which must pass through these four stages. To enable innovation to happen, a school needs to ensure it has capability and capacity at each stage, together with the strategic and organizational frameworks required to ensure linkage between each stage and also to the overarching strategy and mission of the school. Now the challenge has been framed, we can discuss the implications for staff, the campus infrastructure and the external network of partnerships and suppliers.

Staff

In the words of Lou Gerstner, previous CEO of IBM, innovation "needs to be engrained in the DNA of the organization. The performance of exceptional innovators and teams should be rewarded, but the responsibilities and opportunities for innovation are everyone's." (Dodgson & Gann, 2018: 110). In the mature state of the hybrid school, all categories of staff are engaged in all four stages of the innovation process. However, the journey toward this state results in a number of process hurdles that are introduced here through consideration of three categories of staff, specialist EdTech staff, the faculty and the professional staff.

TABLE 4.1 Example tasks across the SSIC Innovation mode

Process	Example tasks
Search	Sourcing ideas. For example:
	• Strategy formation activities
	• Market analysis and scouting
	• Alliances
	• Networking activity. Internal and external events
	• Consultation with student groups and active users
	• Commercial partnerships and venturing activity
	Development of ideas. For example:
	• Experimentation with emerging technology
	• Prototyping, pilot projects and educational research
	• Advocacy: building support, encouraging engagement
	• Business case development and project planning
Select	• Evaluation against strategic frameworks and assessment criteria
	• Forming and organizing decision-making structures and processes
	• Risk assessment exercises, knowledge gathering and forecasting
Implement	• Project management
	• Staff development: training faculty, professional staff and students
	• Technical development: software programming
	• Creation of digital courseware: production of digital learning activities and media
	• Learning design
	• Revision of policy, quality assurance, and governance frameworks
Capture	• Evaluation tasks: project reviews, analysis of feedback
	• Knowledge management tasks: identifying, codifying, protecting, and disseminating capability
	• Exploitation tasks: application of new capability to related areas

We first consider the nature of the work to be performed across the four stages of search, select, implement and capture. Example tasks are illustrated in Table 4.1.

The question now becomes how should these tasks be allocated? In an ideal world, who should do what? The answer to this will depend on context and will also change over time. Work done by specialists now will become part of the routine work conducted by faculty and professional staff later. Tasks conducted by suppliers now may be brought inhouse later and vice versa. However, broad principles do apply and these are now considered for three different categories of staff.

Specialist staff: the educational technology team

Some of the tasks identified above will require a school to secure new capabilities in areas such as web development, media production, educational research, and learning design. Other tasks, such as horizon scanning and project management may not constitute new capabilities but are sufficient in volume to demand increased capacity. Even if largely outsourced to external vendors, internal staff are likely to be required if only to secure the expert knowledge required to manage these external resources in an intelligent manner. Thus, a range of specialist EdTech roles emerge and a logical development is for these roles to be gathered together in an EdTech team, as many business schools have done. The Imperial College Business School and the SDA Bocconi School of Management now have such teams which bring together a diverse range of roles including enthusiasts, evangelists, project staff, learning designers, technical developers, media teams, educational researchers, and support staff.

A key question for schools is where such teams should be placed within their organization. Should they be kept as a separate entity, a so-called "skunk works," or embedded within the operations of the school? If the former then how can a scenario be prevented in which this team eventually becomes a "school within a school," perhaps competing with the mainstream operations or at least duplicating tasks? If the latter then should the reporting line be into innovation, IT, administration, or education? This choice will determine the orientation of the team and thus should be informed by the primary strategic goal.

A further management challenge is that the nature of work demanded from the EdTech team will continually evolve. Such teams often start life as a group of enthusiasts championing educational innovation. However, if successful, then new educational programs will emerge, for example a portfolio of digital educational modules, that need to be delivered and maintained on an ongoing basis. Such teams then either need to become adept at operational work or at managing the migration of such work to other teams within the school.

These evolving demands are compounded as EdTech moves from a niche to a mainstream activity. Work that was previously considered the work of specialists becomes embedded in roles across the school. Faculties start to create their own media, administrators manage online course areas, and the management of educational software moves into mainstream IT support. To remain effective, specialist teams need to be in a continual state of flux, shedding some tasks and acquiring others.

Looking forward, the nature of some of these new tasks will become increasingly technical and this may demand more formal attention to R&D. As discussed earlier in this chapter, the technologies likely to initiate future cycles of innovation will be more complex than the Web 2.0-based collection of technologies that prompted the present growth in digital education. As we move toward the "digital education system," initiatives are likely to require complex coding, sophisticated mathematics, and, potentially, the incorporation of concepts from specialist fields such as neuroscience. Engaging with such technologies will demand knowledge, thought, exploration, development, implementation, and evaluation. To create the space needed for such activity, business schools may need to engage with more formal R&D processes, perhaps for first time. Companies in industries such as pharmaceuticals and IT commonly spend over 10% of their annual sales on R&D (Dodgson et al., 2008) however, systematic programs of R&D relating to teaching delivery are not common within business schools, perhaps reflecting the fact that the core method of teaching delivery has had to change little, until recently. Such R&D teams do exist, one example being the BUILT (Bocconi University Innovations in Learning and Teaching) initiative at Bocconi University that is focused on exploring and exploiting the educational innovation for both learners and faculty members.

A particular approach to conducting educational R&D and one suited to higher education is to incorporate structured programs of educational research and, as institutions of social science, business schools are well-placed to conduct such activity. Programs of educational research facilitate the exploration of complex technical topics and also the development of new technology and educational models. The resulting knowledge also enables a move toward more evidence-based practice in management education (see Briner et al., this volume). Such emerging activity has been termed the "Science of Learning" movement (Chasse, Auricchio, & Liebert, 2017), an approach now well-established in medicine, where it is known as evidence-based medicine (Sackett, Rosenberg, Gray, Haynes, & Richardson, 1996), and now gaining currency in education. Making decisions relating to the design of educational experiences based on evidence will result in a more precise and effective model of management education. At present, however, the impact of learning initiatives across the education sector has not been well examined (Kim & Maloney, 2020).

Faculty

In their roles as school leaders, administrators, and instructors, faculty will be primary actors across the four stages of the SSIC Innovation process and also in the ongoing development and delivery of digital education. This activity places unique challenges on the traditional faculty role. The contemporary university model, which business schools now subscribe to, is one of a community of scholars within which individual faculty are given considerable autonomy. This comes under pressure as schools engage with digital education in a number of ways. The data trail left by digital education, for example via online discussions and class recordings, increases opportunities for, likely unwanted, monitoring and supervision. Teaching often ceases to be a solo activity and may require a teaching team comprising faculty, learning designers, teaching assistants, and other support staff. Course development may require investment, which draws faculty into additional administrative gatekeeping processes such as ROI calculation, KPI measurements, and risk assessments. The notion of faculty retaining the IPR in their course materials is deeply ingrained within the culture of management education, but this becomes problematic once the creation of such materials becomes a team effort requiring investment from the school. Finally, learning to teach well using technology is often not intuitive and experienced instructors may find themselves sitting on the other side of the classroom for the first time in many years.

Together, these demands represent a significant cultural shift in the nature of the faculty position, perhaps leading to the creation of new types of roles, many or some of which will not generally be welcomed. Incentivizing faculty to engage in digital transformation requires a balance to be struck between the collective interests of the school and the individual interests of the faculty who understandably prize the tradition of autonomy.

Professional staff

In the hybrid school, professional staff too will become engaged across the SSIC Innovation process. The transition will impact the roles of all professional staff involved in supporting and enabling the educational provision. This can be illustrated by consideration of the value chain on a typical campus-based program. Figure 4.3 illustrates the value chain for a traditional MBA.

Consider how the tasks required to deliver the components within this value chain change when, for example, an MBA migrates to an online format. Finding students may require recruiting from a wider, perhaps global geographical area and competing against more and different schools. Marketing and recruitment teams may require new skills in areas such as digital marketing and may need to establish broader, global relationships. Housing and feeding students becomes unnecessary or may become a logistical exercise, involving multiple, perhaps short-term, locations. The nature of supporting teaching changes significantly when students are not physically present, becoming less passive and more active and involving the use of digital technologies. The provision of space and technology relates to the virtual rather than physical campus, requiring technical designers and developers rather than architects and AV staff. The move to the hybrid school model thus impacts the majority of existing professional staff roles and is likely to lead to both the creation of new roles and the abandonment of others.

That concludes our consideration of how staff roles may need to evolve during the transition to the hybrid school model. We now turn our attention to the campus, both the physical and the virtual.

The Campus

When considering digital education, it is helpful to think of the business school campus comprising both the physical buildings and also the online environment, or virtual campus. Students continually enter and leave both the physical and virtual campuses, sometimes residing in one and sometimes both simultaneously.

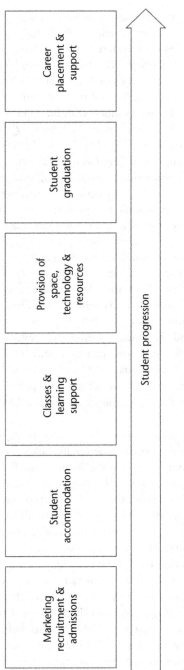

FIGURE 4.3 Business school value chain (MBA) – adapted from Peters et al. (2018)

The virtual campus: the poor relation

On a university campus, the business school building is usually instantly recognizable. Business schools invest heavily in their physical buildings frequently engaging prominent and expensive architects such as Noman Foster (Yale School of Management, Imperial College Business School), Franck Gehry (UTS Business School, Weatherhead School of Management), David Adjaye (SKOLKOVO) and Sanaa (SDA Bocconi School of Management) to create statement buildings that appear as concerned as much with brand creation as with function. Oxford's Saïd Business School is currently investing £60m to refurbish one building for use in executive education. The Tepper School of Business recently spent $201m on a new campus building (Moules, 2019).

When the full student experience is considered, students are now likely to spend more time studying out of class than in-class and increasingly this time is spent in the virtual campus. A module comprising 20 hours of in-class study may require twice this time for out-of-class activities. Data relating to expenditure on the virtual campus is hard to find; however, this is likely to be negligible compared to investments in physical buildings and the experience is generally far from glitzy. While the technology landscape outside universities has evolved, the EdTech inside has not changed at the same pace and is largely centered on the ubiquitous Learning Management System (LMS). The standard format of the LMS, comprising an online course site with functional areas for files, quizzes, discussion boards, and administration tools was developed in 1996 at the University of British Columbia, subsequently commercialized as the WebCT system (Goldberg, Salari, & Swoboda, 1996) and acquired by Blackboard Inc in 2006. And while the Internet and the affordances provided by EdTech have evolved significantly since this time, the format of the LMS has not evolved at the same pace.

The LMS format was created to enable faculty to develop online areas to support campus-based classes at a time when online and blended education was in its infancy and just emerging as a possibility. As such, the format is not well suited to support the new pedagogies and technologies that have developed since. As Kim and Maloney (2020: 33) state, the LMS is "a problematic technology that reinforces many of the least effective parts of the faculty-student engagement." Phil Hill (2015), an EdTech analyst, more colorfully, describes the LMS as the "minivan" of education suggesting that "everyone has them and needs them, but there's a certain shame having one in the driveway."

The question arises as to why the virtual campus has not evolved at the same pace as the technology world outside of academia. Beyond reasons such as mimetic isomorphism (DiMaggio & Powell, 1983) and the role of historical narratives and identities (see Foster & Hibbert, this volume), one important reason is historical. Before the onset of cloud based computing schools were required to host and maintain systems and there were strong incentives for

CIOs to pursue a single platform policy in order to reduce duplication and support overhead. Despite this rationale, the approach stunted schools' ability to experiment with new technology. The argument weakens in the cloud model where the primary role of inhouse IT teams moves to integrating rather than maintaining systems. However, the instinct to advocate a single platform, preferably one that is in common use elsewhere, persists and this has led to rather stagnant ecosystem for learning platforms and a lack of innovation. In 2020, during what should be a period of experimentation, just four technology platforms hold 89.3% of this market (Edutechnica, 2020) and the average age of these systems is 18.5 years.

To paraphrase Darwin, without heterogeneity there can be no evolution and the present lack of diversity not only impedes innovation but also results in a sub-optimum student experience. Few schools would advocate the same classroom specification being used for each of the learning experiences they offer. Classroom layouts differ according to cohort, they also differ according to cohort size and purpose. For example, executive education classrooms differ to those used for undergraduate teaching. A classroom used for case study discussions differs to a room used for group work which differs to a classroom used for computer-based tutorials. The student experience is optimized by choosing the most appropriate physical space for a particular experience. In digital education, MOOC type technology driven courses, online executive education facilitated by human instructors and hybrid undergraduate courses all require a different form of virtual campus and it is unlikely that one system will be optimal in each case. An approach in which a number of different systems are managed and promoted in a structured manner will enable the virtual campus to evolve and result in more optimal student experiences.

The physical campus

While the online platform infrastructure supporting digital education rightly garners most of the attention, its adoption also has implications for the physical campus. Developing and delivering digital education requires dedicated physical studios and study space will be required as some students will want to conduct their online studies on campus

First, we consider the facilities required to create digital materials. Imperial College and the BI Business School in Oslo have created flexible, creative studio spaces which enable faculty, learning designers and others to sit together and work creatively on course design. Once an online or blended learning course has been designed then physical studios are required for the recording of media and these can evolve far beyond the common format of a green screen room. For example, the BI Business School has built a suite of recording rooms with different "sets" akin to a movie studio. These sets are designed to enable the recordings of debates, fireside chats, announcements and the recording of podcasts.

Once created, the delivery of digital education can also be enhanced with digital first teaching rooms such as those developed by Harvard Business School, IESE, and IE. These classrooms include a wall of screens featuring the remote students which enables a faculty member to engage with students in a more dynamic and interactive manner than, for example, conventual webinar software.

An alternative approach is the concept of a "hyflex" classroom. The Fuqua School of Business, IE, and the Imperial College Business School have implemented this style of classroom which enables remote students to attend campus-based classes, together with physically present students, via screens located at the rear of the classroom. The Imperial College Business School and SDA Bocconi School of Management have also removed the raked, fixed seating from such classrooms to enable a more flexible classroom layout.

The move to a digitally enhanced education provision can also lead to greater demand for student study areas. Online students studying programs with campus-based components will require the space to do so and online students local to a university will want to come to campus putting more pressure on available student study space. Blended learning approaches, such as the "flipped classroom" which include online out of class components both lead to a requirement for more flexible teaching classrooms and also increase the demand for student study areas for the out-of-class activities.

When considered collectively, these requirements can represent a significant change to the usage of a school's physical space. From the outside, the physical campus may remain recognizable however the internal configuration will be noticeably different.

Accessing External Capability: Collaboration, Networks and Suppliers

An external network of suppliers and collaborators will form a critical component of the hybrid school's capability. As Dodgson et al. (2008: 134) report "A generation of research on the innovation process has shown that innovators rarely innovate alone. They are embedded in dense networks and external relationships that propel, generate, and sometimes limit opportunities for innovation." External capability will also be required to support the ongoing operations of digital education. Unlike the traditional "chalk and talk" teaching model, often requiring primarily a member of teaching faculty and a physical classroom, securing all the resources and capabilities needed to deliver a digital education project is more complex. Schools are not generally well placed to maintain the technology infrastructure required without the support of external vendors, nor are they able to secure internal specialist capability in emerging areas such as learning analytics and VR. A network of suppliers and partnerships will form an essential component of any successful digital education strategy and a growing network of such suppliers now make it possible to outsource tasks across the SSIC innovation process and across all components in the value chain introduced in this chapter. Schools have options as to which tasks are performed internally to and externally to their organization.

One particular type of supplier is the *Online Program Management company* or OPM. These firms offer a range of services relating to the provision of online degree programs and shorter courses, typically in return for a share of the subsequent fee revenue. These services include funding, marketing, recruitment, technology provision, course development, student support, and even supplying instructors. OPMs remove a number of hurdles business schools face when embarking on online education initiatives and enable them to do so with reduced risk. They also provide schools with market intelligence, access to specialist expertise in areas such as digital marketing, access to additional capacity and also access to a global footprint that would be uneconomic for a single institution to maintain. As such OPMs have gained traction across the sector. HolonIQ, a market intelligence company has compiled a dataset relating to more than 4,900 online programs supported by OPMs across more than 300 universities in the United States and elsewhere (HolonIQ, 2019).

However, there are disadvantages to OPM engagements, the most conspicuous being the loss of a significant proportion of the fee revenue. However, perhaps more significant in the longer term is that outsourcing the delivery of teaching, a core service, has a different character to outsourcing a peripheral service such as catering. Schools forego the advantages of online projects, gaining little with regard to internal capability, capacity and digital assets that could be utilized elsewhere in its teaching provision. Reputational risk requires consideration when the influence schools have on the design and delivery of their education is shared. And it is more difficult to differentiate the school's offer to the market as OPM products are necessarily generic to a number of schools.

OPMs represent one type of supplier and the hybrid school will require an evolving network of supplier relationships. In order to develop and influence the nature of the supplier ecosystem, schools can be pro-active and assume some responsibility for nurturing this network. For example, by engaging the services of early-stage start-ups and providing support for pilot projects. Some schools have taken this notion further. BI Business School in Oslo has created an incubator space on their campus and offers this to EdTech start-ups rent free. IE Business School in Madrid secured its "WOW room," a digital classroom technology, by nurturing a start-up to build it for them. Imperial College Business School in London has now launched two successful EdTech spin-out firms, Epigeum and Insendi, in order to secure the technology it requires. Bocconi University in Milan has launched "Bocconi for Innovation" designed to invest the expertise and resources of the wider Bocconi community to supporting selected EdTech, and other, start-ups to grow and succeed (Bocconi, 2021).

The final component to external capability considered here is the role of alliances and institutional partnerships (see also Hommel & Vandenbempt, this volume). Business schools are enthusiastic participants in the concept of "coopetition" (Brandenburger & Nalebuff, 1996), that is collaboration with potential competitors to secure shared benefit. A range of consortia exist including the FOME Alliance, the Global Network for Advanced Management, the Global Alliance in Management Education, and the Global Business School Network. Such networks enable schools to secure access to knowledge and resources they do not possess internally, provide clues regarding emerging opportunities and accelerate problem solving through knowledge sharing and collective brain power.

That concludes our discussion on how schools can evolve to embrace EdTech and how the notion of the hybrid school has implications for a school's staff, its campus infrastructure and the external network of partnerships and suppliers. Thus, also brings us to the end of this chapter.

Conclusion

The introduction to this chapter asked to what extent the present acceleration in the adoption of EdTech will result in the emergence of additional, technology driven paradigms for ME? Consideration of the educational landscape suggests that we are part way thorough a decade-long innovation cycle initiated by the emergence of Web 2.0 technologies. Although this cycle has been accelerated by COVID-19, developments are still in a fluid state. However, Abernathy and Utterback's (1978) model suggests that this activity will settle and form one or a number of dominant designs which will represent new technology driven paradigms for management education. We argued that further cycles of innovation will be initiated by emerging mathematical and computing based technologies enabling a move toward "precision education" and potentially a new era of digital education systems supported by AI. Such developments will be based on increasingly complex technology requiring schools to secure specialist capability and conduct structured R&D programs, perhaps for the first time.

This chapter then introduced the notion of hybrid school. A school in which EdTech has permeated across all operations and with the expertise to deliver a spectrum of both digital and analogue education. The hybrid school will require a reconsideration of organizational structures and roles, a reconfiguration of both the virtual and physical campus and the nurturing of an extensive external network of suppliers and partnerships. This long-term transition represents a not insignificant challenge for incumbent schools however those that are successful will find themselves riding a new wave of management education, a more flexible, engaging and precise format of education which all stakeholders will want to embrace.

References

AACSB. 2018. *Technologies with potential to transform business and business education: Virtual and augmented reality.* Accessed February 12, 2021, at https://www.aacsb.edu/-/media/aacsb/publications/research-reports/virtual_reality_primer_final.ashx

AACSB. 2020. *Business school data guide.* Accessed December 15, 2020, at https://www.aacsb.edu/-/media/aacsb/publications/data-trends-booklet/2020.ashx

Abernathy, W. J., & Utterback, J. M. 1978. Patterns of industrial innovation. *Technology Review,* 80: 40–47.

Bocconi, 2021. *Bocconi for innovation.* Accessed February 2021 at https://www.b4i.unibocconi.it

Brandenburger, A. M., & Nalebuff, B. J. 1996. *Co-opetition.* New York: Currency Doubleday.

Chasse, R. P., Auricchio, G., Liebert, K-H. 2017. *Digital age learning – A point of view from the EFMD special interest group.* Accessed February 2021 at https://www.efmdglobal.org/ww-content/uploads/PoV_Learning_in _the_digital_age_vFINAL.pdf

Dawes, W. 2020. *Business school leaders research: The future of technology in management education.* Accessed February 2021 at associationofmbas.com/wp-content/uploads/2020/02/Report_v9.pdf

DiMaggio, P. J., & Powell, W. W. 1983. The iron cage revisited: Institutional iso-morphism and collective rationality in organizational fields. *American Sociological Review,* 48(2): 147–160.

Dodgson, M., & Gann, D. 2018. *Innovation: A very short introduction.* Oxford: Oxford University Press.

Dodgson, M., Gann, D. M., & Salter, A. 2008. *The management of technological innovation: Strategy and practice.* Oxford: Oxford University Press on Demand.

Edutechnica. 2020. *8th annual LMS data update, December 9, 2020.* Accessed December 2020 at https://edutechnica.com/tag/market-share

Goldberg, M. W., Salari, S., & Swoboda, P. 1996. World wide web – course tool: An environment for building WWW-based courses. *Computer Networks and ISDN Systems,* 28(7–11): 1219–1231.

Govindarajan, V., & Srivastava, A. 2020. What the shift to virtual learning could mean for the future of higher ed. *Harvard Business Review,* March 31, 2020.

Harvard Business School. 2019. *Annual report.* Accessed December 2020 at https://www.hbs.edu/about/annualreport/2019/

Harvard Business School. 2020. *A campus built on philanthropy.* Accessed December 2020 at https://www.hbs.edu/about/campus-and-culture/campus-built-on-philanthropy/Pages/aldrich-hall.aspx/

Hill, P. 2015. *LMS is the minivan of education (and other thoughts from #LILI15).* Accessed December 2020 at eliterate.us/lms-is-the-minivan-of-education-and-other-thoughts-from-lili15/

Holon, I. Q. 2019. *The anatomy of an OPM and a $7.7B market in 2025.* Accessed December 2020 at https://www.holoniq.com/news/anatomy-of-an-opm/

Ive, J. 2011. *Tribute to Steve Jobs from Apple's celebration of Steve October 19, 2011.* Video re-cording. Accessed December 2020 at https://www.youtube.com/watch?v=GnGI76__sSA

Kim, J., & Maloney, E. 2020. *Learning innovation and the future of higher education.* Baltimore: Johns Hopkins University Press.

Lederman, D. 2017. *Cross-country (and credit-bearing) collaboration.* Inside Higher Ed. Accessed December 2020 at insidehighered.com/digital-lerning/article/2017/02/06/boise-state-offeres-credit-bearing-digital-course-harvard

Lieberman, M. 2018. *Furore over blended and active learning.* Inside Higher Ed. Accessed December 2020 at insidehighered.com/digital-learning/article/2018/09/21/blended-learning-model-university-central-florida-draws-business

LSE. 2021. *MBA essentials.* Accessed February 2021 at https://www.lse.ac.uk/study-at-lse/Online-learning/Courses/MBA-essentials

Maderer, J. 2016. *Artificial intelligence course creates AI teaching assistant —Students didn't know their TA was a computer.* Georgia Tech News Centre. Accessed December 16, 2020, at news.gatech.edu/2016/05/09/artificial-intelligence-course-creates-ai-teaching-assistant

MIT. 2021. *MITx MicroMasters programs.* Accessed February 2021 at https://micromasters.mit.edu

Moules, J. 2019. Business schools are building boldly for the future. *Financial Times,* May 10, 2019. https://www.ft.com/content/248727a4-6bff-11e9-80c7-60ee53e6681d

Peach, R. L., Yaliraki, S. N., Lefevre, D. L., & Barahona, M. 2019. Data-driven unsupervised clustering of online learner behaviour. *NPJ Science of Learning,* 4(1): 1–11.

Peters, K., Smith, R. R., & Thomas, H. 2018. *Rethinking the business models of business schools: A critical review and change agenda for the future.* Emerald. 10.1108/9781787548749

Poets & Quants. 2010. *Accredited online MBA programs.* Accessed December 2020 at https://poetsandquants.com/2010/12/04/accredited-online-mba-programs/

Sackett, D. L., Rosenberg, W. M. C., Gray, J. A. M., Haynes, R. B., & Richardson, W. S. 1996. Evidence based medicine: What it is and what it isn't. *BMJ,* 312: 71–72.

Strauss, V. 2013. How online class about online learning failed miserably. *The Washington Post.* Accessed December 2020 at washingtonpost.com/news/answer-sheet/wp/2013/02/05/how-online-class-about-online-learning-failed-miserably

Tidd, J. B. J., & Bessant, J. R. 2018. *Managing innovation: Integrating techno-logical, market and organisational change.* London: Wiley.

University of the Highlands and Islands. 2021. *Our mission & values.* Accessed February 2021 at https://www.uhi.ac.uk/en/about-uhi/our-mission--values/

Useem, J. 2014. Business school, disrupted. *New York Times,* May 31, 2014.

Wharton School. 2020. *History of Wharton.* Accessed December 2020 at https://www.wharton.upenn.edu/history

5

MANAGEMENT EDUCATION AND EARLY CAREER ACADEMICS: CHALLENGES AND OPPORTUNITIES

Olivier Ratle, Alexandra Bristow, and Sarah Robinson

Introduction

In this chapter, we draw on the literature on ECAs and on our own research (Bristow, Robinson, & Ratle, 2017, 2019; Ratle, Robinson, Bristow, & Kerr, 2020; Robinson, Ratle, & Bristow, 2017) to explore this predicament. We met during our doctoral studies, and upon starting our respective careers we discovered gaps between our expectations and the realities of working in contemporary business schools. Our program of research was therefore triggered by these early experiences, and also by our own questioning of the mixed ways in which ECAs are often portrayed in the literature. ECAs can be seen as a vulnerable group that has limited capacity to resist the growing neoliberalism of higher education and its effects (Laudel & Gläser, 2008). These early years can also be seen as a time of liminality (Smith, 2010) that implies an active process of identity construction for new entrants. This process is fraught with challenges and anxiety (Henkel, 2004; Trowler & Knight, 2000) but also presents many opportunities for ECAs to make positive differences in their working lives and beyond (e.g., Archer, 2008a, 2008b; Bristow, 2012; Harris, 2005; Smith, 2010).

While each of the publications we refer to has its own methodological characteristics, overall our research draws on a dataset of 38 semi-structured interviews with ECAs from 15 countries. Specifically, we studied Critical Management Studies (CMS) ECAs for a number of reasons. One is that our own affiliation to this group means that we have a vested interest in its experiences and future. Another consideration is methodological: in that studying a specific group of ECAs contrasts with most existing studies that treat the category "ECA" as a generic phenomenon. Finally, CMS ECAs often occupy a doubly marginalized

DOI: 10.4324/9781003095903-6

position: they are newcomers in a field where the ethos is more aligned with the tenets of neoliberal capitalism than with its critique.

Below, we discuss five different challenges, and what can be done about them. These challenges do not constitute an exhaustive list of what ECAs may have to face but are representative of the themes emerging from our research over the years. For individual academics, how they engage with these challenges will shape their future: whether or not they endure within the profession, and the extent to which they thrive professionally. These are also challenges for the future of the profession as a whole if it is to escape the narrowing of its horizons. The collective response to these challenges will determine whether or not management education can be a field characterized by pluralism, diversity, and the possibility of critique – something we come back to in the discussion section, before concluding the chapter with some reflections on the need for collective actions and solutions for shaping the future of the early-career experience, and therefore the future of management education.

Challenge 1: Transitioning from PhD Student to University Employee

In becoming a university employee, an ECA experiences a serious change from being on the receiving end of management education for many years to actually delivering it. What happens when these tables are turned and ECAs find themselves the transmitters of management education to incoming cohorts of students? How do ECAs learn to become management educators? Is the transition a smooth natural extension of their doctoral studies or is it fraught with dilemmas, identity struggles, and learning shocks? It is pertinent to pause to consider how the experiences of these incoming management educators might effect and shape the future of management education.

Of course, this is not always a sudden transformation: PhD students often engage in teaching as graduate teaching assistants and are socialized into being an academic through PhD programs (Prasad, 2013). Indeed, the PhD journey has often been referred to as an apprenticeship for an academic career (Austin, 2009; Bansel, 2011). Even so, the transition from PhD to ECA has been characterized as a liminal and often painful period of transition (Bristow, 2012; Prasad, 2015; Raineri, 2015). Our research into the experiences of CMS ECAs conveys how despite PhD socialization, many early career experiences are filled with shock, disorientation and disillusionment. In studying this transitional period and the disjunctures between ECAs' expectations of academia and the lived experience of working in the neoliberal business school, we have drawn on Bourdieu's notion of hysteresis (Bourdieu, 2002) to demonstrate how ECAs struggle to modify their (PhD) habitus (Bourdieu, 1990) to align with the expectations of their schools (Robinson et al., 2017).

Such disjuncture between expectations and practice sometimes leads to what we term "starting pains" (Robinson et al., 2017), characterized by a mismatch between realities such as: work overload and conveyer belt mentalities versus notions of vocation and nurturing teaching; lack of agency versus notions of academic freedom; and lack of support and mentorship from senior colleagues versus notions of collegiality. Dealing with the amount and type of teaching can be both a shock and a draining experience for many. ECAs talked of spending day and night including weekends marking, just sleeping briefly on the sofa, falling asleep at the dinner table, and having to develop three new courses in one semester (Robinson et al., 2017). This "conveyer belt" approach worked against their sense of responsibility as educators (Bristow et al., 2019; Robinson et al., 2017). Others talked of being bored with what they had been given to teach and not wanting to do the same thing for the next 20 years (Bristow et al., 2017). Initially not knowing what working conditions were acceptable and negotiable was a challenge for ECAs who lacked the experience and background knowledge to contest them. This was also impacted by often extremely heavy probationary targets (Ratle et al., 2020).

While the transition from PhD student to university employee can be a serious challenge, we found evidence that it is a time that can provide ECAs with opportunities to reappraise their expectations, reaffirm their convictions, and trace the path to their future. It is also a time for "job crafting," creating an opportunity to reflect on how they can do their work, and how they relate to it. Over time our participants developed what, following Bourdieu, we term a "critical habitus" where CMS ECAs put their critical credentials to good use finding ways of challenging unreasonable workloads and adapting mainstream courses by stealth to suit their own politics and preferences, or by reacting to the Zeitgeist to make their courses more critical when they see an interest or need from their students (Bristow et al., 2019). Our data highlighted an absence of good mentoring from senior colleagues, yet encouragingly it also showed much information-sharing amongst ECAs. Forming social networks thus allowed ECAs to share tips and tricks and build up courage to challenge managerial excesses (Bristow et al., 2017; Robinson et al., 2017).

Taken together, such practices amount to "small spaces of hopefulness" (Archer, 2008a: 282), which help ECAs individually and collectively to achieve acceptable teaching conditions but also to gain confidence to develop and change teaching approaches to fit their own sense of vocation and preferences. Such practices also help ECAs in the development of their own academic identities. Processes of academic identity development will be discussed in the following section.

Challenge 2: Crafting an Identity and Finding Meaning

The second challenge for ECAs is how to craft a professional identity for themselves and find meaning in their work as management educators. This necessitates developing and balancing all aspects of an academic role (teaching, research, and administration), as these are not always mutually supportive (Bristow et al., 2019). Crafting an academic identity is not an easy task as such identities tend to be insecure and fragile (Grey, 2010; Knights & Clarke, 2014). The audit and excellence cultures of the neoliberal business school have many mechanisms in place to measure "academic excellence" and judge academics on all aspects of their performance (Butler & Spoelstra, 2012, 2014; Jones et al., 2020). Trying and often failing to be the "ideal academic" (very narrowly defined), where one is never better than one's last publication or teaching evaluation is often in sharp contrast with trying to find meaning in academic work (Clarke, Knights, & Jarvis, 2012; Miller, Taylor, & Bedeian, 2011). Not surprisingly, performance anxiety and mental health issues have been growing in academia over the past decade (Morrish, 2019; Smith & Ulus, 2019) with universities being labeled "anxiety machines" (Hall & Bowles, 2016).

For ECAs, it could be argued that such identity challenges are exacerbated by the transitionary and precarious nature of the ECA experience which often involves fulfilling challenging probation criteria and being on a series of short-term contracts (Laudel & Gläser, 2008). Archer draws our attention to the plight of ECAs trying to be both "authentic" and "successful" academics who must negotiate on a daily basis not only their attempts at "becoming" but also the threat of "unbecoming" (Archer, 2008b: 385). How then do ECAs craft their academic identities and what identity work do they have to undertake in order to establish identities in line with their own ambitions and values but also which are in line with the exigencies of their multi-faceted roles?

In Bristow et al. (2017) we investigated academic identity creation and its interplay with resistance and compliance and demonstrated that ECAs use multiple and diverse ways of negotiating and developing their academic identities in response to strong normative pressures to conform – what could be interpreted as institutional identity regulation (Alvesson & Willmott, 2002). However, our research has shown that ECAs are not passive and docile worker-bodies who become inscribed with dominant managerial discourses (Thomas & Davies, 2005). Instead, they demonstrate considerable autonomy over their identity construction (Ezzamel, Willmott, & Worthington, 2001), actively engaging in "self-determined action and alternative subject positions" (Nentwich & Hoyer, 2013: 559).

ECAs went through a reflexive process of reproducing, maintaining, contesting, and transforming their sense of self (Alvesson & Willmott, 2002) in which they posed the questions "who am I?" and "who do I want to be?" in their working lives (Bristow et al., 2017). Such identity work becomes particularly important as the disjunctures between expectations and ambitions and life in contemporary business schools that we saw in Challenge 1 hit home for incoming academics. The following example shows the tensions between what sort of meaningful management educator/researcher an ECA wanted to be and the stark realities of the business school:

> I always wanted to become a teacher, and I enjoyed reading and researching. Being an academic meant being able to do both at the same time... I am doing teaching because we are raising the new generation; we are giving them something. And we are doing research to create something new... But a year ago, I realised we are doing teaching to get money ... and we are doing research because of the stupid REF which in the end means nothing. (Interviewee 2 *in* Bristow et al., 2017: 1198)

Much identity work would be needed to reconcile these two positions. What gave us hope was the energy ECAs put into picking themselves up following such disappointments and how they worked to forge their own paths through the system in ways which made them neither powerless victims of the system nor careerists fully capitulating to it (Clarke & Knights, 2015). Rather what we saw was ECAs engaging in a complex and nuanced dance between compliance and resistance (see also Challenge 3).

Several tactics were employed in developing their educator identities. One important manifestation of identity forging was their ability to develop themselves as CMS educators largely through micro-political practice. Examples include using critical questioning to challenge students firmly held beliefs through a sort of "micro-emancipation" (Alvesson & Willmott, 2002). This can come at a cost as speaking truth to power entails "risk and danger and threat" (Fournier & Smith, 2012: 467). One participant recounted a row with a senior colleague as she tried to change assessment to bring it more in line with her pedagogic values. Although she felt she had gone too far and suffered a sleepless night, she subsequently received an email from the colleague in question saying that he appreciated her taking a principled stand (Bristow et al., 2017 and interview data). Sometimes ECAs hid behind their perceived newness to do things that more seasoned colleagues would not dare to do. Others initially followed the normative paths pointed out to them, but at points in their journey had moments of epiphany where they realized, they needed to develop an academic identity they were more comfortable with. Such trigger points included, for example, being bored and unhappy with what they were teaching and researching, not finding meaning, or not getting the success they expected. Resolving such issues sometimes involved changing institutions, forging solidarity with other colleagues, or taking on stimulating external roles such as journal editing. So such apparent moments of crisis could be an opportunity for reflexivity, reassessment, and the making of important and positive career decisions, in other words: an opportunity for crafting identity.

Challenge 3: Finding a Balance between Resistance and Compliance

The challenges experienced by ECAs in transitioning from PhD to their first academic jobs (Challenge 1) and their struggles to construct meaningful academic identities (Challenge 2) led us to probe the extent of their agency. Given their struggles to establish themselves, what opportunities do ECAs actually have to make a difference and shape their field? And at what cost – to the ECAs and to management education – does this shaping currently occur?

From our own ECA experiences, from conversations with colleagues and from the ECA literature, we became aware of the tendency to construe ECAs as passive and helpless victims of the damaging effects of the HE system (Laudel & Gläser, 2008). This included even the best-meaning senior colleagues, who advised us to avoid speaking out and to keep a low profile. "Wait until you are more established," they would say, "then you can take a stand." We felt strongly, however, that such an approach underplays and, in some ways, even erodes ECA agency. Postponing ECA agency risks "domesticating" ECA critique, making it more "toothless" as junior scholars become enculturated into the norms and practices of the neoliberal "Brave New Higher Education" and less willing to initiate radical change (Bristow, 2012).

This links to the paradox of embedded agency, and in particular marginal actors being more willing but less able, and central actors being more able but less willing to institute change, which is a persistent conundrum in organizational and social theory (Hardy & Maguire, 2008; Seo & Creed, 2002). We explored this conundrum empirically (Bristow et al., 2017) by looking at CMS ECAs as a poignant "extreme case" because of their double marginality. Moreover, their critical orientation, which calls for reflexivity, de-naturalization, non-performativity, and anti-managerialism (Alvesson, Bridgman, & Willmott, 2009; Fournier & Grey, 2000) places them at odds with performative, neo-managerialist HE, and makes them acutely aware of this dissonance, and willing to challenge the established conventions and practices.

This is where the opportunity for agency lies. We found that this dissonance translates into an ongoing struggle to find a balance between resistance – in its subversive but also in its constitutive and transformative sense (Courpasson, Dany, & Clegg, 2012; Thomas & Hardy, 2011) of trying to make a difference and (re)shape the field – and compliance (keeping to existing norms and expectations). Due to their position, ECAs can avoid neither compliance nor resistance but have to engage in a continuous, tension-filled, contingent, and nuanced working out of their relationships to the conflicting manifestations of forces at the intersection of which they find themselves. To do this, they make use of the complexity and contradictions in the discourses and practices constituting the neoliberal business schools and their regime of "excellence" (Butler & Spoelstra, 2014). ECAs develop multiple strategies including a mixture of diplomatic compromise, radical heroism, and authentic idealism through which they navigate the complex power relations on a daily basis. Through this effort they produce more tensions and contradictions but also make use of overlaps between conflicting discourses and practices and create new alliances. In these every day, micro-emancipatory (Alvesson & Willmott, 2002) and micro-compliant ways they actively shape not only themselves but also the business schools in which they work.

The field-shaping willingness and capacity of CMS ECAs, which are in a particular challenging position due to their critical orientation, highlight the role of ECAs more generally in constituting the future of business schools and management education. Yet this role is currently perilous and comes at a great cost. Getting the balance between resistance and compliance wrong can have grave consequences, including alienation, mental and physical ill health, and loss of employment or voluntary departure from academia. Even where ECAs avoid those consequences, the sheer effort of the daily balancing act can be debilitating. We explore these issues in more depth in the sections on Challenges 4 and 5.

Challenge 4: Setting the Pace and Finding a Rhythm

A recurring theme emerging from our research is that starting an academic career in a contemporary business school is particularly challenging because of the ways in which academia and academic labor have changed over the last few decades. Much has been written about the commercialization, consumerization, marketization, and McDonaldization of academia (Fitzgerald, White, & Gunter, 2012; Furedi, 2002; Hayes & Wynyard, 2002; Huzzard, Benner, & Kärreman, 2017; Slaughter & Rhoades, 2004), which is now driven by a neoliberal new-managerialist governmentality characterized by the audit culture with its pervasive mechanisms of measuring and managing academic productivity and performance (Mingers & Willmott, 2013; Strathern, 2000; Tourish, Craig, & Amernic, 2017). One of the aspects of this "New Higher Education" (Jary & Parker, 1998) is the growing intensification and complexity of academic work.

In Bristow et al. (2019), we drew attention to the challenge this poses for ECAs in terms of trying to establish working rhythms and pace. Considering this challenge through Lefebvre's (2004) sociological notions of polyrhythmia, eurhythmia, and arrhythmia helps to appreciate its extent and implications. Lefebvre wrote of the pervasiveness and importance of rhythms in social and physical lives, and of the *polyrhythmic* nature of social and physical bodies. Polyrhythmia refers to the ways in which social and physical lives are organized through multiple and diverse rhythms, which sometimes coexist in harmony (i.e., *eurhythmically*) with each other and sometimes clash and conflict with each other, producing the dissonant state of *arrhythmia*. Similarly to medical arrhythmia (a life-threatening condition in which the heart beats with an irregular rhythm) sociological arrhythmia is a debilitating condition affecting the future of management education.

Comparing older literature on academic labor (e.g., Frost & Taylor, 1996) and our data, we found that academic lives are becoming increasingly polyrhythmic and arrhythmic, making eurhythmia increasingly elusive. In particular, changing prioritization of certain rhythms (typically those to do with the narrow notion of academic "excellence") over others; increasing temporal rigidity of deadlines and performance measures; fastening and intensifying pace of work; encroachment of previously "senior" rhythms (e.g., those of external funding applications and significant administrative roles) into the early-career years; and growing polyrhythmic complexity mean that there is an increasing proliferation of academic rhythms coexisting and vying for ECAs' attention and that these rhythms continually clash with each other. ECAs are thrown into the deep end of this rhythmic cacophony, faced with the expectations to deliver simultaneously on multiple fronts at the levels previously expected from much more senior academics and with no time to learn the multiple facets of academic work while trying to orchestrate this complexity.

In this context, we found that ECAs are faced with what we call a *vicious circle of arrhythmia*. Struggling to juggle many clashing rhythms and unbearable workloads, they attempt to develop coping strategies. These include embracing polyrhythmia (throwing themselves into everything and working at an unsustainable pace while hoping that this is a temporary measure before they become established), reducing polyrhythmia (knowingly and strategically abandoning some rhythms at the expense of others), creating eurhythmia (reshaping conflicting rhythms so as to make them more harmonic with each other) and escaping arrhythmia (moving universities or leaving academia altogether). These strategies can be brave and inventive, but with the exception of leaving academia (which creates a loss to the future of the profession) and strategically abandoning rhythms (which can create problems for career development, alienate ECAs, and erode the notion of the complete academic engaging in all aspects of scholarship (Boyer, 1990), they tend to have the effect of piling further rhythmic and workload burdens on already overloaded individuals, therefore making the problems worse. It is striking that the most promising and field-shaping strategy of finding ways of making conflicting rhythms more eurhythmic is also the most time-consuming, labor-intensive, and mentally and emotionally demanding for ECAs. Struggling to cope with arrhythmia adds its own new set of rhythms and arrhythmias to the rhythms and arrhythmias they are attempting to address. For these reasons, with the exception of leaving academia, it is hard for individuals to fundamentally break out of the vicious circle of arrhythmia.

Systemic time-related issues are notoriously difficult for individuals to resolve (Perlow, 1999), and it is therefore crucial that a more collective and radical approach is taken to addressing the vicious circle of academic arrhythmia if business schools and management education are to have a sustainable future. Current support mechanisms (e.g., training, mentorship schemes) are seen by many ECAs as largely ineffective, because they are mostly experienced as yet another demand on their time and yet another burden to bear. Rather than curing the underlying condition of arrhythmia they merely and superficially treat its symptoms; because they do not address the systemic issues, they end up contributing to them. What is needed instead is a bottom-up approach to ECA support and a much more gradual and realistic scaffolding of what is expected from ECAs during the early career stage in order to enable them to learn, grow, and develop. This approach needs to engulf all levels of university structures and processes and be supported through wider HE policy in order to effect a noticeable and sustainable change. This should go hand-in-hand with a deep reimagining of academic work, business schools, and management education. At its core, it links to rethinking what matters in society.

There are latent opportunities here to address the unsustainable pace, temporal constraints, and complexity of business school lives, reconsidering the effects of relentless neoliberal capitalist productivity and competition that are becoming even more apparent in the context of the 2020 pandemic. At this unique historical moment, when both global and local social, economic, mental, emotional, and physical resources are stretched ever further beyond their limits, the fundamentally unhealthy condition of academia places its people and institutions at an increasing risk of collapse. Now is the make-or-break time – an opportunity to make use of the widespread questioning of the "normal" ways of doing things to consider what truly matters and what should be set aside in rethinking the purpose of management education and its role in society. If this opportunity is not wasted, it could pave the way to a much more eurhythmic future.

Challenge 5: Dealing with Adverse Contexts

While the previous section depicted academia as an exhausting and potentially unhealthy place for many ECAs, here we add to this portrait by exploring how for some it can be a place characterized by fear, violence, and domination – key concepts we used in Ratle et al. (2020) to understand ECAs' experience of target-driven cultures. We wanted to problematize the audit culture within universities (Chandler, Barry, & Clark, 2002; Strathern, 2000; Tourish et al., 2017) and specifically business schools (Huzzard et al., 2017; Willmott, 2011), and to explore how, for ECAs whose careers are set against the background of externally imposed target-focused cultures (Jones et al., 2020; Mingers & Willmott, 2013), the inculcation of fear through processes of domination is a significant feature of their lived experience.

We draw on Bourdieu (1976, 1980, 2016) to distinguish modes of domination and their related forms of violence: *inert*, *overt*, and *symbolic*. Bourdieu argues that contemporary societies are generally characterized by "soft" forms of power. A lasting and stable social order requires the "dominated" to acquiesce in their own domination, thus domination must either be objectified and stabilized through impersonal institutional mechanisms – what Bourdieu (2016: 212) calls the inert violence of institutions – or mediated through close interpersonal encounters between the dominant and the dominated (2016: 212–213). Those interpersonal modes of domination operate through two forms of violence: overt violence (Bourdieu, 1980: 217–218) and symbolic violence.

Inert violence was something present in the discourse of most of our participants, who viewed the university systems as being imposing, impersonal, and largely incomprehensible. This inert violence of institutions is enacted in a variety of places, such as: workload models skewed to generate heavy workloads, rules around work visas that render foreign citizens vulnerable to abuse and exploitation, or contractual rules asymmetrically imposed that legitimize exploitative arrangements. The negative effects of this inert violence were many and included: feelings of isolation and confusion; feelings of being crushed, undervalued, and bullied by the system; feeling constantly under surveillance; fear of failure to perform adequately and having no recourse to appeal; or fear of losing their jobs for arbitrary and unjustified reasons.

Overt or economic violence involves the direct enforcement of power relations through "physical threat or the threat of economic ruin" (Bourdieu, 1976: 1990). This is relevant to academia given the widespread precarity to which ECAs are particularly vulnerable (Bataille, Le Feuvre, & Kradolfer Morales, 2017). Our participants experienced how the impersonal exigencies of the audit systems were mediated through interpersonal relations with line managers, members of evaluation committees, or deans. We heard many times the "shifting goalposts" story, where the slipperiness of targets and the lack of clear guidelines led to distressing situations. One participant was told that while the targets set to pass probation and achieve permanence of employment had been met, that was invalid, as the targets were too low in the first place. Another was told that under previous rules, the publication targets had been met, but that under brand new rules, the worth of those publications was demoted, and that the targets were now unmet.

Overt violence requires more effort for the dominant to enact, and as such, is less "efficient" than the "softer," more subtle and seductive strategies of *symbolic violence* (Bourdieu, 1976: 191; Kerr & Robinson, 2012), which can be understood as the imposition and misrecognition of arbitrary power relations as natural and legitimate (Bourdieu, 1976). In Ratle et al. (2020), we argue like Roumbanis (2018) that it is well embedded within university cultures, and we show how this subtle form of violence is exercised through line management relationships and other day-to-day governance mechanisms. For example, personal development reviews can be more about hitting targets (Tourish et al., 2017) than supporting, nurturing, and guiding new entrants into the profession. Some participants pointed out that mentoring relationships can have two sides:

mentors can genuinely help the development of ECAs, but they can also enforce the demands of the system. While we set out to draw attention to symbolic violence, ultimately, we were astonished by how important inert and overt violence were in the accounts of ECAs. This can suggest that symbolic violence goes unrecognized, but also that academia may rely more on inert and overt violence, making it (from a Bourdieusian point of view) a relatively ineffective machine of domination. This offers another glimmer of hope, and an opportunity for agency.

We also sought to account for how ECAs dealt with such adverse contexts using those opportunities for agency. The emerging theme here is similar to those highlighted in Challenges 3 and 4 – namely that ECAs are far from being passive recipients of violence but rather strive to make a positive difference to their own working lives. However, they are also constrained and impacted by the pervasive violence of the system, which has consequences for the extent and effects of their actions. We explored this tension using Meyerson and Scully's (1995) notion of tempered radicals, who are "individuals who identify with ... their organizations and are also committed to a cause, community or ideology that is ... at odds with the dominant culture of the organization" (Meyerson & Scully, 1995: 586). Such individuals are "radicals" because they challenge the status quo, but they are also "tempered" in the sense that they seek moderation, and like steel in a fire, are strengthened by experience while retaining their temper (or anger) against the dominant culture. Seeing ECAs as tempered radicals enabled us to identify many individualized small acts of resistance against a powerful regime, but we also saw a danger that those acts of resistance ultimately reinforce the system they are meant to fight against. This is because in dealing with adversity, ECAs often end up being violent toward themselves, as well as being violent toward the system that exerts violence upon them. The hope for a better future of management education, by contrast, is to eradicate its violence much more radically – the opportunity for which lies in collective action and approaches.

Discussion

After nearly a decade of studying the predicament of ECAs, our solution to many of the problems they face is simple: ECAs need structures of support that are genuinely and sincerely aimed at developing and nurturing their careers. This would be in contrast with many existing structures which, under the appearances of promoting personal development, are merely elaborate disciplinary mechanisms. A measure of success would be that those structures, rather than instilling the fear and anxiety described in Challenge 5, would create something like joy and genuine enthusiasm, and a sense that one has control and freedom over their own career and academic practice. In fact, those feelings should ideally characterize the entire experience of working in a university – something that still has the potential to be a wonderful and meaningful occupation, as many of our research participants highlighted. So how can we get there?

First, we wish to reemphasize the importance and the opportunity of academic activism, and the potential role ECAs can play. By simple virtue of being newcomers, ECAs do not have the same stakes in the "old ways" of doing, and they can be the catalyst for real changes in management education. Society is confronted with crises on different fronts – economic, social, political, environmental, and the multi-faceted consequences of the 2020 pandemic. Echoing Jones et al. (2020), we refuse to give-in to pessimism, as crises often reconfigure power relations and create opportunities for agency. This is a moment to seize for radical reforms on all these fronts, and within the different spheres of academic work. As *teachers*, we see an opportunity for ECAs to privilege values-based education, replacing the technocratic agenda of mainstream management education with a search for purpose and meaning. As *scholars*, we see an opportunity for a deeper and more public engagement with societal issues (in the UK context, "impact" is exactly what national research policies profess to want to achieve). And as *colleagues*, we see an opportunity for ECAs to exemplify and enact a different way of being an academic, and to be the agents of this much needed transformation.

Second, as we have argued in each and all of our collective writings (Bristow et al., 2017, 2019; Ratle et al., 2020; Robinson et al., 2017), how ECAs individually respond to the pressures and the challenges they face can often be contributing to reproducing or even worsening those pressures. For example, we have discussed how ECAs' commitment to the profession can lead them to accept more hardship than they should (Robinson et al., 2017), and the individual strategies developed to deal with unbearable workloads can create a vicious circle of arrhythmia (Bristow et al., 2019), rendering the problem even more acute. We have seen also how, by trying to deal with adversity and deal with a system that exerts violence upon them, ECAs can end up being violent toward themselves. We hope that this chapter and our work preceding it will contribute to raising consciousness about the limitations of individual strategies and coping mechanisms.

This brings us to our *third* point, derived from the previous one: if the effectiveness of individual strategies is limited, collective and concerted action is essential. Who is meant to be part of this "collective action" is the final question we wish to discuss here. We are tempted to say: "Everyone!," and it is probably true that different stakeholders have a role to play: ECAs themselves, but also their colleagues, and middle and senior academic managers. Deep structural and radical change does not happen easily, and ECAs could benefit from as many allies as they can enlist. However, it is also clear to us that such transformation cannot happen without ECAs, and that their senior colleagues cannot solely be relied upon, even with all the best intentions in the world. While we have discussed in Challenge 3 the paradox of embedded agency (marginal actors are more willing but less able to institute change, while central actors are more able but less willing), here we wish to turn our focus on the question of ECAs diversity, and what it could mean for the future.

Conclusion

Taking stock of the five challenges described in this chapter, one can feel that starting a career can be a real obstacle course. A few will survive and thrive, some will merely survive, and some will not survive at all. We are concerned about the possibility that each of these challenges, if not addressed, could contribute toward the homogeneisation of academia. Individuals who thrive in academia can appear as a relatively homogeneous group of individuals who are willing and able to make great personal sacrifices, and to find a narrow niche to publish within, ideally in large quantity. In relation to this homogeneous group, there is a second group which, everything suggests, is becoming bigger: those who merely survive, or who simply leave academia. Whether or not this section of academia has a voice will be indicative of what the future holds.

We are concerned that this disadvantaged group appears to come from so-ciodemographic groups that are already underrepresented within academia. It has always been the case that, for example, being a woman, a single parent, or not being white, all bring additional challenges to being an academic. Speaking from a UK context, we could add to that list speaking with a regional accent or having studied in a non-elite institution (Śliwa & Johansson, 2013), or simply being perceived as "a foreigner." We are seeing Brexit reshaping society, and some of us have been called upon to understand its profound impact (Bristow & Robinson, 2018). In society at large, we may wonder who is welcome in this post-Brexit era, and who becomes marginalized and excluded. In the work-place, many accounts are emerging of non-native workers suffering new forms of discrimination in a context where those holding nativist or xenophobic views feel emboldened to express them. Considering that in the UK, over a quarter of the academic workforce (28% in 2014/2015) are non-UK nationals (Royal Society, 2016), universities could become foci of new forms of hostilities and exclusion, both from the inside (Johnson & Joseph-Salisbury, 2018) and from the outside, where a potent mixture of racism, xenophobia, colonial mentality, and anti-intellectualism all participate in silencing from the public sphere voices that are traditionally more critical.

While this is a bleak picture, times of upheaval also offer opportunities, and we find hope in seeing colleagues taking the mantra of "intellectual activism" (Contu, 2017, 2020; Rhodes, Wright, & Pullen, 2018) to call out and challenge racism and exclusion in the business school (Dar, Liu, Dy, & Brewis, 2020). Fighting against exclusion and toward diversity in the University is traditionally associated with student activism (Rhoads, 2016), and as we advocate for a more public engagement from scholars (Bristow & Robinson, 2018), we cherish the hope that ECAs will also seize this opportunity to ensure that it is them – as a plurality of voices – who are shaping the future.

References

Alvesson, M., Bridgman, T., & Willmott, H. 2009. Introduction. In M. Alvesson, T. Bridgman, & H. Willmott (Eds.), *The Oxford handbook of critical management studies*: 1–26. Oxford: Oxford University Press.

Alvesson, M., & Willmott, H. 2002. Identity regulation as organizational control: Producing the appropriate individual. *Journal of Management Studies*, 39: 619–644.

Archer, L. 2008a. The new neoliberal subjects? Young/er academics' constructions of professional identity. *Journal of Education Policy*, 23: 265–285.

Archer, L. 2008b. Younger academics constructions of authenticity, success and professional identify. *Studies in Higher Education*, 33: 385–403.

Austin, A. E. 2009. Cognitive apprenticeship theory and its implications for doctoral education: A case example from a doctoral program in higher and adult education. *International Journal for Academic Development*, 14: 173–183.

Bansel, P. 2011. Becoming academic: A reflection on doctoral candidacy. *Studies in Higher Education*, 36: 543–556.

Bataille, P., Le Feuvre, N., & Kradolfer Morales, S. 2017. Should I stay or should I go? The effects of precariousness on the gendered career aspirations of postdocs in Switzerland. *European Educational Research Journal*, 16: 313–331.

Bourdieu, P. 1976. Les modes de domination. *Actes de la Recherche en Sciences Sociales*, 2: 122–132.

Bourdieu, P. 1980. *Le sens pratique*. Paris: Minuit.

Bourdieu, P. 1990. *The logic of practice*. Stanford, CA: Stanford University Press.

Bourdieu, P. 2002. *Le bal des célibataires. Crise de la société paysanne en Béarn*. Paris: Seuil.

Bourdieu, P. 2016. *Sociologie générale, Volume 2. Cours au Collège de France (1983–1986)*. Paris: Raisons d'agir/Seuil.

Boyer, E. L. 1990. *Scholarship reconsidered: Priorities of the professoriate*. The Carnegie Foundation for the Advancement of Teaching, New York: John Wiley and Sons.

Bristow, A. 2012. On life, death and radical critique: A non-survival guide to the brave new higher education for the intellectually pregnant. *Scandinavian Journal of Management*, 28: 234–241.

Bristow, A., & Robinson, S. 2018. Speaking out: Brexiting CMS. *Organization*, 25: 636–648.

Bristow, A., Robinson, S., & Ratle, O. 2017. Being an early-career CMS academic in the context of insecurity and 'excellence': The dialectics of resistance and compliance. *Organization Studies*, 38: 1185–1207.

Bristow, A., Robinson, S., & Ratle, O. 2019. Academic arrhythmia: Disruption, dissonance and conflict in the early-career rhythms of CMS academics. *Academy of Management Learning and Education*, 18: 241–260.

Butler, N., & Spoelstra, S. 2012. Your excellency. *Organization*, 19: 891–903.

Butler, N., & Spoelstra, S. 2014. The regime of excellence and the erosion of ethos in critical management studies. *British Journal of Management*, 25: 538–550.

Chandler, J., Barry, J., & Clark, H. 2002. Stressing academe: The wear and tear of the new public management. *Human Relations*, 55: 1051–1069.

Clarke, C., Knights, D., & Jarvis, C. 2012. A labour of love? Academics in business schools. *Scandinavian Journal of Management*, 28: 5–15.

Clarke, C. A., & Knights, D. 2015. Careering through academia: Securing identities or engaging ethical subjectivities? *Human Relations*, 68: 1865–1888.

Contu, A. 2017. '...The point is to change it' – Yes, but in what direction and how? Intellectual activism as a way of 'walking the talk' of critical work in business schools. *Organization*, 25: 282–293.

Contu, A. 2020. Answering the crisis with intellectual activism: Making a difference as business schools scholars. *Human Relations*, 73: 737–757.

Courpasson, D., Dany, F., & Clegg, S. 2012. Resisters at work: Generating productive resistance in the workplace. *Organization Science*, 23: 801–819.

Dar, S., Liu, H., Dy, A. M., & Brewis, D. N. 2020. The business school is racist: Act up! *Organization*, Epub ahead of print July 2. 10.1177/1350508420928521

Ezzamel, M., Willmott, H., & Worthington, F. 2001. Power, control and resistance in the factory that time forgot. *Journal of Management Studies*, 38: 1053–1078.

Fitzgerald, T., White J., & Gunter, H. 2012. *Hard labour? Academic work and the changing landscape of higher education.* Bingley, WYK: Emerald Group Publishing.

Fournier, V., & Grey, C. 2000. At the critical moment: Conditions and prospects for critical management studies. *Human Relations*, 53: 7–32.

Fournier, V., & Smith, W. 2012. Making choice, taking risk: On the coming out of CMS. *Ephemera*, 12: 463–474.

Frost, P. J., & Taylor, M. S. 1996. *Rhythms of academic life: Personal accounts of careers in academia.* Thousand Oaks, CA: Sage.

Furedi, F. 2002. The bureaucratization of the British university. In D. Hayes & R. Wynyard (Eds.), *The McDonaldization of higher education*: 33–42. Portsmouth, NH: Greenwood Press.

Grey, C. 2010. Organizing studies: Publications, politics and polemic. *Organization Studies*, 31: 677–694.

Hall, R., & Bowles, K. 2016. Re-engineering higher education: The subsumption of academic labour and the exploitation of anxiety. *Workplace: A Journal for Academic Labor*, 28: 38–47.

Hardy, C., & Maguire, S. 2008. Institutional entrepreneurship. In R. Greenwood, C. Oliver, T. B. Lawrence, & R. E. Meyer (Eds.), *The Sage handbook of organizational institutionalism*: 198–217. London: Sage.

Harris, S. 2005. Rethinking academic identities in neo-liberal times. *Teaching in Higher Education*, 10: 421–433.

Hayes, D., & Wynyard, R. (Eds.). 2002. *The McDonaldization of higher education.* Portsmouth, NH: Greenwood Press.

Henkel, M. 2004. Current science policies and their implications for the formation and maintenance of academic identity. *Higher Education Policy*, 17: 167–182.

Huzzard, T., Benner, M., & Kärreman, D. (Eds.). 2017. *The corporatization of the business school: Minerva meets the market.* London: Routledge.

Jary, D., & Parker, M. (Eds.). 1998. *The new higher education: Dilemmas and directions for the post-dearing university.* Stoke-on-Trent, UK: Staffordshire University Press.

Johnson, A., & Joseph-Salisbury, R. 2018. 'Are you supposed to be in here?' Racial microaggressions and knowledge production in higher education: Racism, whiteness and decolonising the academy. In J. Arday & H. Mirza (Eds.), *Dismantling race in higher education: Racism, whiteness and decolonising the academy*: 143–160. Cham: Palgrave Macmillan.

Jones, D. R., Visser, M., Stokes, P., Örtenblad, A., Deem, R., Rodgers, P., & Tarba, S. Y. 2020. The performative university: 'Targets', 'terror' and 'taking back freedom' in academia. *Management Learning*, 51: 363–377.

Kerr, R., & Robinson, S. 2012. From symbolic violence to economic violence: The globalizing of the Scottish banking elite. *Organization Studies*, 33: 247–266.

Knights, D., & Clarke, C. A. 2014. It's a bittersweet symphony, this life: Fragile academic selves and insecure identities at work. *Organization Studies*, 35: 335–357.

Laudel, G., & Gläser, J. 2008. From apprentice to colleague: The metamorphosis of early career researchers. *Higher Education*, 55: 387–406.

Lefebvre, H. 2004. *Rhythmanalysis: Space, time and everyday life*. London: Continuum.

Meyerson, D. E., & Scully, M. A. 1995. Tempered radicalism and the politics of ambivalence and change. *Organization Science*, 6: 585–600.

Miller, A. N., Taylor, S. G., & Bedeian, A. G. 2011. Publish or perish: Academic life as management faculty live it. *Career Development International*, 16: 422–445.

Mingers, J., & Willmott, H. 2013. Taylorizing business school research: On the 'one best way' performative effects of journal ranking lists. *Human Relations*, 66: 1051–1073.

Morrish, L. 2019. *Pressure vessels: The epidemic of poor mental health among higher education staff*, HEPI Occasional Paper 20. London: Higher Education Policy Institute. https://www.hepi.ac.uk/wp-content/uploads/2019/05/HEPI-Pressure-Vessels-Occasional-Paper-20.pdf

Nentwich, J., & Hoyer, P. 2013. Part-time work as practising resistance: The power of counter-arguments. *British Journal of Management*, 24: 557–570.

Perlow, L. A. 1999. The time famine: Toward a sociology of work time. *Administrative Science Quarterly*, 44: 57–81.

Prasad, A. 2013. Playing the game and trying not to lose myself: A doctoral student's perspective on the institutional pressures for research output. *Organization*, 20: 936–948.

Prasad, A. 2015. Liminal transgressions, or where should the critical academy go from here? Reimagining the future of doctoral education to engender research sustainability. *Critical Perspectives on Accounting*, 26: 108–116.

Raineri, N. 2015. Business doctoral education as a liminal period of transition: Comparing theory and practice. *Critical Perspectives on Accounting*, 26: 99–107.

Ratle, O., Robinson, S., Bristow, A., & Kerr, R. 2020. Mechanisms of micro-terror? Early career CMS academics' experiences of 'targets and terror' in contemporary business schools. *Management Learning*, 51: 452–471.

Rhoads, R. A. 2016. Student activism, diversity, and the struggle for a just society. *Journal of Diversity in Higher Education*, 9: 189–202.

Rhodes, C., Wright, C., & Pullen, A. 2018. Changing the world? The politics of activism and impact in the neoliberal university. *Organization*, 25: 139–147.

Robinson, S., Ratle, O., & Bristow, A. 2017. Labour pains: Starting a career within the neoliberal university. *Ephemera*, 17: 481–508.

Roumbanis, L. 2018. Symbolic violence in academic life: A study on how junior scholars are educated in the art of getting funded. *Minerva*, 57: 197–218.

Royal Society. 2016. *UK research and the European Union: The role of the EU in international research collaboration and researcher mobility*. https://royalsociety.org/-/media/policy/projects/eu-uk-funding/phase-2/EU-role-in-international-research-collaboration-and-researcher-mobility.pdf

Seo, M. G., & Creed, W. E. D. 2002. Institutional contradictions, praxis, and institutional change: A dialectical perspective. *The Academy of Management Review*, 27: 222–247.

Slaughter, S., & Rhoades, G. 2004. *Academic capitalism and the new economy: Markets, state and higher education*. Baltimore and London: John Hopkins University Press.

Śliwa, M., & Johansson, M. 2013. Playing in the academic field: Non-native English-speaking academics in UK business schools. *Culture and Organization*, 21: 78–95.

Smith, C., & Ulus, E. 2019. Who cares for academics? We need to talk about emotional well-being including what we avoid and intellectualize through macro-discourses. *Organization*, Epub ahead of print August 12. 10.1177/1350508419867201.

Smith, J. 2010. Forging identities: The experiences of probationary lecturers in the UK. *Studies in Higher Education*, 35: 577–591.

Strathern, M. (Ed.). 2000. *Audit cultures: Anthropological studies in accountability, ethics and the academy*. London: Routledge.

Thomas, R., & Davies, A. 2005. Theorizing the micro-politics of resistance: New public management and managerial identities in the UK public services. *Organization Studies*, 26: 683–706.

Thomas, R., & Hardy, C. 2011. Reframing resistance to organizational change. *Scandinavian Journal of Management*, 27: 322–331.

Tourish, D., Craig, R., & Amernic, J. 2017. A mania for assessment: How an audit culture undermines the purpose of universities. In T. Huzzard, M. Benner, & D. Kärreman (Eds.), *The corporatization of the business school: Minerva meets the market*: 34–55. London: Routledge.

Trowler, P., & Knight, P. T. 2000. Coming to know in higher education: Theorising faculty entry to new work contexts. *Higher Education Research & Development*, 19: 27–42.

Willmott, H. 2011. Journal list fetishism and the perversion of scholarship: Reactivity and the ABS list. *Organization*, 18: 429–442.

PART II

Prospects and Perspectives of ME

6

MANAGEMENT EDUCATION AND INTERPERSONAL GROWTH: A HUMANIST TRANSCENDENTAL-PERSONALIST PERSPECTIVE

Kleio Akrivou, Manuel Joaquín Fernadez Gonzalez, Germán Scalzo, and Ricardo Murcio Rodriguez

Introduction: Why Renew Management Education?

The COVID-19 pandemic has made it evident that the ecological, health, and societal challenges we face in the twenty-first century are now, without doubt, a shared global concern. Presenting significant challenges for businesses and management education (ME) alike, this reality offers both the opportunity to renew their sense of purpose toward fomenting the sustained good life for all beyond profitability, i.e., contributing to the common good. And, indeed, all kinds of organizations, including commercial ones, have stepped up to contribute to public health maintenance and improvement. We believe this moment provides the opportunity for future ME, along with management and economics more broadly, to go forward as human activities that intend to facilitate purposive, goal-oriented actions for promoting the common good (Lutz, 2018; Tirole, 2017).

At the beginning of the twenty-first century, awareness of the necessity of revisiting the purpose of management education to avoid unethical or amoral management and leadership was aroused by corporate scandals in the United States and elsewhere. Given the key role of ME in shaping leaders' ethical behavior (Conrad, 2018), business schools and ME practices increasingly came under question regarding their role, relevance, and purpose (e.g., Bennis & O'Toole, 2005), being accused of dallying in surface-level social transformation and lauding uninspiring and unfulfilled promises that perpetuate "the triumph of the market" and replicate market managerialism (Khurana, 2010).

Many managers and management educators have taken these critiques to heart. Interest in business ethics and in corporate social responsibility has notably increased among managers (Conrad, 2018; Ghoshal, 2005), giving rise to an

DOI: 10.4324/9781003095903-8

impressive movement that advocates for corporate humanistic responsibility (Arnaud & Wasieleski, 2014) and in favor of more humanistic, people-oriented approaches to business and management, including global professional networks (e.g., Grassl & Habisch, 2011; Melé, 2016; Rocha & Miles, 2009).

Mirroring managers' concern, some management educators have started to move away from the mechanistic paradigm in which business schools are simply considered a professional training ground that prioritizes the teaching of "useful" content, and have started seeing humanistic ME as the way forward (Amann, Pirson, Dierksmeier, Von Kimakowitz, & Spitzeck, 2011; Gagliardi & Czarniawska, 2006; Fukami et al., this volume; Lepeley, Von Kimakowitz, & Bardy, 2016). As a result, ethics, responsibility, and sustainability (ERS) are being integrated into all aspects of business education, and most of the 16,000 business and management programs worldwide have introduced or significantly re-inforced the provision of business ethics and humanistic concerns in under-graduate and graduate programs and core courses, often as a key compulsory offering in MBA programs. In addition, business school accreditation bodies currently include ERS criteria in accreditation standards and reviews (Cho, Dyllick, Falkenstein, Killian, O'Regan, & Reno, 2014), and humanistic ME has also reached the field of management theory (Pirson, 2019; Hommel et al., this volume; Bryant et al., this volume).

This response is quite impressive in terms of effort and investment. But how efficient is it for eradicating the ethical problems that provoked it? And how sustainably can it foresee and deal with future ethical issues? To address these questions, we must look in more detail at the current approaches involved in humanistic ME.

Humanism in ME: Current Approaches and Their Shortcomings

In the scientific literature, two main approaches to humanist management and ME can be distinguished: the human dignity approach and the sustainability approach. The former focuses on the promotion of human dignity and well-being (Dierksmeier, 2016; Pirson, 2017, 2019). In this view, those values make life worthwhile, and while they cannot be traded on markets they are nonetheless seen as an important tool for protecting dignity and contributing to well-being. This perspective offers a humanistic alternative to more dominant practices that commodify human experience and prioritize profit and productivity and pro-poses the integration and use of human dignity and human rights governance as a new management education paradigm (Albareda & Aguado, 2015).

Humanistic impulses in ME have largely been embraced with a second approach, i.e., Sustainability in Management Education (SiME). About 15 years ago, the idea of sustainability entered the field of ME and research (Stead & Stead, 2010; Wankel & Stoner, 2009) and, since then, SiME has developed rapidly, adopting the Sustainable Development Goals (SDG). The SDG contain deeply humanistic concerns (Herrmann & Rundshagen, 2020) such as fighting poverty and hunger, and pursuing good health and well-being, quality education and gender parity in education. The relevance of this trend is reflected in the increasing amount of SiME-related scientific publications, including academic books (Kassel & Rimanoczy, 2018), handbooks (Arevalo & Mitchell, 2017), benchmark studies (Wymer & Rundle-Thiele, 2017) and systematic literature reviews (Figueiró & Raufflet, 2015). This trend is also visible among practitioners – currently, there are some 650 management-related higher education institutions that formally adhere to the Principles of Responsible Management Education (PRME), a UN-supported initiative founded in 2007 that aims to provide future leaders with skills for balancing economic and sustainability goals. The PRME has also been the object of an increasing body of research (for a recent review, see Parkes, Buono, & Howaidy, 2017).

These two approaches (management for human dignity and SiME) are interconnected (Aguado & Albareda, 2016) in that both promote a kind of purposeful management that serves human dignity and the planet; for example, the 2030 Agenda for Sustainable Development (DESA UN, 2016) seeks to guarantee that the dignity, equality, and full potential of all human beings can be fulfilled.

Against this backdrop, it would seem reasonable to think that the humanistic movement in ME is enhancing future managers' awareness of what it means to be human, and how to lead a good life that does not damage the earth. However, according to Tourish (2020: 99), "[m]ore management scholars than ever are expressing concern about the state of our field." The effectiveness of humanistic ME, in its current form, in helping students and professors understand the deeper ethical meaning of the business world, and to foresee future ethical issues, is up for question (Rivera, 2019). It is therefore timely and relevant to look critically at the foundations of current approaches in humanistic ME, and provide a more profoundly humanistic perspective to future ME students, empowering them to work with increased awareness of and a more robust commitment to the good of society and human flourishing.

Humanistic ME is based on a certain understanding of what human beings are or, as Conrad put it, on "the image of humans" (2018: 47) underlying it. Pirson (2017: 26) argued that "one of the critical stepping-stones to better management theory and practice is a better and more accurate understanding of who we are as people." In this context, a number of voices contend that anthropology should be more relevant in business schools (Rivera, 2019). For example, the SiME approach acknowledges the importance of philosophical and anthropological knowledge in ME regarding sustainability (Vidal & da Silva Martins, 2017) and facilitates the development of a deeper capacity for reflection on the transcendence of management activity.

The need for anthropology in ME is well established, but *what concept of human beings underlies the humanistic discourse in ME today? Should it be challenged?*

When looking at the way anthropology is currently addressed in humanistic ME, two main shortfalls emerge, namely in some cases, the implicit presence of a "mechanistic humanism"; in other cases, an eclectic and partial view of human beings. We address them in more detail below.

Even if, as explained in the introduction, humanistic management in ME is progressively replacing mechanistic management, a relevant trend in humanist management still psychologically articulates the human factor and treats it mechanistically like an engineering component whereby scientific management remains unquestioned. Most dominant theories of responsible management set normative expectations for the role of management, whereby groups or persons are not considered per se priority stakeholders, but rather groups/agents in a synergistic relationship geared mainly toward the organization's benefit (Phillips, Freeman, & Wicks, 2003). However, according to Derksen (2014), human management is found in the articulation of freedom and responsibility as the essence of the human factor (p. 164). "Mechanistic humanism" is also influential in ME – in many cases, humanistic concern is presented as a means of avoiding future economic crises, rather than a way of prioritizing human beings (Rivera, 2019). Therefore, according to Dierksmeier (2020), we must still transition from mechanistic ME to true humanistic management learning, going "beyond the current conception of the human being as a maximizer of preferences" (Vidal & da Silva Martins, 2017: 151).

Several recent anthropological proposals (unconvincingly) address the shortcomings of the "mechanistic humanism" anthropological approach. For example, Pirson (2017), echoing many other voices, questions the traditional paradigm of the *homo oeconomicus* and its successor, Jensen and Meckling's (1994) REMM (the Resourceful, Evaluative, Maximizing Model), and sketches a humanistic description of human beings which, among other insights, includes evolutionary biology theory, stressing the biological roots of human sociability, empathy and emotionality, morality and altruism. However, this anthropological proposal seems quite eclectic and incomplete – Pirson's (2017: 26–57) sketch of human nature is in fact a collection of insights from the natural and social sciences and from the humanities, and fails to provide a unifying picture of human beings. Other (incomplete) proposals are based on ME students' need to meet social expectations, or on the promotion of personal and societal flourishing (Vidal & da Silva Martins, 2017), but they do not holistically address students' self identity and sense of purpose.

In short, these alternative anthropological proposals for ME lack a comprehensive and unifying conception of human beings and would benefit from an overarching humanistic philosophical framework that integrates selfhood, morality, action theory and social concern toward a new humanistic sense of economic activity. The case of Jensen is illustrative of the need for a more radical shift regarding ME's underlying anthropological paradigm. Up to 2002,

Jensen held an extreme mechanistic position that rebuked ME's teaching values, but more recently changed his views (Erhard & Jensen, 2011, 2013), stressing that management studies' main function is found in empowering students to give authentic expression to their personal values in their professional lives. However, "[h]is remaining within a positivistic framework ultimately impedes the kind of progress Michael Jensen envisions for business studies" (Dierksmeier, 2020: 73). We thus argue that current anthropological perspectives in ME should be enlarged with a sounder, more comprehensive understanding of the main economic actor, namely *the human person*. For this task, the transcendental personalist perspective, which is presented in the next section, offers a unified understanding of human beings as persons from which ME curricula could benefit.

Transcendental Personalism and Features of Personalist Management

This section addresses what it means to be a *manager with a transcendental personalist mindset*. Transcendental personalist anthropology, developed by Leonardo Polo (1998, 2003), is based on realist personalist philosophy (Mounier, 1936; Spaemann, 2006; see Burgos, 2018, for an introduction), which builds on Aristotelian virtue ethics and sees the human being as an end in itself. Polo's most relevant insight for this chapter is his answer to the question "What is the most profound reality (that characterizes us) as human beings?"

According to him (Polo & Corazón, 2005: 10), at least "as far as the West is concerned ... there have been ... three ways of focusing or accentuating the most important thing in human beings," what he called "human radicals," namely the "classical radical" which stresses our common human nature and its perfectibility through the acquisition of virtues, the "modern radical" which highlights human subjectivity as the locus of the autonomous self and of freedom, and the "personal radical" which underlines the person's uniqueness, relationality, and transcendence of her actions.

Among these three radicals (from "radix" or roots), which capture human facets from different philosophical traditions (the Greek, the modernist, and the Christian ones, respectively), Polo identifies the personal radical as the most complete one because it synthesizes and redirects the insights of the other radicals into a higher, personalistic form. In a personalist understanding, the person freely opens her selfhood and intimacy to an interpersonal, caring relationship with others, which is manifested through virtuous actions. Transcendental personalism's understanding of human beings and its implications regarding what it means to be a manager can be condensed into three points: (1) the person's intimacy and the manager's selfhood, (2) the person's transcendence and the manager's interpersonal growth, and (3) the person's manifestative actions and the manager's activity.

Personal Intimacy and Managers' Selfhood

Each person possesses intimacy, which is the source of her dignity and makes her unique and absolutely original. Therefore, personalist managers are cognizant of others' and their dignity and worth, transcendence and uniqueness; they genuinely care for every human being affected by their managerial activity.

The person's intimate selfhood is a complex whole of emotions, intentions, agency, decisions, and understandings, but each person has a *telos*, i.e., a potentiality and a call to grow as a human being, and this purpose marks her personal path in life. In this regard, personalist managers are called to put the richness of their intimacy into managerial work and to seek to integrate their professional vocation and activity into a more general life purpose. This also requires honest self-inquiry to avoid moral hypocrisy (Batson, Thompson, Seuferling, Whitney, & Strongman, 1999), i.e., the tendency toward preserving self-esteem by convincing ourselves of our morality and goodness.

Given the strong relational dimension of the managerial vocation, personalist managers' sense of self is close to what has been referred to as the "relational-self-of-virtue" (Fernández González, 2019), understood as a deep disposition toward virtuous growth in communities of virtue. This also entails a sense of personal and professional vocation that aspires to use one's freedom and socioprofessional role as a service to the other (Akrivou, Orón, & Scalzo, 2020), rather than for personal profit.

The Person's Transcendence and Managers' Interpersonal Growth

According to transcendental personalism, the person's moral development is per se transcendental, in the sense of transpersonal and interpersonal.[1] Humans are relational beings whose intimacy is open to other intimacies. Every human person is intrinsically called to live and to grow for someone and with someone rather than for herself and by herself, and therefore, moral development is catalyzed in coexistence: expansive two-way interpersonal relations are the locus (context) that witnesses the growth of all persons involved. Therefore, transcendental personalist managers freely engage in genuine, radical care (and not the appearance thereof) for the flourishing of all those who are influenced by their work, directly and indirectly. They are "virtuous leaders" (Havard, 2018) who seek to grow in virtue by focusing on the moral growth of their followers, whose dignity they willingly acknowledge. Furthermore, in the firm, they try to create an atmosphere of mutual respect and appreciation and a culture of mutual support and healthy emulation rather than of competitiveness.

Interpersonal relations are not established automatically – they are premised upon each person's transcendental freedom. In transcendental personalism, freedom is conceived of as a "freedom-*for-self-giving*" to another person.[2]

Accordingly, personalist managers use personal agency (freedom-*for*) to create opportunities for cultivating interpersonal friendship and engaging in effusive two-way self-giving relationships, and they freely orientate their decision-making power toward the enhancement of others' well-being. For example, when figuring out the best place for an employee in the enterprise, they prioritize his/her flourishing as a human being over maximization of benefits for the organization.

Acting in this self-giving way entails a source of motivation that draws from the perception of the intrinsic, transcendent value of every person. Personalist managers freely serve others with the best of themselves, guided by altruistic motives and genuine empathy (Batson & Moran, 1999), not from a "psychological need to serve," as is the case of so-called servant leadership (Greenleaf, 1977; Spears, 2010; Van Dierendonck, 2011). This transcendental motivation enables, at the same time, personal and interpersonal growth.

The Person's Manifestative Action and Managers' Activity

Human actions manifest the person's intimacy and transcendence in a concrete space and time and have the potential to become a self-giving endeavor that perfects the person and allows for interpersonal growth. Therefore, personalist managers see their management activity as a concrete opportunity for manifesting their intimate selfhood (sense of call to moral growth) and transcendence (readiness to interpersonal growth). Their willingness to engage in interpersonal, caring relationships, and their orientation toward others' flourishing and the common good, appears firstly in their concern for social justice and responsibility. Accordingly, in their economic and managerial activity, they are inspired by the logic of the gift (Scalzo, 2017; Schrift, 2014) and tend to create networks of giving and receiving (Bernacchio, 2018). Personalist managers look at the firm as a resource for human development, instead of seeing others as "human resources" for the firm.

Intentional loving service to others, which characterizes the transcendental personalist view of any truly human activity (be it economic, aesthetic, political, intellectual or of any other kind), also becomes apparent in a personal commitment to the fulfillment of high standards. This quest for quality, which aims at better serving others through work, is the natural arena for the development of virtues, and in particular of practical wisdom. In this regard, in recent years, Neo-Aristotelian virtue ethics (MacIntyre, 2007) has emerged the field of business ethics (Moore & Beadle, 2006; Sison, Ferrero, & Guitián, 2018), particularly through the lens of the virtue practical wisdom (Conrad, 2018; Sison & Hühn, 2018). Personalist managers approach their work as an arena for developing the virtues and personal qualities inherent in the management activity, e.g., effort and diligence in displaying high levels of professionalism at work, the prudential ability to make and set goals with the future in mind, and timely, honest, thoughtful, and good decision-making. They also pay particular attention to the virtues involved in interpersonal relationships (Fontrodona, Sison, & de Bruin, 2013), such as humility and openness when listening to colleagues and subordinates, magnanimity, generosity in serving others, friendliness, etc.

Personalist practical wisdom attributes to the person the integration of the cognitive, affective, decisional, and ethical dimensions involved in a wise course of action. Personalist wisdom is displayed in thoughtfully considering how a situation can be handled or transformed consistently with one's interiority and relationally in order to bolster intimacy and relationality among all persons involved, while serving the common good (Akrivou & Scalzo, 2020). Analytic and modern understandings of practical wisdom are at odds with this understanding. The meaning of this cardinal virtue has been degraded throughout time (Aubenque 1999; Scalzo & Alford, 2016), becoming a merely protective, self-interested, rationality seeking and clever form of action. Cognitivist approaches reduce practical wisdom to an individual cognitive skill unrelated to interpersonal relations. In turn, behaviorists see it as a protective practical skill of individual actors. Recovering an understanding of phronesis consistent with realistic personalism requires an appropriate moral psychology of action and the self.[3]

In the field of management, this means that action related choices ("What should I do?") are inseparable from questions of being ("Who am I?") (Weaver, 2006: 344) and of moral identity ("How does this action affect who I am and who I am becoming?"). This personalist practical wisdom coordinates the different dispositions involved in the network of virtues previously mentioned.

The above has implications for how ME should contribute to the formation of managers across three domains, corresponding to the three dimensions found in transcendental personalism, which we detail in the next section.

Educating Future Managers for Interpersonal Growth

In this section, we explore how our understanding of transcendental personalist managers can be translated into future ME practices. The person's dimensions (intimacy of selfhood, interpersonal transcendence, and manifestation in prudent, self-giving activity) correspond to three personal aptitudes that should be developed in the education of the future managers. They include, as developed within this chapter, self-reflection, interpersonal relationality, and virtuous habits, in particular personalist practical wisdom.

Self-Reflection and the Enrichment of Selfhood

Transcendental personalist ME focuses on managers as persons, taken holistically in their singularity and complexity, as well as in their unity and self-understanding as interpersonal moral agents. To develop self-awareness and enrich selfhood, we suggest that management educators and students should engage in reflective practice (Schön, 1987; McLaughlin, 1999; Loughran, 2002). While reflection can take many forms (individual silent reflection, question-guided reflection, journaling, dialogue-based peer discussion etc.), written reflection is most suitable for enriching one's intimacy: reflective logs act as a "mirror of the mind" (Moon, 2010: 4) and help "to find one's own voice," using words that capture one's unique personal "sound" in a language that is "more like the language of thought" (Moon, 2010: 6). In a transcendental personalist framework, this goes beyond traditional focus on reflection regarding practitioners' environment, behavior, competencies and beliefs, and forays into what Korthagen and Vasalos (2005) called "core reflection," that is, a more fundamental form of reflection at the level of identity and mission. Reflective activities allow future managers to embrace their chosen profession as a true vocation and engage with it as a meaningful personal calling. Reflection also helps students and educators to grasp the purpose and meaning of economic activity itself from an interpersonal perspective, and to question the role students will have as managers who engage in interpersonal relations of mutual personal growth.

Interpersonal Relationality

In our view, the future of ME should be seen as a process that includes both teachers and students' interpersonal growth, as well as emotional, ethical, and cognitive aspects (Orón, Akrivou, & Scalzo, 2019). Rooted in a transcendental personalist understanding of human beings, interpersonal moral growth in ME should be rooted in a view that the person herself is a free moral actor who is endowed with a singular intimacy and who can personally commit to mutual moral growth in interpersonal relations.

One paradigmatic example of a personalist pedagogical approach to interpersonal growth can be found in the "pedagogy of gift" (Martín-García, Gijón-Casares, & Puig-Rovira, 2019), which shifts focus from the '*homo oeconomicus*' to the '*homo donator*' (Godbout, 2000), and could therefore be used to embed transcendental personalism in future ME. Indeed, the logic of gift has emerged as a new alternative for overcoming both individualism and holism in social sciences (Caillé, 2000: 46), based on its potential to integrate the relationship between concrete people and human nature as a common project (Hittinger, 2002). The theory of gift positions the core of personhood and society on 'the gift', defined as a free provision of goods or services made without guarantee of return, and with a view toward creating, nurturing, or recreating the social bond between people (Godbout, 1997). The gift is seen as beyond the logic of the normative social contract, and is found at the origin of conviviality, personality, and community (Caillé, 2003). It is not a specific act, but rather a cycle that is made up of three elements—giving, receiving, and giving back. The pedagogy of gift includes a two-way gift cycle: from teachers to students and from students to the community. Two different methodological tools can be used in each gift-cycle: (1) personal tutoring and (2) service learning (Martín-García et al., 2019).

Interpersonal growth in ME can be facilitated by using pedagogical methods that feature interpersonal relationships, such as the shared case study and conversational learning. These methods help scaffold both personal and common knowledge, however, paradigmatic case studies should be rewritten with an eye toward enabling interpersonal growth, and the Socratic method (questions and dialogue) should be used to facilitate the sharing of personal narratives and sense-making stories. Personal feeling complements cognition and informs a worldview that integrates personality, community, and interpersonal relationships in a very personal, singular way (Orón Semper, 2018). Other institutional members (facilities and administrative staff, senior management, etc.) should also engage in the experience of creating an institutional culture of interpersonal mutual growth. This "ethos" is of great importance: the practice context in which ME learners are situated will influence them both during learning and while applying what they have learned.

Personalist Practical Wisdom

The development of *personalist* practical wisdom undergirds future ME toward personal development (Akrivou & Scalzo, 2020). Those who advocate for teaching practical wisdom in ME (Bachmann, Loza Adaui, & Habisch, 2014; Naughton, Habisch, & Lenssen, 2010) argue that new managers "are generally missing … what Aristotle calls 'wisdom,' to be understood as interpersonal capabilities and practical knowledge" (Conrad, 2018: 64). In a transcendental personalist paradigm, future managers learn to grow in interpersonal relationships, and to be practically wise for and with those whose lives are implicated in their actions.

In this line, Bachmann, Habisch, and Dierksmeier (2018) recently suggested that forward-looking management studies and the discipline of business ethics should promote the study, internalization, and realization of practical wisdom as a virtue that is integral to management. They claim that practical wisdom is no longer a forgotten virtue in management, and that it is a valuable resource for management that might counteract contemporary management failures. Their "conciliatory conception" of practical wisdom is close to personalism and includes, among others features, an orientation toward human flourishing, a consideration of human sociality, and self-awareness, humility, and acknowledgment around human vulnerability.

This view of practical wisdom will inspire new visions for future ME in terms of enlarging and expanding how knowledge is approached and how students as future managers learn to know; it involves a shift from "knowing what" and "knowing how" to "knowing why" and, most importantly, "*knowing for whom.*"

Thus, teaching within and across the ME curriculum should not just focus on the transmission of knowledge and technique, but rather on understanding what human beings are and how to build interpersonal relationships that contribute to mutual growth. This also requires transformation in how the "technical" subjects that pertain to ME are taught; rather than being taught as an amoral, technical kind of knowledge, they must also embrace genuine concern for ethics and a pro-social orientation.

Broader Discussion and Practical Implications for ME

Beyond the practical implications that transcendental personalism has for future managers, a basic question remains, namely why should human beings be seen in a transcendental personalist view? Or more simply, why should the person be at the center of the future of management education?

First of all, the current reductionism found in the modern radical, which stresses human subjectivity as the locus of the autonomous self and of individual freedom, must be overcome. Slowly, scholars and practitioners have started to realize the limitations inherent in this radical, with its focus on external results, including money and power. In that sense, the classical radical has begun to reemerge; therein, human beings are seen as naturally sociable and rational with a common human nature, which can be perfected or improved upon by developing virtues. This position is at the center of communitarian (Etzioni, 1993) or naturalistic-ecological approaches (O'Riordan, 1981; Purser, Park, & Montuori, 1995), and especially of the Neo-Aristotelian virtue ethics approach to business (MacPherson, 2015; Sison et al., 2018).

Yet, human beings (as persons) are more complete than what Aristotle had in mind, and less dualistic and fragmentary than what modern anthropologies purport. Neo-Aristotelian virtue ethics fails to capture the deepest notion of the human person because she is neither conceived of in a profound way as a being with a transcendental dimension, nor as an end in herself. This cannot be proven; it is a first principle of practical reason (for Kant, a *faktum*). Although its absence (considering the person as a means) has caused significant social and political problems throughout history, today a common agreement exists regarding human dignity and equality expressed in the form of human rights (Taylor, 1989). The personalist understanding of human beings synthesizes and redirects into a higher form the insights those radicals put forward. In a personalist understanding, it is the person who freely opens her own self and intimacy to an interpersonal caring relation with others, which is manifested through virtuous actions. This personalist understanding stands in marked contrast to much of traditional ME. Approaches to educating and developing managers and leaders that adopt and practice from a person-oriented stance can help address the limitations of both traditional, mechanistic conceptions of ME and management practice, and the more recent, similarly reductionistic modern alternatives that place excessive value on separateness and thus over-individualize through valuing difference as an end in itself.

According to the logic of gift, personal relationships are the natural condition of personal growth, since they manifest a certain dynamic that is a substantial aspect of the person, namely accepting and offering what has been received in the interpersonal sphere (Polo, 2007). Every act of giving implies a "giving-of-oneself" (*freedom for*); in other words, this giving, which is a giving of ourselves and proper to the gift that we are, transforms us at the same time that it transforms others. Hence, this notion "unifies two things which are so often split apart in modern political and social thought: first, what man claims as his own, and second, what man has to give as a gift of service" (Hittinger, 2002: 391).

Thus, the transcendental personalist approach is the best alternative we have for sustainably addressing contemporary challenges. In this view, the person is not a mere "factor" in the equation of effective management, but rather an end in herself and the basis of all social and organizational institutions; hence, management activity (business, public management, etc.) is oriented *toward the service of the person*. It goes beyond the fact that the person should be considered as an end in herself, *à la Kant* and Humanistic Management Theory, and also argues that her intimacy should be acknowledged in the process of inter-relational growth, which is the ontological foundation of a transcendental (personalist) anthropology.

At this point, some might think, and not without reason, that it will be challenging to teach this understanding to business school students, and even more challenging to transfer it into management practice. To start, this understanding can certainly seem like a distant dream from today's institutional realities and requirements. ME institutions depend, after all, on market demands, in part because they receive funds and "educational mandates" from the business field. In addition, many business students may sign up for ME to get a degree for their future career, rather than to challenge their identity and the way they relate with others.

The anthropological basis of this ME proposal first requires a profound shift toward an overall person-based approach that aims to develop *managing persons* with purpose to support their flourishing, rather than just impersonal managers. Concrete proposals for facilitating this shift should start by developing a shared concern for personalist interpersonal growth at all levels of the *institution's culture* by sending consistent messages to the educational community through presentations, board meetings, student assessment practices, and in relationships with alumni, donors and employers. For its practical implementation, it will require a core team of *faculty members and students* who can jointly *identify what is* already *enhancing* interpersonal growth, what is currently *hindering* it, and initiatives for boosting it at each business school. This work could be done at different levels, including the whole institution, curricular content, examination of the methodology used within a concrete discipline, etc. That concern for personalist interpersonal growth should be *embedded in different disciplines* by sharing key messages about its importance among management educators, students, and practitioners. Business schools should become places where faculty, students, and alumni co-create and imagine future paths toward interpersonal growth within and outside of the school.

Indeed, teaching this understanding to business school students and transferring these ideas into management practice – taking into account the culture, governance, leadership and pedagogy of business schools, and ME – is not an easy task. Clearly, a personalist virtue ethics approach to the future of ME will require bold transformation of current practices and patient planning. Efforts to shift toward personalist ME may find serious obstacles with ME's current and predominant focus on marketization and commercialization (Khurana, 2010) and the status quo in many ME institutions. Pragmatically, that may mean that both individual management educators and, more importantly, ME institutions and other stakeholders such as accreditation and ranking organizations must start to "educate their market" about the value of transformational ME approaches and practices that invest in the full person. Realistically, it will require considerable investment and effort to create sufficient recognition of the differential value that can arise out of a move toward a more transcendental, personalist approach to ME.

However, and although relatively new to many ME settings, looking more widely, an ontological turn is taking place in higher and professional education (e.g., Dall'Alba, 2009; Dall'Alba & Barnacle, 2007; Fellenz, 2016) that supports the underlying approach proposed here. In addition, as we mentioned in the introduction, reason for hope is found in that both management practice and ME are attempting movements away from the mechanistic paradigm toward that of humanistic ME; in addition, the personalist approach to humanistic management has recently become a topic of interest in business ethics (Acevedo, 2012; Melé, 2009), as well as in corporate integrity theory (Chennattu, 2020).

Conclusion

In this chapter, we have argued that future ME would benefit significantly from a radical shift toward incorporating a humanistic personalist approach. Although a number of approaches already advocate for a humanistic ME, we suggest that they fall short in terms of a deeper and more profound anthropological foundation. Instead, we suggest that ME should be renewed with a profound, more realistic, and comprehensive understanding of the main economic actor, namely *the human person*, which represents the philosophical-anthropological root of our humanistic proposal for future ME centered on transcendental personalism.

To address this task, we relied upon this transcendental personalist understanding to discuss management with an orientation toward persons as ends in themselves as opposed to instrumental resources or "factors" in the quest for managerial effectiveness. Accordingly, we highlighted implications for a professional ethos *at the service of the person* (all persons who partake in the common good inside and outside the businesses) and offered a view of what managers should be in correspondence with the three dimensions of personhood identified herein. Moreover, we showed how incorporating a transcendental personalist vision can profoundly change management education, offering practical implications for how ME can shift toward educating for interpersonal growth. Enriching the selfhood of future managers, as well as their interpersonal relationality and personalist practical wisdom requires a focus on teaching and learning, and education centered on personalist self-reflection.

We aimed to show that such a shift would facilitate the practice of management as a force for rehumanizing business, society, and work and for promoting the flourishing of all involved, including managers. These paths have the potential to profoundly renew ethical ME beyond traditional "know-what" and "know-how" content, by shifting ME and knowledge toward more profound ethically informed "know-why" and "know-for-whom" types of knowledge that enable practically wise action. Within the broader scholarship that argues for a revival of humanistic management as the future of ME, this contribution highlights the profound notion of personhood and personalist approaches to management and ME. It further emphasizes personal intimacy through the "logic of gift," which requires cultivating future managers' disposition for interpersonal ethical growth. This vision gives management and economics the tools to shift their social purpose, fulfilling their ends as spheres that promote the common good and serve all human beings involved in organizational life with a concern for each one as a human person.

Funding Support

This work project is partially co-financed by the European Regional Development Fund postdoctoral grant No 1.1.1.2/VIAA/1/16/071.

Notes

1 In this chapter, we understand transcendence as a transhuman, horizontal form of transcendence that includes openness to the other, gratitude and humor, vulnerability, compassion, and caring, loving relationships. However, it should be noted that Polo's transcendental anthropology also includes vertical – spiritual transcendence. According to him, horizontal transcendence is based on each person's unique, transcendent and vertical relationship with God, which is at the origin of each human person. This vertical transcendence is both the basis of our shared humanity and the uniqueness that characterizes our action. Focusing on horizontal transcendence in this chapter is a methodological choice and does not rule out the possibility of vertical transcendence toward ideal values (Kristjansons, 2016) and toward the divine (MacPherson, 2015; Taylor, 2007).
2 *Freedom-for* should be distinguished from what Isaiah Berlin (1966) called "freedom to" or positive freedom as opposed to "freedom from" or negative freedom (absence of coercion,

"freedom-from-that-which-hinders-one's-development"). Berlin's "freedom-to" is closely related to Aristotle's understanding of freedom as "self-mastery," which is reached through the acquisition of virtues. Transcendental personalist freedom-for assumes the classical understanding of *freedom-to,* but elevates it teleologically toward the establishment of interpersonal self-giving relationships.

3 A recent effort in this direction is the "Inter-Processual Self" (IPS) theory (Akrivou, Orón, & Scalzo, 2018), which considers that the person's selfhood evolves through intentional relations with others (Akrivou, Orón, & Scalzo, 2018; Trowbridge, 2011).

References

Acevedo, A. 2012. Personalist business ethics and humanistic management: Insights from Jacques Maritain. *Journal of Business Ethics,* 105(2): 197–219.

Aguado, R., & Albareda, L. 2016. A new approach to humanistic management education based on the promotion of justice and human dignity in a sustainable economy. In M. T. Lepeley, E. Von Kimakowitz & R. Bardy (Eds.), *Human centered management in executive education:* 182–201. London: Palgrave Macmillan.

Akrivou, K., Orón, J. V., & Scalzo, G. 2020. How differing conceptions of integrity and self-integration influence relationships: Implications for management, personal and professional development, *Archives of Psychology,* 4(1): 1–26.

Akrivou, K., Orón Semper, J. V., & Scalzo, G. 2018. *The inter-processual self. Towards a personalist virtue ethics proposal for human agency.* London: Cambridge Scholars Publishing.

Akrivou, K., & Scalzo, G. 2020. In search of a fitting moral psychology for practical wisdom: The missing link for virtuous management. *Business Ethics: A European Review,* 1–12 (in press). 10.1111/beer.12295

Albareda, L., & Aguado, R. 2015. Integrating human dignity and human rights governance as a new management education paradigm. In G. Atinc (Ed.), *Academy of management proceedings,* 1:1376. Briarcliff Manor, NY: Academy of Management.

Amann, W., Pirson, M., Dierksmeier, C., Von Kimakowitz, E., & Spitzeck, H. 2011. *Business schools under fire: Humanistic management education as the way forward.* London: Palgrave Macmillan.

Arevalo, J. A., & Mitchell, S. F. 2017. *Handbook of sustainability in management education: In search of a multidisciplinary, innovative and integrated approach.* Cheltenham: Edward Elgar Publishing.

Arnaud, S., & Wasieleski, D. M. 2014. Corporate humanistic responsibility: Social performance through managerial discretion of the HRM. *Journal of Business Ethics,* 120(3): 313–334.

Aubenque, P. 1999. *La prudencia en Aristóteles,* trad. Mª José Torres Gómez-Pallete, Barcelona: Crítica.

Bachmann, C., Habisch, A., & Dierksmeier, C. 2018. Practical wisdom: Management's no longer forgotten virtue. *Journal of Business Ethics,* 153(1): 147–165.

Bachmann, C., Loza Adaui, C. R., & Habisch, A. 2014. Why the question of practical wisdom should be asked in business schools: Towards a holistic approach to a renewal of management education. *Humanistic Management Network, Research Paper Series,* 2460665.

Batson, C. D., & Moran, T. 1999. Empathy-induced altruism in a prisoner's dilemma. *European Journal of Social Psychology,* 29(7): 909–924.

Batson, C. D., Thompson, E. R., Seuferling, G., Whitney, H., & Strongman, J. A. 1999. Moral hypocrisy: Appearing moral to oneself without being so. *Journal of Personality and Social Psychology*, 77(3): 525–537.

Bennis, W. G., & O'Toole, J. 2005. How business schools have lost their way. *Harvard Business Review*, 83(5): 96–104.

Berlin, I. 1966. *Two concepts of liberty. An inaugural lecture delivered before the University of Oxford on 31 October 1958.* Oxford, UK: Clarendon Press.

Bernacchio, C. 2018. Networks of giving and receiving in an organizational context: Dependent rational animals and macintyrean business ethics. *Business Ethics Quarterly*, 28(4): 377–400.

Burgos, J. M. 2018. *An introduction to personalism.* Washington: The Catholic University America Press.

Caillé, A. 2000. *Anthropologie du don. Le tiers paradigm.* Paris: Desclée de Brouwer.

Caillé, A. 2003. *Critique de la raison utilitaire.* Paris: La Découverte.

Chennattu, A. 2020. *Managing with integrity: An ethical investigation into the relationship between personal and corporate integrity.* Minneapolis, MN: Augsburg Fortress Publishers. *Project MUSE* muse.jhu.edu/book/73880.

Cho, C., Dyllick, T., Falkenstein, M., Killian, S., O'Regan, P., & Reno, M. 2014. *Ethics, responsibility, and sustainability (ERS) in business school accreditation: Peer-learning perspectives. Discussion draft 7.0 globally responsible leadership initiative-50+ 20 values in action group-management education for the world.* http://grli.org/wp-content/uploads/2017/12/Values-in-Action_Draft-20140920.pdf

Conrad, C. A. 2018. *Business ethics: A philosophical and behavioral approach.* New York, NY: Springer.

Dall'Alba, G. 2009. Learning professional ways of being: Ambiguities of becoming. *Educational Philosophy and Theory*, 41(1): 34–45.

Dall'Alba, G., & Barnacle, R. 2007. An ontological turn for higher education. *Studies in Higher Education*, 32(6): 679–691.

Derksen, M. 2014. Turning men into machines? Scientific management, industrial psychology, and the "human factor." *Journal of the History of the Behavioral Sciences*, 50(2): 148–165.

DESA UN – Department of Economic and Social Affairs, United Nations (2016). *Transforming our world: The 2030 agenda for sustainable development.*

Dierksmeier, C. 2016. *Reframing economic ethics: The philosophical foundations of humanistic management.* London: Palgrave Macmillan.

Dierksmeier, C. 2020. From Jensen to Jensen: Mechanistic management education or humanistic management learning? *Journal of Business Ethics*, 166(1): 73–87. 10.1007/s1 0551-019-04120-z

Erhard, W., & Jensen, M. 2011. *A positive theory of the normative virtues.* Working paper no. 12-007, Harvard Business School NOM Unit.

Erhard, W., & Jensen, M. C. 2013. *Creating leaders: A new model. An evening with Werner Erhard and professor Michael C. Jensen.* SSRN Electronic Journal. 10.2139/ssrn.2352280

Etzioni, A. 1993. *The spirit of community: Rights, responsibilities and the communitarian agenda.* New York: Crown Publishers, Inc.

Fellenz, M. R. 2016. Forming the professional self: Bildung and the ontological perspective on professional education and development. *Educational Philosophy and Theory*, 48(3): 267–283.

Fernández González, M. J. 2019. Relational-self-of-virtue: Classical, modern and Christian perspectives in moral education. In L. Daniela (Ed.), *Human, technologies and quality of education. Proceedings of scientific papers*: 22–32. Rīga: Latvijas Universitātes Akadēmiskais apgāds. 10.22364/htqe.2019.02

Figueiró, P. S., & Raufflet, E. 2015. Sustainability in higher education: A systematic review with focus on management education. *Journal of Cleaner Production*, 106: 22–33.

Fontrodona, J., Sison, A. J. G., & de Bruin, B. 2013. Editorial introduction: Putting virtues into practice. A challenge for business and organizations. *Journal of Business Ethics*, 113(4): 563–565.

Gagliardi, P., & Czarniawska, B. 2006. *Management education and humanities.* Cheltenham: Edward Elgar.

Ghoshal, S. 2005. Bad management theories are destroying good management practices. *Academy of Management Learning & Education*, 4(1): 75–91.

Godbout, J. T. 1997. *El espíritu del don.* México: Siglo Veintiuno Editores.

Godbout, J. T. 2000. Homo donator versus homo oeconomicus. In T. Vandevelde (Ed.), *Gifts and interests*, vol. 9: 23–46. Leuven: Peters Publishers.

Grassl, W., & Habisch, A. 2011. Ethics and economics: Towards a new humanistic synthesis for business. *Journal of Business Ethics*, 99(1): 37–49.

Greenleaf, R. 1977. *Servant leadership: A journey into the nature of legitimate power and greatness.* New York: Paulist Press.

Havard, A. 2018. *From temperament to character. On becoming a virtuous leader.* New York: Scepter Publishers.

Herrmann, B., & Rundshagen, V. 2020. Paradigm shift to implement SDG 2 (end hunger): A humanistic management lens on the education of future leaders. *The International Journal of Management Education*, 18(1): 100368.

Hittinger, R. 2002. Social pluralism and subsidiarity in catholic social doctrine. *Annales theologici*, 16: 385–408.

Jensen, M. C., & Meckling, W. H. 1994. The nature of man. *Journal of Applied Corporate Finance*, 7(2): 4–19.

Kassel, K., & Rimanoczy, I. 2018. *Developing a sustainability mindset in management education.* Abingdon-on-Thames, Oxfordshire, UK: Routledge.

Khurana, R. 2010. *From higher aims to hired hands: The social transformation of American business schools and the unfulfilled promise of management as a profession.* Princeton, NJ: Princeton University Press.

Korthagen, F., & Vasalos, A. 2005. Levels in reflection: Core reflection as a means to enhance professional growth. *Teachers and Teaching*, 11(1): 47–71.

Kristjánsson, K. (2016). *Aristotle, emotions, and education.* Abingdon-on-Thames, Oxfordshire, UK: Routledge.

Lepeley, M. T., Von Kimakowitz, E., & Bardy, R. 2016. *Human centered management in executive education.* London: Palgrave Macmillan UK.

Loughran, J. J. 2002. Effective reflective practice: In search of meaning in learning about teaching. *Journal of Teacher Education*, 53(1): 33–43.

Lutz, D. 2018. Leadership, management, and the common good. In A. Örtenblad (Ed.), *Professionalizing leadership: Debating education, certification and practice*: 237–250. Cham: Palgrave Macmillan.

MacIntyre, A. 2007. *After virtue: A study in moral theory* [1981]. London: Duckworth.

MacPherson, D. 2015. Cosmic outlooks and neo-Aristotelian virtue ethics. *International Philosophical Quarterly*, 55: 197–215.

Martín-García, X., Gijón-Casares, M., & Puig-Rovira, J. M. (2019). Pedagogía del don. Relación y servicio en educación. *Estudios Sobre Educación*, 37: 51–68.

McLaughlin, T. H. 1999. Beyond the reflective teacher. *Educational Philosophy and Theory*, 31(1): 9–25.

Melé, D. 2009. Integrating personalism into virtue-based business ethics: The personalist and the common good principles. *Journal of Business Ethics*, 88(1): 227–244.

Melé, D. 2016. Understanding humanistic management. *Humanistic Management Journal*, 1(1): 33–55.

Moon, J. 2010. Learning journals and logs. *Assessment – UCD Teaching & Learning/ Resources*: 1–23. https://ar.cetl.hku.hk/pdf/ucdtla0035.pdf.

Moore, G., & Beadle, R. 2006). In search of organizational virtue in business: Agents, goods, practices, institutions and environments. *Organization Studies*, 27(3): 369–389.

Mounier, E. 1936. *Manifeste au service du personnalisme*. Paris: Montaigne.

Naughton, M., Habisch, A., & Lenssen, G. 2010. Practical wisdom in management from the Christian tradition. *Journal of Management Development*, 29(7-8). 10.1108/jmd.2010. 02629gaa.002

Orón, J. V., Akrivou, K., & Scalzo, G. 2019. Educational implications that arise from differing models of human development and their repercussions for social innovation. *Frontiers in Education*, 4: 139. 10.3389/feduc.2019.00139.

Orón Semper, J. V. 2018. Educación centrada en el crecimiento de la relación inter-personal. *Studia Poliana*, 20: 241–262.

O'Riordan, T. 1981. Environmentalism and education. *Journal of Geography in Higher Education*, 5(1): 3–17.

Parkes, C., Buono, A. F., & Howaidy, G. 2017. The principles for responsible manage-ment education (PRME). The first decade – what has been achieved? The next decade – responsible management education's *challenge* for the sustainable development goals (SDGs). *The International Journal of Management Education*, 15(2): 61–65.

Phillips, R., Freeman, R. E., & Wicks, A. C. 2003. What stakeholder theory is not. *Business Ethics Quarterly*, 13(4): 479–502.

Pirson, M. 2017. *Humanistic management: Protecting dignity and promoting well-being.* Cambridge, UK: Cambridge University Press.

Pirson, M. 2019. A humanistic perspective for management theory: Protecting dignity and promoting well-being. *Journal of Business Ethics*, 159(1): 39–57.

Polo, L. 1998. *Antropología transcendental*, vol. 1. Pamplona: EUNSA.

Polo, L. 2003. *Antropología transcendental*, vol. 2. Pamplona: EUNSA.

Polo, L. 2007. *Persona y libertad*. Pamplona: EUNSA.

Polo, L., & Corazón, R. 2005. Lo radical y la libertad. *Cuadernos de Anuario Filosófico*: 179. Pamplona: Servicio de publicaciones de la Universidad de Navarra.

Purser, R. E., Park, C., & Montuori, A. 1995. Limits to anthropocentrism: Toward an ecocentric organization paradigm? *Academy of Management Review*, 20(4): 1053–1089.

Rivera, C. A. 2019. How can we empower a new generation of business leaders through ethical management education? *Journal of Character Education*, 15(1): 39–52.

Rocha, H., & Miles, R. 2009. A model of collaborative entrepreneurship for a more humanistic management. *Journal of Business Ethics*, 88(3): 445–462.

Scalzo, G. 2017. A genealogy of the gift. In J. D. Rendtorff (Ed.), *Perspectives on philosophy of management and business ethics, Ethical economy*. Studies in economic ethics and philosophy, vol. 51: 31–45. Cham: Springer.

Scalzo, G, & Alford, H. 2016. Prudence as part of a worldview: Historical and conceptual dimensions. In K. Akrivou & A. Sison (Eds.), *The challenges of capitalism for virtue ethics and the common good. Interdisciplinary perspectives*. Aldershot: Edward Elgar.

Schön, D. A. 1987. *Jossey-Bass higher education series. Educating the reflective practitioner: Toward a new design for teaching and learning in the professions*. San Francisco, CA: Jossey-Bass.

Schrift, A. D. 2014. *The logic of the gift: Toward an ethic of generosity*. London: Routledge.

Sison, A. J. G., & Hühn, M. P. 2018. Practical wisdom in corporate governance. In A. J. G. Sison, I. Ferrero, & G. Guitian (Eds.), *Business ethics*: 165–186. London: Routledge.

Sison, A. J. G., Ferrero, I., & Guitián, G. 2018. *Business ethics: A virtue ethics and common good approach*. London: Routledge.

Spaemann, R. 2006. *Persons: The difference between 'someone' and 'something.'* Oxford: Oxford University Press.

Spears, L. C. 2010. Character and servant leadership: Ten characteristics of effective, caring leaders. *The Journal of Virtues & Leadership*, 1: 25–30.

Stead, J. G., & Stead, W. E. 2010. Sustainability comes to management education and research: A story of coevolution. *Academy of Management Learning & Education*, 9(3): 488–498.

Taylor, Ch. 1989. *Sources of the self: The making of the modern identity*. Cambridge, MA: Harvard University Press.

Taylor, Ch. 2007. *A secular age*. Cambridge, MA: Harvard University Press.

Tirole, J. 2017. *Economics for the common good*. Princeton, NJ: Princeton University Press.

Tourish, D. 2020. The triumph of nonsense in management studies. *Academy of Management Learning & Education*, 19(1): 99–109.

Trowbridge, R. 2011. Waiting for Sophia: 30 years of conceptualizing wisdom in empirical psychology. *Research in Human Development*, 8(2): 149–164.

Van Dierendonck, D. 2011. Servant leadership: A review and synthesis. *Journal of Management*, 37(4): 1228–1261.

Vidal, A., & da Silva Martins, G. 2017. The importance of philosophical and anthropological knowledge in management education regarding sustainability. In J. Arevalo & S. Mitchell (Eds.), *Handbook of sustainability in management education*: 151–170. Cheltenham: Edward Elgar Publishing.

Wankel, C., & Stoner, J. A. 2009. *Management education for global sustainability*. North Caroline: Information Age Publishing.

Weaver, G. R. 2006. Virtue in organizations: Moral identity as a foundation for moral agency. *Organization Studies*, 27(3): 341–368.

Wymer, W., & Rundle-Thiele, S. R. 2017. Inclusion of ethics, social responsibility, and sustainability in business school curricula: a benchmark study. *International Review on Public and Nonprofit Marketing*, 14(1): 19–34.

7

IN SEARCH OF DIVERSITY IN MANAGEMENT EDUCATION

Kiran Trehan and Clare Rigg

Introduction

Diversity has achieved the status of shibboleth in management education (ME), a social good, a source of richness, a resource to be welcomed, worked with and managed. Similarly, diversity studies are well covered in critical management studies (Gotsis & Kortezi, 2014). Over recent years, education and research in university business schools has mirrored societal attention to issues of diversity and social inclusion with an increasing interest in understanding the importance, relevance, and impact of developing a diverse workforce, particularly in relation to organizational effectiveness (Roberson, 2019; Sharma, Moses, Borah, & Adhikary, 2020). The message advocated is that diversity can enhance performance and make the classroom and workplace more socially inclusive. However, the premise of this chapter is that contrary to such rhetoric, working with diversity in ME continues to be a challenge. The chapter investigates the ways in which the synthesis of critical management education (CME) and systems psychodynamics shed new light on the complex and nuanced experience of working with diversity in the classroom and helps us to identify and articulate new implications for CME. We explore the potential of CME to advance the theory and practice of diversity in ME by engaging more critically with lived experiences of students through alternative critical pedagogical approaches and methods, and in the process highlighting the social, political, and moral aspect of management and ME practice.

CME aspires to address the limitations of traditional managerial perspectives, while also seeking to address structural inequalities. The interconnection between diversity – whether of gender, nationality, culture – and CME is seen as important for stimulating critical thinking in relation to diversity and power issues

DOI: 10.4324/9781003095903-9

(Hibbert, 2013). When expedited through participative educational methodologies, such linking is equally important for us to understand educational experience as exemplifying society in microcosm (Reynolds & Trehan, 2013).

In this chapter, we first outline the drivers for CME to encompass diversity. Second, we introduce critical action learning as an approach to illuminate the ways in which diversity in the classroom interconnects in encounters where the participants have different biographies, trajectories, and linguistic histories, paying particular attention to questions of power, emotions, and learning spaces. The chapter presents two illustrations of practical ways in which diversity initiatives have been utilized in ME and concludes by demonstrating how a synthesis of psychodynamic and critical action learning (CAL) sheds new light on the complex and nuanced experience of working with diversity in the classroom and helps us to identify and articulate new implications for CME.

Diversity in Critical Management Education: Theories in Use

This section considers the drivers for CME to encompass diversity. It argues that while some inroads have been made with respect to bringing gender into CME, comparatively little attention has been paid to race and ethnic diversity.

Educational institutions are faced with the challenge of how to ensure that the diversity of perspectives of different student groups are effectively heard, incorporated, and managed. A key aim of diversity has been to promote knowledge, recognition, and respect for different cultural traditions (Bonnet, 2000). However, CME can offer more than simply recognizing difference, given its concern with "working towards democratic values and practices both in organisations and in management learning and education" (Reynolds & Vince, 2020: 136). Ayikoru and Park (2019: 416) see the purpose of CME as "transformation of society in the direction of social justice, disrupting ... practices that reproduce inequality and oppression." This focus of CME on addressing structural inequalities would suggest a foregrounding of issues associated with diversity. In principle, interculturality, diversity, and difference are potentially central resources for any discussion of contemporary CME. However, contrary to the rhetoric, ME seems to have largely ignored differences that surface in the classroom, or contributed to its suppression (Reynolds & Trehan, 2001), and CME has been criticized for failing to appreciate diversity and difference (Perriton & Reynolds, 2018). This is further echoed by Thompson and McGivern's (1995) exploration of "sexism in the seminar"; Sinclair's (2000) outline of similar resistance in discussing issues of gender in the context of CME, and Reynolds and Trehan's (2001) demonstration of how "difference" is engaged with in the critical classroom, often in ways that undermine the intent of the educators themselves.

Consequently, if issues of gender remain problematic for CME, it has been even more negligent in addressing racial and ethnic diversity issues, not least in the ways in which ME is expedited within international business schools and in the teaching of international students within UK higher education (e.g., Perriton & Reynolds, 2018). This is not to deny that within CME there have been genuine well-intentioned attempts to advance equality, nevertheless, underlying them is an assumed intercultural homogeneity (Ellsworth, 1989). Trehan and Rigg (2015) argue the challenge in CME is to explore and actively engage in the broader question of what it takes to create a learning environment that facilitates diversity in an intersectionally diverse, multinational context. As Reynolds and Trehan (2013) highlight, diversity requires a removal of the fear and intolerance associated with difference and the capacity to focus on the micro-politics in order to create spaces in which diversity exchange can occur, as the next section elaborates.

In Search of Diversity in Management Education

This section explores some of the sources of cultural and ethnic diversity in contemporary business and management schools, particularly in the context of increasing internationalization of the student body. We argue that diversity is not empty multiculturalism, in which all are deemed welcome but differences are denied, but it raises challenge for a pedagogy that recognizes and encompasses difference.

Within CME, questions of diversity are ever more important in a context where the contemporary classroom is now often so intersectionally diverse (Perriton & Reynolds, 2018) and with increasing pressures from such factors as teacher ratings, fees, and student evaluations. The desire for more inclusive pedagogy has never been in such high demand, in part driven by a need to cultivate contemporary skills in students to enable them to respond to the changing social, political, and economic demographics of the world in which they will work. As a result, attention to inclusion represents a shift away from "managing diversity" in favor of proactive approaches which involves "managing for diversity" (Andrews & Ashworth, 2015). To do this, Trehan (2019) argues critical pedagogy needs to challenge the status quo, enable creativity, be innovative, and entrepreneurial.

While CME has attempted to respond to racial and ethnic diversity (e.g., Boje and Al Arkoubi, 2009; Ellsworth, 2005), the literature concerning issues of race and ethnicity in the context of CME is limited compared to the issues and debates on gender (Perriton & Reynolds, 2018).

In exploring the future of critical management education, discussions on race, decolonizing, and diversifying the curriculum provide an opportunity to explore how diversity is stimulated or deterred through the practices of teaching and learning. In CME practices that foster diversity are those that, through their inclusive approach, nurture difference as a positive force for learning, while practices that reduce diversity are seen as those that lead toward the reduction of difference. CME has an opportunity to explore to what extent are its practices conducive either to the reduction or the fostering of difference. The question of diversity in CME requires that we look at what is being taught, that is, the knowledge content, as well as how knowledge is being taught, namely the process of teaching and learning. The question of what is being taught looks toward the curriculum that is being used, while the question of how leads toward the pedagogies in which teaching and learning is happening. The nurturing of diversity in CME requires a transformation of both what is being taught and how it is being taught.

However, taking a decolonial and intersectional approach reveals that diversity-poor practices are monocultural and one of the main problems here appears to be that university business schools across the globe have been moulded into adopting Western models of teaching and practice – they adopt English as the language of teaching and tend to celebrate Western models/cultural hegemony. As a result, local identities – including the social, cultural, economic, and political concerns within these societies – appear to be marginalized at the expense of promoting a corporate professional identity that reflects Western ideology and culture (Boje and Al Arkoubi, 2009). This is problematic because as opposed to celebrating cultural, racial, and ethnic diversity within the context of CME, it would appear that this is being eroded. A pedagogy of positionality that promotes diversity is not only directed toward the recognition of marginalized positions, it also requires the recognition of the default position. It requires the unmarked positions in the practices of knowledge, in particular the intersectional positions of privilege, to be spelled out and recognized as particular historical and contextual formations. Exercises that reveal the positionality of Western centrism of whiteness, masculinity, ethnicity, and gender have proven to be fruitful to the transition toward inclusive practices of learning in which difference can thrive.

In exploring difference, the work of radical and feminist educationalists provides some important insights, with feminist pedagogies in particular contesting the fiction of equal relationships implied in propositions of "classical liberatory" forms of education (Weiler, 1991: 450). Similar challenges are made in critiques of idealized claims for equality in communication (Fraser, 1994), and of concepts of community (Young, 1986) in which differences "in the sense of the basic asymmetry of subjects" are denied (Young, 1986: 10), as in the likelihood of voices of the other becoming "lost or silenced." Earlier propositions for dialogue based on trust and a commitment to social equality had met with similar criticism for discounting the destructive effects of asymmetrical relations on aspirations for democratic classroom "dialogue," not least in discounting the consequences of differences in power and influence between students and tutors (Ellsworth, 1989). As Lather (1991: 124) points out, "…to deconstruct authority is not to do away with it but to learn to trace its effects, to see how authority is constituted and constituting." If not addressed, differences and their relationship to interculturality may well undermine possibilities for equal dialogue. If they are confronted, and space protected for marginalized discourses (Beyer & Liston, 1992), a common interest in learning may be sufficient for respect, understanding, and dispute to coexist. From this point of view, rather than from the perspective of critical theorists, and in stark contrast to the psychologizing traditions of much ME, it becomes important to know how the interculturality impacts the education process, on what basis, of what kind, and with what consequences for an individual's experience and subsequent action – whether as student or tutor. In the next section, we illuminate these ideas in action.

Critical by Design: Working with Diversity in Critical Management Education

ME can be critical in content, in process, or in both (Reynolds, 1998). In respect to diversity, attempts to decolonize the curriculum, or to explicitly explore gender or race within organizations, would constitute critical content. Our objective in this section, however, is to illustrate how critical process methods of teaching and learning can create the space to work with and learn from diversity in the management classroom. We do this by providing two practical illustrations of a synthesis of CAL and psychodynamic, which places encounters center stage where the participants have different biographies, trajectories, and linguistic histories. These shed new light on the complex and nuanced experience of working with diversity in the classroom and identify future implications for CME. First, we outline the key ideas of CAL and of systems psychodynamic.

Critical Action Learning (CAL)

CAL, a development of action learning (Revans, 1982; Rigg & Trehan, 2004) is distinctive in its theory and practice, including:

- Its emphasis on the way that learning is supported, avoided and/or prevented through power relations
- The linking of questioning *insight* to complex emotions, unconscious processes and relations
- A more active facilitation role than implied within traditional action learning (Mughal, 2021; Vince, 2008)

CAL attempts to supplement an individual's experiences of action (learning from experience) with the reflection of existing organizational and emotional dynamics created in action (learning from organizing). The latter process is an explicit recognition of the role that politics and emotions can play in facilitating, and constraining, the scope for learning, (Vince, 2001).

Willmott's (1997) endeavor to promote a synergy between critical thinking and critical management learning is often presented as the genesis of the CAL approach. Willmott (1997: 169) contended that "the task of *critical action learning* is to present and command an alternative to the seeming neutrality and authority of orthodox management theory as a means of opening up and facilitating a transformation of management practice."

Trehan and Ram (2010) argue this approach aims to inflect the practical stance of action learning (Revans, 1982) with a more sociological perspective drawn from critical theory. In this view, CAL represents a shift from the traditional technicist approaches to learning which have been characterized by the presumption that management knowledge and practice is objective and value free. CAL challenges this position and argues for the need to deconstruct the discourse of policy and practice. As Edwards (1993: 155) argues "… 'Practice' is already informed by overt or covert discursive understandings and exercises of power." Hence, the "problem-solving" and "self-development" orientation of traditional action learning is contrasted with CAL's more explicit engagement with the tensions, contradictions, emotions, and power dynamics that inevitably exist both within a group and in individual learners' lives. CAL, as a pedagogical approach, emerges when these dynamics are treated centrally as a site of learning about managing and organizing.

Systems Psychodynamic

Psychodynamic refers to the unconscious and conscious impulses and emotions that underlie people's behaviors. The value of a psychodynamic perspective is that it reveals the irrationalities of management and the psychic defenses, fears, and needs behind organization interactions and cultures (French & Grey, 1996). One common psychodynamic model in UK ME derives from the Tavistock Institute, which particularly emphasizes the function of anxiety in management (Vince, 2010). The French psychodynamic tradition couples this with a greater interest in the material and social constraints experienced by employees at work (Dashtipour & Vidaillet, 2020).

Trehan and Rigg (2015) advance the practice of CAL by foregrounding emotion, power, and diversity (see also Mughal, 2021; Mughal et al., 2018; Pässilä et al., 2015). They argue that action learning sets are environments within which the emotion, politics, and social power relations that are integral to organizing can be viewed, discussed, and (potentially) transformed. Learning sets can be seen as diverse and specific identity groups (Vince, 2008), where identity is shaped and defined both through social power relations (e.g., race and gender dynamics) and by organizing processes (e.g., engagement and/or avoidance of difference and diversity). Critical reflection on individual and collective emotions that are mobilized in action learning sets may help to reveal the contradictions of experience that are integral to managerial roles:

The dynamics of learning sets – their processes of organising, often provoke emotions. Attending to and making sense of these is a rich source of experiential learning about organisational behaviour … The process of critical reflection provides language and concepts which help people acknowledge and make sense of feelings they may have long carried, but ignored, for example over tensions or contradictions they experience. (Rigg & Trehan, 2004: 167)

Though elaborated by the authors cited above, the seminal work by Vince (2004) exemplifies the ways in which politics, emotion, learning, and organizing interact in the context of action learning. He discusses the notion of "organizing insight" and illustrates how action learning is also a reflection of existing organizational dynamics created in action. He argues that organizing insight provides a link between CAL and organizational learning, and organizing insight becomes possible when there is an examination of the politics that surround and inform organizing. In addition, to comprehend these politics it is often necessary to question these political choices and decisions, both consciously and unconsciously (Vince, 2004: 74).

Encouraging "critical reflection" is a further distinguishing feature of CAL. Reynolds (1998: 183) distinguishes between reflection and critical reflection by suggesting that, "… whereas critical reflection is the cornerstone of emancipatory approaches to education, reflection as a management learning concept is expressed primarily as a key element of problem solving." The questioning of taken-for-granted assumptions is emancipatory and central to the ideals of CAL and critically reflective practice. Reynolds (1998) emphasizes the social aspect of this questioning and the need to encourage participants to confront the social and political forces which provided the context of their work. Vince (1996) highlights the importance of moving away from reflective models that lead to reflection on experience being constructed or interpreted as managers "thinking about their experience," emphasizing the rational nature of reflective processes rather than engaging with the emotional and political dimensions. Thus, critical reflection blends learning through experience with theoretical and technical learning to form new knowledge constructions, and new behaviors or insights (Hibbert, 2013; Rigg & Trehan, 2008).

But what can this mean in practice? How is a synthesis of psychodynamic and CAL actually implemented? The next section provides two illustrations of how we applied a CAL perspective through the design, content, and process in our work with students on a part-time master's program in a management school in the United Kingdom. The program illustrates how educational practices can integrate working with diversity through the social and political dimensions of learning. CAL is apparent because, as a matter of design, "content" and "process" issues are accorded equal importance.

Illustration One – Bringing Diversity into Critical Management Education

In this illustration, a conceptual design for management learning is presented which elucidates the experiences of integrating diversity into CME. The program is designed and embedded within CAL and systemic psychodynamic traditions, where the open space design and pedagogical process is as significant as the content for management learners. The theoretical advances highlighted facilitate how ME needs to rethink and re-engage with notions of space, emotions, and power dynamics within management and organizational learning. A key aim of this illustration is to develop our practical understanding about how to implement a systems psychodynamic open space design which supports learning about difference, diversity, power dynamics, authority, leadership, and organizational processes in action. Furthermore, the example aims to highlight how a psychodynamic approach allied with CAL can stimulate new thinking in the theory and practice of CME.

Psychodynamic-Designed Space for Learning

What is a psychodynamic-designed space for learning? A psychodynamic-informed open space is a temporary educational institution made up of management learners and academic staff who come together to study the organization they enact as it forms, develops, and comes to an end. In this context, the primary task is for them to learn about diversity, power dynamics, authority, and leadership.

Context for Creating Psychodynamic Learning Spaces

The context for this discussion of CAL intertwined with psychodynamic learning spaces is a three-year part-time MBA program in a management school in the United Kingdom. First created around 1980, the program is designed and run on the principles of a learning community approach with participation integral to the design. The program illustrates how educational practices can integrate the social and political dimensions of learning. Psychodynamic learning space is explicit because, as a matter of design, "content" and "process" issues are accorded equal importance. In the next section, we provide an insight into the site of study in order to illuminate the core psychodynamic learning spaces, which underpin the program, including assessment. Participants on this part-time program are professionals ranging in age from mid-20s to early 60s with most in their 30s and 40s. Generally, there is an equal spread of participants from the public, private, and voluntary sectors, and a roughly equal gender balance, with representation of black, Asian, and ethnic minority students increasing over the years.

All of the participants on the program attend three residential workshops spaced throughout the first two years and in between the workshops they work in action learning sets comprising, on average, five to eight students plus one facilitator. The intended purpose for the sets is to provide support for each individual to choose, plan, and write course assignments, including a number of group projects, as well as to discuss matters of interest arising from either the program itself or from people's work or career experience. The sets are also part of the assessment process of the program, which is collaborative and involves peer, self, and tutor assessment of each assignment. Participants choose during the first workshop (held near the start of the program) who and which set of people they will work with. The groups meet weekly for the duration of the program. Participants attend for a total of six hours per week. Two of these hours are given over to lecture inputs; the remaining four are dedicated to work in action learning sets.

Program Design

The program is designed on CAL principles and focuses on the meaning participants make of themselves and their social worlds or learning about the knowledge they possess from a careful study of their practice. It is complex and variable, posing problems in relation to diversity, race, power, control, and emotions not prevalent in more traditional models of education and does not conform to participants' expectations of themselves as passive learners and tutors as the expert givers of knowledge (Reynolds & Trehan, 2001; Trehan & Rigg, 2015). The approach is informed by three key assumptions about learning. Firstly, of encouraging participants to become aware of their theories-in-use (Argyris & Schön, 1974); secondly, to think critically, as Carr and Kemmis say of action research: "... a deliberate process for emancipating practitioners from the often unseen constraints of assumption, habit, precedent, coercion and ideology" (1986: 192), thirdly, informed by Bateson's (1973) and Belenky, Clinchy, Golderger, and Tarube's (1986) theories on levels of learning, tutors also encourage participants to value their own experience and insights and to develop their own models; in other words, to create knowledge from practice.

The educational principles upon which the program is based are in many ways familiar to andragogical approaches and can be broadly summarized as set out below:

1. Participants should have as much choice as possible over the direction and content of their learning.
2. They are responsible for "managing" their own learning and for helping others in theirs (The notion of the "learning community" is generally invoked to denote this).

3. Work on the program integrates the idea of critical thinking, central to the academic tradition, with the day-to-day professional experience of participants.
4. The opportunities presented to students on the program should be equally for learning about and developing themselves in their professional role as for engaging with relevant ideas and concepts in the public domain and academic literature.
5. The marked degree of participation inherent in the design assumes a commitment to take collective responsibility for attending to the "process" of the community; in other words, reviewing and modifying the design, procedures and ways of working.

In practice these principles mean that the responsibility for the spaces for learning is a collective one and activities are organized/planned on a collective basis. Topics that arise emerge from the interests of staff and participants, as do choice of methods and choice of the action learning sets. The topics for course assignments are the choice of each student and assessment is done collaboratively within each set.

Inherent in the design of our program was a structure that ensured a collective responsibility for attending to the "process" of the group; in other words, reviewing and organizing insights, in order for the action learning set to modify the design, procedures, and ways of working. Within the program we actively pursued a review of the emotional and political bases of experience and how they impacted on wider micro-political processes and power relations in and between members and their organizations.

Psychodynamic Learning Spaces in Action

Learning from experience is central to psychodynamic traditions (French & Vince, 1999). When action learning groups are diverse in membership, this inevitably means the potential to learn from that diverse experience. At the heart is the understanding that work groups, relationships, and institutional ways of working more broadly are shaped by organization members' psychic projections as they unconsciously set up defenses against feelings of anxiety, and also love, guilt, and other emotions. In the next section, we illustrate the potential to learn from diversity within the psychodynamic learning spaces created in initial residential workshop of this MBA program.

A key space our MBA participants experience is a five-day residential workshop held in the first month of the program. Informed by Tavistock group relations training, the week is carefully designed to combine plenary and small group sessions in which participants will experience the power and emotion that lie at the heart of a psychodynamic understanding of organizations and organizing. Based on a T-group model (Miller, 1990), the purpose of this is to learn experientially about aspects of organizational behavior, interpersonal relations, group processes, leadership, and management practices and perspectives. Participants (40–60 in number) are tasked to come prepared to work on particular work-related issues. Prior to arrival, their expectation is that they are learners, consuming expert inputs led by lecturers, who they cast in the role of expert givers of knowledge. Instead, after an opening activity late on Monday morning in which groups of four exchange their hopes, fears, and concerns for the week, when the plenary re-assembles after lunch in a room layout deliberately hier-archical with a row of staff chairs facing several rows of students, the staff team remains silent and expressionless, deliberately disrupting the convention of the room. Momentarily, silence and uncertainty reign in the student group. The anxiety is palpable. But always, into that vacuum, someone will step in when they cannot bear their own anxiety any longer, and organizational dynamics will unfold as other members compete, explode with anger, feel relieved, follow, take responsibility for themselves, and so on.

The week progresses with small group and plenary times and the staff team barely speak until Wednesday evening. Participants quickly grow accustomed to making their own decisions on how to fill the time as they conform to the week's learning objectives. But Wednesday evening is another particular space in which each group, including the staff team, sends a representative to negotiate with each other for how to use time on the Thursday and final Friday sessions. In a fishbowl format, the inner circle of representatives is watched by others sitting around. An empty chair in the inside group allows others to come in to contribute and in doing so to undermine their representative or display their own competitiveness (issues that will be revisited within the small groups on the following day). There is no time limit on this negotiation activity, which often goes on for four or five hours. As the evening progresses, the outer ring is able to observe Bion's (1998) theories of group dynamics in practice within the inner group, namely its si-multaneous functioning at both the task level as a work group engaged in a given brief and at the process level, as a group subject to one of three primitive basic assumptions: fight/flight, dependency, or pairing.

The final psychodynamic space we want to highlight in this week is the "Creative Session" invariably secured as one of the slots for Thursday morning by the staff negotiator. Various representational forms are used by groups to capture how they see themselves, their group, and the whole temporary or-ganization of the week, including short plays, songs, and body sculptures. A "Freedom Square" is also often used, as a physical space within the room in which students are told that they can do anything that is (1) legal and (2) won't incur damages to the venue.

Below we include a number of student comments that illustrates the capacity of the psychodynamic space within the first residential week to provoke learning about power. These comments are collected as part of the critical reflective process during the workshop. Vince (1996) highlights the importance of moving away from reflective models that lead to reflection on experience being constructed or interpreted as management learners "thinking about their experience," emphasizing the rational nature of reflective processes rather than engaging with the emotional and political dimensions. Thus, critical reflection blends learning through experience with theoretical and technical learning to form new knowledge constructions, and new behaviors or insights (Rigg & Trehan, 2008).

One participant described this as the "total refusal, well not so much refusal, more slippery than that, an avoidance of allowing the students to inscribe the tutors as knowledge bearers or themselves as empty vessels to be filled with knowledge."

Another said, "The loose style of the [course] acts more rigidly upon the student … because I had to pace out and set my own boundaries upon my learning."

One woman said, "It was like a great jolt. It made me sit up and think what I want to do with my life. I'm drifting along in a job I don't enjoy and nobody else is going to sort it out."

Another highlighted: "I can recall incidents when my own uncertainty, that feeling of being on the edge of change, created the conditions for risk and it was in these situations that I think I learned most."

As indicated above, the purpose of this residential week was to create a temporary organization from which participants could learn about diversity, difference, groups, systems, power, and influence from their emotional experiences and observations. Readings and assignment briefs helped provide structure for such learning. Invariably one of their most powerful lessons was the realization that people differed in their perceptions of the week and responded variably. As such the recognition of diversity and difference was made central. A second insight came when the action learning groups reflected on psychodynamic questions such as "where does the power lie?," "who has influence in this group?," and "who are you drawn to in this group?." These typically unleashed emotive discussions about inclusion, silence, recognition, and difference, as the second illustration below elucidates.

Illustration Two – Grasping the Nettle: Working with Diversity, Inclusion, and Cultural Difference

The example below illuminates how the principles of CAL, which encouraged participants, through facilitation, to reflect on how they wished to work together and by what processes the learning and development would be shared, can create feelings of fear and anxiety. Risks are many and varied in learning groups, the expressions of powerful feelings such as anger, the risk of speaking or not speaking, the risk of leading, fear, and anxiety all have important implications for our program, and as the above illustrations demonstrate, students are actively encouraged to work with these issues as they surface.

This group dialogue, recorded contemporaneously by the group's facilitator, illuminates how engaging with CAL can be a source of learning about diversity, inclusion, and cultural difference. During the dialogue there are challenges to some people's assumptions, while support and validation are offered to others. Action learning groups are imbued with and surrounded by social power relations, which contribute to the construction of individual and group identity as illuminated in this example.

A group of six was a newly formed action learning set. The members were Nirmal, a Sikh man, Wolè, from Nigeria, Dave, a white man, Sally, a white woman, Geoff, a white man, and Mohamoud, a Somali refugee. The group's facilitator was a white woman. After four weeks of meeting and just prior to going on a one-week residential, Mohamoud told the other group members he was likely to have to withdraw from the course because he could not finance the course fees, so he wouldn't be attending the residential.

On the residential Sally joined the group, transferring from a different set. As they all sat talking one afternoon, Geoff told Sally of the group's history and Mohamoud's probable departure.

GEOFF: So that's why Mohamoud's not here. But it's probably just as well because he wasn't a very good communicator. We couldn't understand him very well.

FACILITATOR: Did the group consider cultural differences?

[There was no answer]

SALLY: Look, it's almost tea-time; shall we stop for a break now?

[There was awkwardness in the room and this suggestion appeared welcomed by most with relief. Despite the attempted avoidance of an uncomfortable issue, after the tea-break the subject was revisited.]

WOLÈ: If I don't say something now, I'm not going to be able to work with this group. It's been said that Mohamoud is a poor communicator. You should consider that he speaks six languages and he does not have a communication problem. If people find it difficult to understand him it's because they're not being patient. I'd say it's them who have the communication problem. If something like this was said at work, I would almost feel obliged to report it to authority because the behaviour displayed was racist. I've been observing over the weeks the body language people show to Mohamoud, how people cut him out when he talks, the ways people look impatient when he starts talking, just because he has a way of expressing something that is different from those who speak English as their first language.

I've been thinking how the way people behave towards him would destroy his confidence. You have no understanding of the structureof Mohamoud's first language, which will influence how he speaks English. And I feel you would have been patient if the person was French or German. So I think the behavior displayed by the listeners was racist.

[The other group members looked taken aback.]

Geoff sat back defensively: I'm not a racist.

FACILITATOR: Wolé didn't say you were a racist as a person; he said that what you said about Mohamoud's communication can be perceived as racist.

WOLÉ: Many small everyday actions and statements can feel racist even though the person might not mean them to be. Take my name for example, you've been finding it hard to say Wolé, so you've just anglicised it to Wally. But my name is very precious to me. I was given it by my parents at birth and it has a real meaning for me. To have a name given is like naming a dog and it's not what I'd want.

Dave to Nirmal: I know I've kept calling you the wrong name and you ended up saying, just call me Norman, because that's what they do at your work.

NIRMAL: Yeh, I would rather you called me my proper name. But it's like there's so many little ways that you get put down, you just give up battling on some things.

SALLY: Do you mean like last night in the bar, when you had to wait ages to get served? And then Matt from that other group just walked up and got served straight off?

Two weeks after the residential the group has met twice more. Mohamoud has continued on the course. The facilitator described Geoff and Dave as visibly trying hard not to repeat their earlier behavior toward Mohamoud. She recounted one incident as illustrative:

[The group was planning a presentation based on what they'd learnt about team building from the residential. Nirmal had written a skit modeling the group on Black Adder, complete with medieval English.]

GEOFF: This is great, but we must remember that not everyone in the group has English as their first language so maybe we shouldn't use the Shakespearean English.

WOLÉ: Yes, although you can't make the assumption that we won't understand. I've read quite a lot of Shakespeare myself.

Typically, groupwork within traditional ME avoids contentious emotional displays and the emphasis is on learning content, rather that learning from the process. The crucial point in the illustration above is that by encouraging a process of collective critical reflection on the cultural and racial assumptions and context of their group formation, participants were able to develop clearer understandings of the political and emotional processes that accompany CAL. Within CAL, facilitation is not solely concerned with supporting the learner in challenging or changing the discourses that generate positions of marginality; equally important is the capacity to illuminate the ways in which participants resist or reinforce power relations that develop from learning inaction.

Concluding Reflections: Possibilities and Challenges for Critical Management Education

The growing revival in CME is an indication of how the changing nature of education is illuminating the importance of working with diversity in the classroom. Our experience of running this MBA program is where the pedagogical process is as significant as the content for management learners. This highlights that *how* knowledge is being taught and learned must be located in the social, cultural, and/or political processes produced in the classroom. The program described above provides an illustrative example of the opportunities to work and imbed diversity into the curricula so that issues of ethnicity and race are adequately addressed while challenging curricula, which have a conventional Western focus through local and institutional developments. CME in the future has an opportunity to grasp the nettle to ensure it avoids the passivity associated with more conventional ME. This requires a process of disruption, which challenges traditional curricula structures and supports creativity and innovation in teaching content and process. It also requires, first, a diversity of knowledge and experience, which seek to broaden academic traditions and mainstream canons that are solely centered on Europe and the United States, by adopting other academic perspectives and approaches to teaching and learning. Second, as a community of scholars we could be more critically reflective of how academic knowledge is influenced by its historical conditions, and of its social and cultural impact, by this we mean exploring what epistemic frameworks are favored and why and who gets to design, lead, and speak in relation to curricula, in the classroom, in textbooks, and on what grounds. Third, as our illustrations highlight, CME in the future has an opportunity not simply to manage diversity but rather to open the canon in a situated way, so as to allow for inclusive approaches in which different perspectives may be expressed and recognized as valuable sources for learning. Management learners from diverse backgrounds often see curricula functioning as a form of exclusion of difference rather than working in a porous way and being open to dialogue and to including diverse perspectives. Our examples have elucidated how you can surface the social and political context of experience in the classroom through CAL, which offers practical insights to engage reflexively with diversity, emotions and power relations that provide the inevitable backdrop to learning both in the classroom and in the world of work about the implications of exclusion through alternative program design and perspectives in the curricula which goes hand in hand with intersectional biases (gender, nationality, class, race, ethnicity, age, disability, and sexuality).

However, while there are important future opportunities for CME, there are also a number of challenges, which needs to be acknowledged and explored. First, through our experience we have learned that working with diversity does not always lead to inclusive pedagogies. Our example highlights how difference can end up reinforcing the monocultural approach as the norm and experienced as a form of discrimination because diversity reinforces exclusion and discrimination by marking certain individuals and knowledges as "the other." We suggest that the recognition of difference has to be radically distinct from the exhibition of difference, in that it should work toward inclusive practices of teaching and learning and not toward the reinforcement of monocultural approaches. Second, for some management learners and tutors it can be difficult to engage in CAL approaches, as such approaches can be counter-cultural to the pressure to conform to organizational ideologies. We have highlighted in the chapter that a diversity-rich and inclusive approach to teaching is one that requires a form of "open expertise," instead of an expertise that is geared to reinforce monocultural approaches. In terms of implications for tutor roles, drawing on the tradition of process consultation (Schein, 1987), the educator-as-facilitator helps the learning group become aware of management/leadership processes and is concerned with passing on the approach, methods and values of process-consultancy to participants. In this way, the teaching/learning strategy seeks to integrate the educational-based activities with the participants' work and personal experiences and, as our earlier examples illustrate, reflects the processual and situated nature of CME. The innovation and transformation happen when tutors have the license to develop and build on the richness and the limits of their own positionality and expertise, working with different sources of knowledge and other perspectives to enrich the dialogue on diversity.

This shift in emphasis reflects how CME in the future needs to move from using individually focused educational methods to methods that place the emphasis on enabling management learners to observe and experience in real time the interactions between students and staff. Specifically, the aim is to understand better the social and political process of diversity and the different ways it is defined, contested, and negotiated between people and the ways this process reflects the history and context of the management learners. If there is an individual focus in this approach, it is because each participant can experience and make sense of the part they play in the process. But diversity as such and its associated dimensions of power and authority is a property of the group more than of a particular individual. Such methods reveal the complexity of the diversity process, one which involves moral and social aspects. Literature, discussions and critical reflection to support such methods would be chosen to reflect this focus.

Conclusion

In conclusion, our proposal for the future of CME is for an approach that is experiential. In contrast to more formal pedagogies which rely on transmitting authoritative "truths," a CAL approach begins with reflecting on experience rather than from accepted theory, and in working in groups rather than as individuals. It allows for what the educationalist John Dewey called "active experimentation," CAL methods have the aim of being able to observe and experience the "what happens if" when a number of people have to work together toward some shared purpose. A CAL learning design can provide an opportunity to be part of and observe in real time the interactional processes we have associated with diversity, authority; power; difference, including gender and race; and the ways these are experienced within study group, practically, emotionally, and conceptually. Furthermore, CAL presents an opportunity to observe, experience, interpret, and to question the assumptions which underpin interpretations. It supports the idea of generating theory through discussion in preference to deferring to received wisdom. As we hope our illustrations have illuminated, CAL methods can provide an opportunity to examine social and political as well as the psychological processes which permeate diversity, work toward an understanding of these events which is collectively constructed and take account of wider social discourses reflected in the microcosm of the classroom. The question is are we ready to grasp the nettle?

References

Andrews, R., & Ashworth, R. 2015. Representation and inclusion in public organizations: Evidence from the U.K. civil service. *Public Administration Review*, 75(2): 279–288.

Argyris, C., & Schön, D. 1974. *Theories in practice*. San Francisco: Jossey Bass.

Ayikoru, H. Y., & Park, M. 2019. Films and critical pedagogy in management education: A tourism studies context. *Academy of Management Learning and Education*, 18(3): 414–432.

Bateson, G. 1973. *Steps towards ecology of the mind*. London: Paladin.

Belenky, F. M., Clinchy, B. M., Golderger, N. R., & Tarube, J. M. 1986. *Women's ways of knowing: The development of self, voice and mind*. New York: Basic Books.

Beyer, L. E., & Liston, D. P. 1992. Discourse or moral action? A critique of post-modernism. *Educational Theory*, 42(4): 371–393.

Bion, W. R. 1998. *Experiences in groups: And other papers*. London: Routledge.

Boje, D., & Al Arkoubi, K. 2009. Critical management education beyond the siege. *The Sage handbook of management learning, education and development*: 104–125. Los Angeles, CA: Sage.

Bonnet, A. 2000. *Anti-racism*. London: Routledge.

Carr, W., & Kemmis, S. 1986. *Becoming critical: Knowing through action research*. Geelong, Victoria: Deakin University Press.

Dashtipour, P., & Vidaillet, B. 2020. Introducing the French psychodynamics of work perspective to critical management education: Why do the work task and the organization of work matter? *Academy of Management Learning and Education*: 131–146. 19(2).

Edwards, P. 1993. *Contested terrain: The transformation of the workplace in the twentieth century*. London: Heinemann.

Ellsworth, E. 1989. Why doesn't this feel empowering? Working through the repressive myths of critical pedagogy. *Harvard Educational Review*, 59: 297–324.

Ellsworth, E. 2005. Multiculture in the making. In C. A. Grant (Ed.), *Multicultural research: A reflective engagement with race, class, gender and sexual orientation*: 24–36. London: Routledge.

Fraser, N. 1994. Rethinking the public sphere: A contribution to the critique of actually existing democracy. In H. A. Giroux & P. McLaren (Eds.), *Between borders: Pedagogy and the politics of cultural studies*: 56–80. New York: Routledge.

French, R., & Grey, C. 1996. *Rethinking management education*. London: Sage.

French, R., & Vince, R. 1999. *Group relations: Management and organisation*. Oxford: Oxford University Press.

Gotsis, G., & Kortezi, Z. 2014. The rhetoric of diversity management: How critical diversity studies explicate organizational appropriation of differences. In *Critical studies in diversity management literature: A review and synthesis*: 23–44. Dordrecht: Springer.

Hibbert, P. 2013. Approaching reflexivity through reflection: Issues for critical management education. *Journal of Management Education*, 37(6): 803–827.

Lather, P. 1991. *Getting smart: Feminist research and pedagogy with/in the postmodern*. New York: Routledge.

Miller, E. J. 1990. Experiential learning in groups: The development of the Leicester model. In E. L. Trist & H. Murray (Eds.), *The social engagement of the social science: A Tavistock anthropology*. Philadelphia: University of Pennsylvania Press.

Mughal, F. 2021. When global meets local: Action learning, positionality and post-colonialism. *Management Learning*, 52(1): 65–85.

Mughal, F., Gatrell, C., & Stead, V. 2018. Cultural politics and the role of action learning facilitator: Analysing the negotiation of critical learning in the Pakistani MBA management learning. *Management Learning*, 49(1): 69–85.

Pässilä, A., Oikarinen, T., & Harmaakorpi, V. 2015. Collective voicing as a reflexive practice. *Management Learning*, 46(1): 67–86.

Perriton, L., & Reynolds, M. 2018. Critical management education in challenging times. *Management Learning*, 49(5): 521–536.

Revans, R. W. 1982. *The origins and growth of action learning*. Bromley: Chartwell-Bratt.

Reynolds, M. 1998. Reflection and critical reflection in management learning. *Management Learning*, 29(2): 183–200.

Reynolds, M., & Trehan, K. 2001. Classroom as real world: Propositions for a pedagogy of difference. *Gender and Education*, 13(4): 91–109.

Reynolds, M., & Trehan, K. 2013. Making sense of intercultural dynamics: Theory and practice. In J. E. Raffaghelli & G. Constantino (Eds.), *On-line learning: Education and globalization: Learning in enlarged cultural contexts*, Venice: Formare Series Venezia.

Reynolds, R., & Vince, R. 2020. The history boys: Critical reflections on our contribution to management learning and their ongoing implications. *Management Learning*, 51(1): 130–142.

Rigg, C., & Trehan, K. 2004. Reflections on working with critical action learning. *Journal of Action Learning*, 1(2): 51–67.

Rigg, C., & Trehan, K. 2008. Critical reflection in the workplace – Is it just too difficult? *Journal of European Industrial Training*, 31(2): 219–237.

Roberson, Q. M. 2019. Diversity in the workplace: A review, synthesis, and future research agenda. *Annual Review of Organizational Psychology and Organizational Behavior*, 6: 69–88.

Schein, E. 1987. *Process consultation: Lessons for managers and consultants*, vol. 2. Wokingham: Addison Wesley.

Sharma, A., Moses, A. C., Borah, S. B., & Adhikary, A. 2020. Investigating the impact of workforce racial diversity on the organizational corporate social responsibility performance: An institutional logics perspective. *Journal of Business Research*, 107: 138–152.

Sinclair, A. 2000. Teaching managers about masculinities: Are you kidding? *Management Learning*, 31(1): 83–102.

Thompson, J., & McGivern, J. 1995. Sexism in the seminar: Strategies for gender sensitivity in management education. *Gender and Education*, 7(3): 241–349.

Trehan, K. 2019. Making diversity our business. *Insider Magazine*.

Trehan, K., & Ram, M. 2010. Critical action learning, policy learning and small firms: An inquiry. *Management Learning*, 41(4): 415–428.

Trehan, K., & Rigg, C. 2015. Enacting critical learning: Power, politics and emotions at work. *Studies in Higher Education*, 40(5): 791–805.

Vince, R. 1996. Experiential management education as the practice of change. In R. French & C. Grey (Eds.), *Rethinking management education*: 111–131. London: Sage.

Vince, R. 2001. Power and emotion in organisational learning. *Human Relations*, 54: 1325–1351.

Vince, R. 2004. Action learning and organizational learning: Power, politics and emotions in organizations. *Action Learning*, 1(1): 63–78.

Vince, R. 2008. 'Learning-in-action' and learning inaction: Advancing the theory and practice of critical action learning. *Action Learning Research and Practice*, 5(2): 93–104.

Vince, R. 2010. Anxiety, politics and critical management education. *British Journal of Management*, 21(1): 26–39.

Weiler, K. 1991. Freire and a feminist pedagogy of difference. *Harvard Educational Review*, 61: 449–474.

Willmott, H. 1997. Critical management learning. In M. Burgoyne & M. Reynolds (Eds.), *Management Learning*: 161–174. London: Sage.

Young, M. 1986. The ideal of community and the politics of difference. *Social Theory and Practice*, 12(1): 1–26.

8

EVIDENCE-BASED MANAGEMENT EDUCATION

Rob B. Briner, Alessandra Capezio, and Patrick L'Espoir Decosta

An Introduction to Evidence-Based Practice

In the following we describe the origins of EBP, what it means, and discuss what we believe to be some of the most common misconceptions of its principles. Next, we discuss how this idea has spread into management and why we believe EBMgt should be taught in business schools.

What Is Evidence-Based Practice and Where Did It Originate?

EBP refers broadly to the idea of incorporating the best available evidence of different types from different sources to make more informed decisions about both specific problems or opportunities at hand and potential solutions or interventions. The term first appeared several decades ago (Sackett, Rosenberg, Gray, Haynes, & Richardson, 1996) in the context of medical practice and medical education. Concerns were and continue to be raised about the quality of decisions taken by medical practitioners and the consequences of poor decisions for patient outcomes. In general, effective decision making is compromised by well-documented biases (e.g., Kahneman, 2011) and even those with considerable expertise may make poor choices and decisions. In the specific case of medicine, doctors may fail to make good quality evidence-informed decisions even though they are highly educated and experienced (Tetlock & Gardner, 2015).

Perhaps the best-known definition of EBP comes from Sackett et al.'s (1996) editorial in the *British Medical Journal* evidence-based medicine: what it is and what it isn't where it is described as "…the conscientious, explicit, and judicious use of current best evidence in making decisions about the care of individual patients" (Sackett et al., 1996: 71). Put simply, "conscientious" implies making effort and

DOI: 10.4324/9781003095903-10

taking care in the use of evidence, "explicit" means making clear the precise content and nature of the evidence being used, and "judicious" refers to making judgments about the quality and relevance of that evidence. This editorial goes on to emphasize that evidence-based medicine is not just about clinical evidence from research but also about the clinical expertise of medical practitioners and, most important, the integration of these forms and areas of knowledge in making clinical decisions. Another key feature of EBP is therefore that it involves the use of multiple sources of information in order to contextualize and triangulate.

Since that time, the idea of EBP has been adopted, to varying degrees, into a number of other fields of practice including policy-making, policing, social work, and more recently management. While these fields are in many ways very different, they have all adopted very similar approaches to and definitions of EBP (see Trinder & Reynolds, 2000).

What Are Some Common Misconception about EBP?

The idea of EBP can provoke strong feelings among proponents and critics alike. Some of the most intense reactions – both positive and negative – are, in our view, based on misconceptions or misapplications of its basic principles. It is worth noting that in medicine and other fields there have been numerous attempts over many years to clarify its meaning. The 1996 *British Medical Journal* editorial mentioned above represents one such effort and debates about what evidence-based medicine is, and is not, continue to the present day (Greenhalgh, 2020). It is also worth noting that the term itself, evidence-based practice, is probably not particularly helpful or descriptive but, given its now widespread use, it seems to make more sense to use the term.

Drawing on our experience of teaching EBP and speaking with colleagues and practicing managers, we list some of the most common misconceptions of EBP in Table 8.1 along with responses that can help clarify how these perceptions are actually misconceptions.

It is worth considering why such misconceptions persist. In the case of the first three listed, these appear to come about through the term "evidence-based" itself which, at least for some, seems to suggest that EBP is about establishing something akin to absolute truth using only certain types of data or evidence. The fourth misconception is in part a consequence of a further misconception of how innovation occurs but also derives in part from the idea that the EBP process is unnecessarily slow and holds back progress. While it is the case that making more-informed decisions takes more time than making less-informed decisions it does not mean the process has to be slow or to get in the way of taking actions. The fifth misconception arises when the general idea of using evidence at all in practice or teaching is seen as the same thing as doing EBP. As we go on to discuss there are essential differences between EBP and using evidence in a general sense.

TABLE 8.1 Addressing some common misconceptions of evidence-based practice

Misconception	Response
1. It's about getting to the truth and establishing certainty.	It's about probabilities and likelihoods based on the quantity, quality, and nature of different types of evidence. Its purpose is not to seek truth but to make better-informed decisions.
2. "Evidence" means scientific evidence above all else.	"Evidence" means *any* form of relevant and trustworthy information including, for example, professional expertise. Looking across multiple sources of evidence is key to EBP. One of these sources is stakeholder concerns, so ethical considerations are also included.
3. "Evidence" means only *some* types of scientific evidence.	Any type of scientific evidence can be relevant depending on the question asked. For example, qualitative data can answer questions which experiments cannot and vice versa.
4. It gets in the way of innovation and creativity.	Innovation and creativity are not arbitrary but draw on existing information. EBP itself also requires creativity.
5. We're doing it and teaching it already.	While it is the case that evidence is always used in management decisions and in management education, using evidence is not the same as EBP.

What Is Evidence-Based Practice in Management?

Since its inception in medicine, several other disciplines and professions have attempted to incorporate EBP into their teaching, training, and continuing professional development. Multiple groups and centers have sprung up throughout the world to promote and support EBP in these professions. One challenge of developing EBP in management is that it is not a profession as such. Although this means there are not shared and agreed on practice standards which often define professions, the EBP principles and the process itself remains the same for managers as it does for traditional professions.

The Center for Evidence-Based Management (cebma.org) was established in 2010 to do the same for management as other centers have done in their disciplines or fields. Some of the earliest publications on EBMgt (e.g., Pfeffer & Sutton, 2006; Rousseau, 2006) tended to focus too heavily on the role of scientific evidence in informing practice. Subsequent writings, drawing on the earliest definitions of EBP in medicine, generally define evidence more broadly to include multiple sources and types of evidence:

> Evidence-based management is about making decisions through the conscientious, explicit, and judicious use of four sources of information: practitioner expertise and judgment, evidence from the local context, a critical evaluation of the best available research evidence, and the perspectives of those people who might be affected by the decision. (Briner, Denyer, & Rousseau, 2009: 19)

Another definition produced by the Center for Evidence-Based Management (Barends, Rousseau, & Briner, 2014) refers to the same multiple sources and to the idea that EBMgt is a *process* containing a number of steps, again drawing explicitly on approaches first developed in medicine (Sackett, Straus, Richardson, Rosenberg, & Hayes, 2000). It also includes a statement about the purpose of EBP in management or any other field which is to "increase the likelihood of a favourable outcome" (Barends, Rousseau, & Briner, 2014: 4). This more comprehensive and practice-oriented definition has been represented as an infographic by the Chartered Institute of Personnel and Development (a UK-based professional association for HRM professionals). A key feature of EBP is that it starts with a question first about the potential organizational problem or opportunity and, once identified through the use of evidence, the next question to be answered concerns the most appropriate solution or intervention.

It is sometimes the case that practitioners and managers and indeed some academics feel this is already what organizational decision-makers do. However, there are *three key differences* between what practitioners, including managers, generally do and EBP (Briner, 2019):

1. EBP emphasizes a particular *approach* to the use of evidence: Namely that it should be conscientious, explicit, and judicious. In other words, it is not just about generally using evidence but doing so in a particular way.
2. A second difference is the deliberate use of *multiples sources* in part to triangulate but equally important to contextualize and interpret evidence from other sources. For example, evidence from the local organizational context is vital to make sense and use of scientific evidence.
3. Another important difference is the attempt to follow a *structured* approach or process. This is important as decision-makers can easily be pushed off track or distracted in a search for and use of evidence.

An Illustration of Taking an EBMgt Approach

Perhaps the best way to convey the meaning of EBMgt is to provide a hypothetical example of the types of questions organizations could ask to gather relevant and reliable evidence. This illustration (Briner, 2019) considers the commonly perceived problem of low employee engagement. While there is much debate about what employee engagement means it is related to constructs such as job satisfaction and organizational commitment and is usually measured in a similar way using a self-report employee attitude survey. It is widely believed to predict a range of employee behaviors relevant to individual and organizational performance (e.g., Kelleher, 2013; Macey, Schneider, Barbera, & Young, 2011; MacLeod & Clarke, 2009). A senior management or HR team may have concerns that the level of employee engagement as measured in their survey is in some way too low and rather than simply assume that this is the case they would, in taking an EBMgt approach, ask the question: do we have a problem with low employee engagement?

With their question in mind, team members would start to gather evidence and information from each of these four sources (scientific literature, organizational data, stakeholder values, and practitioner expertise) to help answer their question and in each case would consider both its relevance to the question and level of trustworthiness. Detailed guidance about how to do this can be found in Barends and Rousseau (2018) (Table 8.2).

Returning to Figure 8.1 and the process it describes, the team would *ask* the questions, *acquire* evidence and information that might answer them, judge its trustworthiness through critical *appraisal, aggregate,* or pull it together and then *apply* it to answering their overarching question about whether or not they have a problem with low employee engagement. The sixth stage involves *assessing* the outcome of the decisions being taken.

When teaching and indeed practicing EBMgt it is essential to have the definition and the process in mind as well as some awareness of the ways in which it is different from what we usually do. At the same time, it is essential to remember that this is not a rigid approach or a recipe that must be precisely followed. Rather, it is an approach based on a set of principles which cannot necessarily always be completely followed. Sometimes only some sources of evidence may be used and not all the steps followed. While this is not ideal, the purpose of EBMgt is not to make perfect decisions but better-informed decisions. Taking an EBMgt approach, even if in some circumstances it is only possible to do so to some extent, is *still* likely to lead to a better decision and increase the likelihood of desired outcomes.

(Why) Should Management Schools Teach Evidence-Based Management?

The answer to this question depends on what one believes the purpose of ME – and indeed university education more broadly – to be. One view is that ME is not so much to equip students with practical skills directly relevant to the work of management (except in areas such as accounting and finance) but rather to inform them about bodies of mostly social science theory and evidence deemed applicable in some way to management and organizations. From this perspective, management is viewed as an academic discipline, just like any other, and therefore teaching something like EBMgt is not so relevant.

TABLE 8.2 Examples of the questions that could be asked to identify a perceived organizational problem

Source	Example questions asked to gather evidence to help identify the problem of low employee engagement (EE)
Scientific literature/ findings	• What do scientific findings suggest are the problems with low EE? • How valid and reliable is our measure of EE? • What do the results of scientific studies tell us about the *effects* of low EE? In what ways might this be a problem or lead to problems? How strong are these effects? • What do the results of scientific studies tell us about the *causes* of low EE? Are these causes amenable to intervention and change? • What theories have been used to explain low EE? • How trustworthy and relevant is this information?
Organizational data	• What do organizational data tell us about the nature of the low EE problem? How much of a problem is it? • What are the numbers? Are there any trends or changes over time? Are there patterns relating to particular parts of the organization or roles or functions? • Do organizational data reveal anything about the effects of low EE? What problems is it causing? • Do organizational data reveal anything about the causes of low EE? • How trustworthy and relevant is this information?
Stakeholders' concerns	• What do stakeholders (e.g., employees, managers, customers and clients, trades unions, shareholders, etc.) believe are the problems with low EE? • Do stakeholders have views about the possible effects of low EE? • What are stakeholders' perceptions of possible causes of low EE? • How trustworthy and relevant is this information?
Professional expertise	• Based on our experiences and expertise, what do we think is the nature of the problem of low EE? • From our experience what are the effects of low EE? • What do we believe, from our experience, are the causes of low EE? • Drawing on our expertise, what are our theories about the causes of low EE? • How trustworthy and relevant is this information?

On the other hand, if we view ME as more vocational then teaching EBMgt, or something very much like it, is essential as it helps students develop the skills required to make better-informed practice decisions. While management

FIGURE 8.1 An evidence–based practice definition and process

Figure devised by the Center for Evidence-Based Management and the Chartered Institute of Personnel and Development

practice involves many skills, a key distinction between managing and other forms of work activity is both the requirement and responsibility to make decisions that affect organizations and their members. As the quote from Mintzberg (1975) at the start of this chapter suggests, the decisions managers make can have profound implications not only for the organizations in which they work but in society more broadly. From this perspective, business schools have a responsibility to produce students who are better able to take on such responsibilities.

These perspectives are of course not mutually exclusive. Some courses within a business school could be taught as traditional academic subjects while others could adopt a more vocational or practice-oriented approach. A single course could include both purely academic and more EBP elements.

Whether business schools should include EBMgt in their curriculum depends also on what students and other ME stakeholder such as employers hope to get from particular programs. Most MBAs and professional doctorates, for example, are quite explicitly focused on post-experience students who are looking for additional knowledge and insight from management research to help them be more effective in their work. The same is true of master's programs aimed at students currently or planning on working in a particular area of management such as marketing or HRM. In these cases, including EBMgt or indeed making it the cornerstone of a program makes considerable sense.

On the other hand, an undergraduate general management program at a highly academically ranked university may attract students who are more interested in studying management as an academic discipline. Teaching EBP on such programs may make rather less sense.

While one can, and indeed must, argue and debate the meanings of evidence, EBP, and what we mean by trustworthy or reliable information we believe it is hard to argue with the idea that all business school students should leave better equipped to collect relevant evidence, understand how to judge its quality in relation to a particular context or question, and use it critically to analyze situations and where necessary identify likely solutions. In this sense, EBP has much in common with teaching critical thinking but with more emphasis on the information and data to which critical thinking is then being applied.

Key Principles for Incorporating Evidence-Based Management Approaches into Teaching

The past decade has seen a steady rise in activity around teaching EBMgt and its role in ME. Such activity includes discussions and symposia at conferences, online resources (see www.cebma.org), publications (e.g., Barends & Rousseau, 2018; special issue of *Academy of Management Learning & Education* 13(3), 2014), critiques (e.g., Morrell & Learmonth, 2015) and the inclusion of EBMgt courses in business school curricula.

Most of this activity has focused on providing practical guidelines about how to teach EBMgt in the context of ME as well as considering how doing so can help to addresses a number of long-standing concerns about ME such as the limited attention paid to critical thinking, ethical issues, and preparing students for their working lives.

Underlying this activity are a number of fundamental principles, which can help guide an individual academic, department, or whole business school interested in designing and delivering EBMgt education. While the eight high-level principles we discuss below is by no means comprehensive, and not all those currently involved in teaching EBMgt would necessarily agree with them all, they provide useful bearing points for those interested in incorporating an EBMgt logic in their teaching, their programs, or their curriculum.

Teach the Skills Needed to Ask and Answer Practice-Relevant Questions Using Critical Thinking and Evidence rather than Transmit Received Management Literature or Case Study Wisdom

Much university and business school teaching is based on a model of education where an expert transmits knowledge based on existing literature to students usually with some practical implications added at the end once the academic knowledge has been communicated. In contrast, a fundamental principle of EBMgt education is to help students learn for themselves by teaching them to ask and answer specific and context-relevant questions or problems faced by practitioners in their everyday work rather than telling them what they need to know or learn. In other words, the emphasis is less on gaining knowledge as such but learning how to gather and *use* knowledge.

At its core, EBMgt education is about learning to learn – how to gather, critically appraise, and use information to answer specific and ideally practice-relevant questions, which helps with the development of critical thinking and metacognitive skills (Ambrose, Bridges, DiPietro, Lovett, & Norman, 2010; Ford, Smith, Weissbein, Gully, & Salas, 1998). One of its goals is to turn students from relatively passive recipients into active consumers and users of knowledge (Briner & Walshe, 2014). This is in part achieved through conducting smaller versions of systematic reviews of evidence to answer practice-relevant questions.

Provide Students with Experience of Some of Our Common Individual and Social Cognitive Biases and Distortions and Ways of Dealing with Them

One important impediment to EBP and, more generally, to making better-informed decisions are the numerous cognitive biases that unconsciously shape the way we process information (e.g., Kahneman, 2011). Typically, students are unaware that such biases exist and can have a profound effect on managerial (and other) decision-making. Providing experience of such biases not only demonstrates that we can be easily fooled and why it's important to think about how we are thinking but also demonstrates the role of EBP in helping to minimize the effects of such biases. By presenting students with a range of examples of both visual and cognitive illusions (for examples of cognitive illusions see Kahneman, 2011, or Pohl, 2016), how these play out in management decision-making (e.g., Rosenzweig, 2014) and what can be done to mitigate some of their effects (Kahneman, Lovallo, & Sibony, 2011) helps to show why EBP is important.

Help Students Develop Sensitivity to Claims and Assumptions and How They Can Be Evaluated

As many have noted (e.g., Collins, 2013; Miller & Hartwick, 2002; Pfeffer & Sutton, 2006), management practice is awash with fads and fashions and extravagant claims about leaders, organizations, and new or cutting-edge techniques. If such claims remain unexamined they can derail attempts to make better-informed decisions. It is likely that, if they become practicing managers, students will be exposed to such claims throughout their career. They are also exposed to such claims during their university education through popular management journals (e.g., *Harvard Business Review*), marketing materials from consultancies and best-selling management books. It is only when the precise nature of the claims being made (about a management technique for example) have been identified that it is possible to consider the types and quantity of evidence required, in principle, to assess the likely validity of such claims. Asking students to spot explicit and sometimes implicit claims made about management practices or leaders can help sensitize students to their widespread presence. Once identified, the process for evaluating claims has many similarities with critical thinking skills sometimes taught in business schools (e.g., Braun, 2004).

Emphasize That the Management Literature Is One But Only One Source of Evidence and That It Is Not Intrinsically Superior to Other Types and Sources of Evidence

Given we are in a university context, there is a danger of privileging scientific or "academic" evidence above other evidence and information. Using numerous small examples and cases it is possible to show how, when it comes to practical management questions, any type or any sources of evidence can be the most valuable and relevant depending, as ever, on the question and context.

Teach Some Practical Techniques for Identifying, Collecting, Aggregating and Judging the Trustworthiness and Relevance of Evidence

When a specific practical question has been established, the skills required for finding, pulling together and critically appraising (judging the trustworthiness of) evidence can then be developed. The exact nature of these skills varies somewhat across the four sources. For instance, identifying and collecting stakeholder perspectives requires different skills to those needed for identifying and collecting scientific evidence. At the same time, the underlying logic of these techniques has many similarities. Judging the trustworthiness and relevance of evidence from any source requires us to ask many of the same questions to better understand what that evidence actually is, how it was collected, the ways it may be biased, and the extent to which it can safely be used to answer our question. Providing students with the opportunity to practice the skills involved in asking and answering such questions can start with examples from outside management such as identifying "fake news" and examining how claims and facts in the news can be checked (e.g., fullfact.org).

"It Depends" Is Usually the Right Answer

Another misconception not previously discussed is the idea that EBP is about getting to the "right" answer. On the one hand, the idea that gathering and using more and better-quality evidence will lead to the correct answer or solution makes sense. But this reasoning assumes that managerial problems are like math problems and have a single correct answer. Typically, the EBP process leads to the identification of a range of possible answers which are more or less likely depending on other considerations such as context and outcome trade-offs. A key principle is to understand and appreciate such contingencies as providing important and actionable knowledge. Hence, rather than searching for universal "truths" or generalizable solutions to problems we can encourage students to identify the various implications of a number of possible solutions.

Doubt and Humility rather than Certainty and Hubris

Some of the currently most-admired styles of leadership and decision-making across many contexts are those that embody unassailable self-assurance and a complete absence of doubt (e.g., Pfeffer, 2010). Students may have come across stories of famous business leaders who seem to share such traits. Senior managers may also, because of their experience and elevation, make judgments with great confidence assuming these have been mostly correct in the past even though learning from experience is actually difficult in complex situations where decision outcomes are quite distal and subject to many other unknown influences. ME should encourage doubt and skepticism along with techniques to help students judge the trustworthiness of evidence and the claims made about such.

Start with a Practical Question or Problem Not with Academic Theory or Evidence

For understandable reasons, many empirical publications in management science start with theories, empirical tests of such theories and then end with practical applications. It is not surprising therefore that much ME replicates this approach. However, EBP does not start with theory or scientific evidence but, rather, with a practical question, problem or issue. So rather than presenting students with bodies of what might be regarded as foundational management knowledge we start with the challenges faced by managers and organizations, unpack the nature of those issues, and identify how management research (along with other types and sources of evidence) can help address such challenges. It is worth noting that many of these challenges do not fit neatly into management sub-disciplines such as HRM or finance or marketing but are more likely to involve several areas of management research.

These eight key principles for incorporating EBMgt into ME can be used to help guide the design of EBMgt education. We now turn to some examples of EBMgt teaching to further illustrate how EBMgt courses can be structured.

Practical Examples of Evidence-Based Management Teaching

Having discussed the origins of EBP, how it applies to management, some commonly-held misconceptions and eight key principles for incorporating EBP into ME we now turn to three concrete examples of EBP in ME based on the authors' own teaching experience at their current and previous institutions.

As mentioned earlier, EBP is not a rigid recipe but rather a flexible approach whose only purpose is helping practitioners make more informed decisions. A similar flexibility is also required when adopting EBP within ME hence we provide multiple examples to illustrate just some of the ways in which it can be taught. Some of these involve single stand-alone modules or courses whereas others show how EBP can be taught across a whole program or curriculum. Each of these examples in different ways and to different degrees follows the eight principles listed in the previous section.

Example 1: Evidence-Based Human Resource Management

This semester-long course is part of a one-year MSc program in International Human Resource Management.

Aims

In addition to providing a broad introduction to the idea of EBP in management, this course also has the following aims which align closely with the eight principles described earlier:

- Demonstrate how management can be approached in an EBP way.
- Identify the costs and benefits of an evidence-based approach.
- Develop skills related to collecting relevant information of different types

including: (1) scientific evidence, (2) organizational data, (3) professional expertise, and (4) stakeholder perspectives and values.

- Develop skills related to critically appraising the quality and relevance of different types of information.
- Give hands-on experience of what practicing in an evidence-based way entails through completing several practical activities including producing a shortened version of a small semi-systematic review which gathers together the best available scientific evidence relevant to answering a specific management practice question.

Structure and Assessment

The first quarter of the teaching sessions provide a relatively brief overview of the principles of EBP and how they can be applied to HRM. The rest of the semester is devoted to the assignment which is a simplified and narrowed version of a systematic review or critically appraised topic (CAT) (see Barends, Rousseau, & Briner, 2017). The course is assessed entirely in relation to this assignment. Students are given a choice of question and some context to each question. For example:

> A healthcare organization has been measuring safety culture for many years and believes it has discovered a consistent (though small) relationship between safety culture and various types of medical error. The senior management team has decided that rather than just measuring safety culture they should now take steps to improve it. They are aware of various interventions healthcare organizations use to try to improve safety culture but are not aware of their efficacy. You have agreed with them that you will answer the following question: *What is known in the scientific literature about the effects of interventions aimed at improving safety culture?*

Reflections

EBMgt is probably more accessible to students on a specialist MSc since many of whom intend to go on and work in that field. The idea of management practice – in this case HRM practice – is more tangible and hence EBP concepts probably make more sense as a result. The assignment is, again, challenging because it is different from other assignments but also because it requires slow and steady work throughout the semester and cannot be crammed.

Example 2: Global Immersion Consultancy Practicum (Tourism Management Course)

This practicum course in the form of a consulting project in cultural heritage and *community-based tourism* is organized as part of a university's global immersion program.

Aims

The main purpose of the practicum is to assist a tourism region in a developing country in identifying areas of priority for the long-term sustainable and responsible vision for tourism growth in light of their present situation of overtourism, increasing population and environmental degradation. To integrate sustainability education (e.g., Cotterell, Hales, Arcodia, & Ferreira, 2019; Stephens, Hernandez, Román, Graham, & Scholz, 2008) as part of the broader response to overtourism, a link was explicitly established between each of the EBMgt-inspired learning outcomes (created at the intersection of Bloom's learning taxonomy and EBMgt functional skills) and the respective standard of the United Nations-supported Principles of Responsible Management Education (PRME).[1] The resulting Evidence-Based Transformational Education Framework (EBTEF) ensured the learning outcomes were aligned with the PRME's vision to realize the Sustainable Development Goals as expressed in the four pillars of the Global Sustainable Tourism Council (L'Espoir Decosta, Matus, Dale, & Wilson-Wünsch, 2020). The EBTEF is of utmost significance as it embeds elements such as learning strategies, critical thinking and the use of metacognitive skills in reflection, that are also part of its research methods.

Structure and Assessment

Before they fly out, students receive intensive training through workshops on tourism sustainability and research methods and they are introduced to the main steps in EBP. They learn research strategies to identify reliable sources of evidence (from academic literature, industry and organizations, and stakeholders such as practitioners), as well as learning strategies, including critical thinking and the use of metacognitive skills in reflection. Students were expected to later employ these elements embedded in the research methods of the Evidence-Based Transformational Educational Framework (EBTEF) to assess the health of the region's tourism industry against the Global Sustainable Tourism Council's (GSTC) destination level criteria. These EBMgt skills and capabilities were deemed critical in the transformative learning of participants as they apply theoretical knowledge, searching skills, critical and analytical skills and reflections to:

- Identify the best evidence for practice and decision making.
- Use different sources of evidence to lead in research, collaboration, and policy proposal.
- Acquire evidence and appraise its relevance and usefulness to the problem under study.
- Obtain practical insights into how to turn evidence into action.

Assessments are multi-pronged. An initial desk search and analysis assignment requires students to identify theories relevant to their subjects of interest (e.g., over-tourism, excess carrying capacity, commodification, erosion of culture, conflicts between communities and tourists, destruction of ecosystems (Dodds & Butler, 2019; Milano, Cheer, & Novelli, 2019). This exercise enables students to focus during the problematization phase and allows them to surface not only their own assumptions about the issues at hand but also those underlying theoretical explanations. A phase 2 practicum in situ assessment requires students to focus on the different pillars of the GSTC destination sustainability criteria to:

- Confirm the list of key stakeholders in the sector based on the exercise carried out in the initial phase.
- Identify the key documents necessary to verify the indicators for assessment through reports and information from GSTC.
- Identify missing evidence/documentation about performance in the sector under each of the four pillars.
- Confirm the research methods identified in phase 1 as part of the triangulation (of methods, respondents, and researchers) process adopted and implemented during the practicum.
- Appraise the literature collected related to key dimensions of tourism, including tourists' motivations, government policy and planning at both the tourism and inter-sectoral levels, host community and socio-cultural impacts, host environment and ecological impacts, and host economy and business and economic impacts.
- Analyze the data and information gathered to assess and evaluate the state of destination sustainability national standards since Indonesia's adoption of the GSTC destination level criteria and indicators.
- Develop a Destination Sustainability Assessment Report for local stakeholders and deliver evidence-based recommendations to the government and community to address areas of priorities in view of the challenges that over-tourism and concomitant problems represent to long-term sustainable and responsible tourism growth.

Ultimately, the groups gather evidence and information by interviewing key local stakeholders, local industry experts, and community leaders and members. Further primary data is collected through participant observation. Secondary data are collected from industry reports, official local and national government reports, previously commissioned consultancy reports, and UNWTO and World Bank reports and on-site evaluation. In the analysis phase, students have to make sense of the data collected to answer questions related to the different GSTC criteria of assessment under each pillar. The groups then critically appraise these answers a using extant scientific literature to ascertain the evidence-based recommendations in the Destination Sustainability Assessment Report, which was finalized upon the students' return to their home university. This is different from a standard case assignment by its emphasis on the systematic evidence-based approach to appraise the different types of evidence available.

Reflections

The faculty members aimed to provide them with research skills to encourage inquisitiveness, creativity, and a thirst for knowledge by requiring them to (1) identify the practical problem and turn it into a question, and (2) search for information and theories of explanation in scientific literature to support their questioning. The practicum thus provided a curriculum employing a combined approach made up of research-methods and EBMgt. This meant students had to be aware of existing research and knowledge in the field to ultimately become reflective practitioners by evaluating both existing and their own research. The post-action course feedback report revealed students would have preferred a longer time for training in EBP skills. An individual reflection part of their final group report revealed students appreciated the opportunity the practicum pro-vided in understanding the relationship between EBP and research. There were several points during the practicum where students were challenged to integrate practical evidence (from literature, stakeholders, organizations and practitioners) under each of the four pillars they were studying (e.g., site interpretation as part of cultural and natural heritage management and water management and waste water as part of environmental conservation).

Example 3: Evidence-Based Practice in Organizations (Capstone)

Aims

This MBA course requires students and practitioners to consolidate, integrate, and apply their knowledge, tools, theoretical frameworks, and EBMgt capabilities ac-quired throughout the MBA program to develop solutions to real world problems, opportunities, and innovation challenges. The course provides students with an integrated learning experience that strengthens all functional and core EBMgt cap-abilities (in particular the Assess & Apply skills), and how to translate knowledge, and practice ethical and responsible management in a research-led or applied project.

Structure and Assessment

After a refresher on EBMgt tools and frameworks, the students individually work on a ten-week self-directed project to develop, design, and implement (if war-ranted and feasible), an evidence-based innovative management decision to ad-dress a complex real-world problem, preferably within their organization.

Students can choose among four different options for the applied project:

1. A piloting and implementation proposal that relies on designing an evidence-based intervention or innovation in collaboration with their own organization or an organization of their choice. The outcome of this option is the proposal of methodological instruments and a well-laid out plan for implementation of the project.
2. A consultancy report that requires the student to act as a consultant working on a real-life management or business problem within an organization, a business, or a department that requires their EBMgt knowledge and skills to propose solutions through a properly structured and presented consultancy project (practicum).
3. A thesis related to an empirical problem within the student's organization, a department, or business of their choice using the school's EBMgt framework (Capezio, L'Espoir Decosta, & Keating, 2016) displaying all the related capabilities to ultimately propose appropriate evidence-based solutions and show academic contributions to the field of EBMgt.
4. An Evidence-Based Intervention or Innovation Proposal. For this option, the student has to write a report, which they will present to their organization. In the report, they are required to design and plan an evidence-based intervention or innovation, in collaboration with their organization, with the purpose of piloting and implementation, to address a complex problem, opportunity, or innovation challenge. The student will be required to develop a detailed implementation plan that (1) incorporates the tenets and principles of EBMgt and Responsible Management, and (2) shows how to evaluate and assess progress and success of the intervention.

Reflections

In the core Evidence-Based Management Course at the start of the program, the students learned how to conduct a Critically Appraised Topic (CAT – see Barends et al., 2017) a smaller version of a systematic review – where they examined the science behind a complex problem in their organizations. In this capstone course, they were required to synthesize the knowledge, skills, and capabilities honed throughout the programs and build upon several pieces of reflections across different disciplines to apply to a management problem (and its related discipline) in an organization. Though students found writing up the final report quite challenging, they appreciated the EBMgt skills and capabilities they acquired in the preceding courses (through assignments like the CAT) as helpful and relieving.

These three examples of EBMgt courses and our experiences of teaching them suggest that EBMgt can play a key role in ME by providing students with opportunities to engage actively with management research through the process of using it to help make decisions about a practical problem. By incorporating the eight principles, these courses not only develop skills around collecting and using information of various types but also help to develop attitudes or frames of mind toward management and managerial work such as accepting "it depends" answers and doubt and humility.

Although such EBMgt courses can play a key role in ME, they are rather different in the ways described earlier, to more traditional ME. For this reason, EBMgt education also raises concerns for academics and students alike. We now discuss some of these along with what we have found to be useful responses.

Responding to Concerns Raised by Teaching Evidence-Based Management

In our experience, and those of others who have introduced EBMgt into ME, it does seem to be the case that such courses can raise a range of concerns for both academic colleagues and students. In the following we consider some of these concerns and possible responses.

As mentioned earlier, teaching EBP in management is somewhat different to most other forms of ME and these differences can play out in the ways in which both academic colleagues and students sometimes react. One of the most striking and most readily apparent differences is that rather than presenting historical and contemporary received wisdom across different fields of management gleaned from research, EBMgt teaching focuses on the *processes* of gaining knowledge and insight. In other words, it focuses on encouraging students to identify and then ask good questions and then equipping them with the skills they need to gather evidence with which to answer them.

Examples of Concerns Raised by *Academics* with Some Responses

Why Are Students Asking Me to Justify My Course Material in Relation to Evidence-Based Practice Principles?

A key feature of EBMgt courses is the emphasis on the idea that claims need to be examined and to do so it is important to evaluate the quality and quantity of evidence needed to support specific claims. Sometimes this learning generalizes to other courses such that they may question the claims implicit in the course materials. For example, students may ask about the evidence for Maslow or organizational change models. While many colleagues welcome such critical questioning, others, in our experience, do not feel such content is part of a historical core curriculum in ME which simply needs to be delivered. This can raise some important and interesting discussions about the content of well-established courses (and their accompanying textbooks) concerning the purpose of ME more generally.

Why Do These EBMgt Courses Privilege Only Certain Types of Scientific Evidence?

From the outside, it can appear that EBP is exclusively about randomized controlled trials and quantitative data. As mentioned above, we regard this as one of the misconceptions of EBP because what constitutes high quality and relevant information depends entirely on the question. Some of these concerns reflect historical and still current tensions with management science. By using different kinds of practical management questions, it is possible to demonstrate that within EBP many different types of scientific evidence are relevant (see also Petticrew & Roberts, 2003).

Examples of Concerns Raised by *Students* with Some Responses

Aren't You Supposed to Be Telling Us What We Need to Know?

Students are, on the whole, used to teaching which delivers received academic wisdom. EBMgt teaching focuses on questioning received wisdom (both practical and academic) and identifying what we don't know or is rather uncertain. This seems to frustrate some students who expect and perhaps want to be told what is "correct." One way of dealing with this is to emphasize that an EBMgt approach improves skills such as critical thinking and evaluating claims which also have practical value at work.

But I Don't Know What to Believe Anymore

This concern is most often raised when an EBMgt course starts to examine evidence for widely used and fashionable management practices. It is, typically, fairly easy to demonstrate that such practices do not have much, if any, support in the scientific literature. Most students are shocked by this – having heard many stories and claims in the popular management literature. Some appreciate the debunking while for others it can create some uncertainty and even frustration. One response to this is, again, to emphasize that an EBMgt course is about learning practical skills, not simply being told what to think and to judge the degree to which claims are likely to be correct. Another response is to give multiple examples of management practices for which there is better-quality evidence in order to illustrate that the point is not to disbelieve everything but rather discover what is more or less believable.

This Course Is Hard Work

Because of the uncertainties, the learning-how-to-learn approach and the more hands-on assessments, students sometimes do report that an EBMgt course is much harder than other courses. Our usual response is that such courses are harder for a good reason: Because such courses are teaching new skills so they are bound to be more difficult than courses in which students can use their existing skills to keep up with the course and complete the assessment. It's also worth pointing out that learning is generally better when faced with more complex tasks that bring higher cognitive loads.

But We Aren't Practicing Managers So How Can We Use the Other Sources of Evidence?

Students sometimes struggle with the idea that EBMgt is about using four sources of evidence but the courses we teach tend to focus only on one source if the students are not also currently practicing managers (as they may be on part-time MBAs for example). In order to deal with this concern it is important, where possible, to give examples of other types of evidence and information students are likely to encounter in the workplace. This can be done through cases which include evidence from the other three sources or business simulations.

Although some of these concerns are based on misconceptions of EBMgt, others represent understandable and indeed desirable responses to ways of teaching which emphasize critical thinking, questioning and independence. Such responses are desirable in that they constitute a form of active and reflexive engagement with the experience of ME which can, if dealt with effectively, be used to better explain the purpose and value of EBMgt courses.

Implications for the Future of (Evidence-Based) Management Education

EBMgt is not now widely or routinely taught in business schools though, as mentioned above, it does seem that the number of institutions teaching EBMgt is slowly increasing. But what of the future? There seem to be three possible futures. The *first* is that EBMgt remains a small or even fringe activity within ME. Given the concerns EBMgt teaching seems to provoke for at least some people, and the fact that such teaching is rather different to and perhaps more demanding than more traditional business school teaching, this possibility seems quite plausible.

Another possible future is that EBMgt becomes a dominant and mainstream approach to ME. At the present time this seems the least likely unless accreditation bodies such as AACSB or AMBA require EBMgt to be taught as part of the accreditation standards. However, the increasing pressure to address issues of global climate change and environmental concerns has highlighted the expanding significance of the UNSDGs and its ramifications in education as more and more of the world's business schools are becoming PRME signatories. As we showed in example two, EBMgt allowed for an efficient integration of these principles, thus taking ME to new levels of growth and socio-economic significance.

It is possible, in a third scenario, that EBMgt gains a much wider acceptance with ME. EBMgt education is itself a model of ethical and responsible decision-making given that problems, opportunities, and their most preferred solutions are identified on the basis of the best available and most trustworthy evidence derived from the triangulation of multiple sources of evidence. Such an approach helps to reduce risk, mitigate problem misdiagnosis and resource wastage in terms of ineffectual interventions, as well as to increase the likelihood of achieving desired outcomes. Incorporating stakeholder concerns as a source of evidence to test claims about problems and their solutions will likely help improve organizational trust, adoption, and implementation of evidence-based practice in the workplace.

Given the increasing availability of certain types of data in organizations and the external demands for managers and leaders to use such data in their decision making we hope, perhaps optimistically, that there will be a concomitant increase in any type of ME that focuses, as does EBMgt, on helping managers and future managers make more-informed decisions for the benefit of business and society more broadly. Addressing what seem to be global political trends around fake news and disinformation may also help accelerate the demand for EBMgt education. External challenges that the SARS-CoV-2 pandemic and its concomitant impacts present to both the private and public sectors have highlighted the need for a generation of managers who can make informed decisions based on data and different sources of evidence. EBMgt education not only promises better informed decision-making processes but also more fundamentally active, rather than passive, processes of knowledge and insight acquisition and application which help business students to make better decisions. In learning EBMgt students develop other core capabilities including metacognitive skills (thinking about thinking), problematization, triangulation, business research methods, probabilistic reasoning, critical thinking, and causal inference.

As the opening quote from Mintzberg (1975) emphasizes, what management does and how well it is done *really* matters. One function of ME is to help future managers be more effective (and more ethical) in their practice. We believe that teaching evidence-based management is one way of doing this.

Note

1 For details about the six principles of the PRME, please go to: https://www.unprme.org/about-prme/the-six-principles.php

References

Ambrose, S. A., Bridges, M. W., DiPietro, M., Lovett, M. C., & Norman, M. K. 2010. *How learning works: Seven research-based principles for smart teaching.* San Francisco, CA: Jossey-Bass.

Barends, E., & Rousseau, D. M. 2018. *Evidence-based management: How to use evidence to make better organizational decisions.* London: Kogan Page Publishers.

Barends, E., Rousseau, D. M., & Briner, R. B. 2014. *Evidence-based management: The basic principles.* Amsterdam: Center for Evidence-Based Management.

Barends, E., Rousseau, D. M., & Briner, R. B. 2017. *CEBMa guideline for critically appraised topics in management and organizations.* Amsterdam: Center for Evidence-Based Management.

Braun, N. M. 2004. Critical thinking in the business curriculum. *Journal of Education for Business,* 79(4): 232–236.

Briner, R. B. 2019. The basics of evidence-based practice. *SHRM Executive Network: HR People + Strategy,* Retrieved from https://cebma.org/wp-content/uploads/Briner-The-Basics-of-Evidence-Based-Practice.pdf

Briner, R. B., Denyer, D., & Rousseau, D. M. 2009. Evidence-based management: Concept cleanup time? *Academy of Management Perspectives,* 23(4): 19–32.

Briner, R. B., & Walshe, N. D. 2014. From passively received wisdom to actively constructed knowledge: Teaching systematic review skills as a foundation of evidence-based management. *Academy of Management Learning & Education,* 13(3): 415–432.

Capezio, A., L'Espoir Decosta, J. N. P., & Keating, B. 2016. "Evidence-based management competency grid." Unpublished internal report. *Evidence-Based Management Curriculum.* Research School of Management, Australian National University.

Collins, D. 2013. *Management fads and buzzwords: Critical-practical perspectives*London: Routledge.

Cotterell, D., Hales, R., Arcodia, C., & Ferreira, J. A. 2019. Overcommitted to tourism and under committed to sustainability: The urgency of teaching "strong sustainability" in tourism courses. *Journal of Sustainable Tourism,* 27(7): 882–902.

Dodds, R., & Butler, R. 2019. The phenomena of overtourism: A review. *International Journal of Tourism Cities,* 5(4): 519–528.

Ford, J. K., Smith, E. M., Weissbein, D. A., Gully, S. M., & Salas, E. 1998. Relationships of goal orientation, metacognitive activity, and practice strategies with learning outcomes and transfer. *Journal of Applied Psychology,* 83(2): 218–233.

Greenhalgh, T. 2020. Will COVID-19 be evidence-based medicine's nemesis? *PLoS Medicine,* 17(6): e1003266. 10.1371/journal.pmed.100326

Kahneman, D. 2011. *Thinking, fast and slow.* New York: Farrar, Straus and Giroux.

Kahneman, D., Lovallo, D., & Sibony, O. 2011. Before you make that big decision. *Harvard Business Review,* 89(6): 50–60.

Kelleher, B. 2013. *Employee engagement for dummies.* Hoboken, NJ: John Wiley & Sons.

L'Espoir Decosta, J. N. P., Matus, S., Dale, N. F., & Wilson-Wünsch, B. 2020. Transformative education: An evidence-based framework as best practice in the age of overtourism. In *Overtourism and tourism education: A strategy for sustainable tourism future* Séraphin, H. & Yallop, A. C. (Eds.), London: Routledge, 155–179. https://www.taylorfrancis.com/books/edit/10.4324/9781003031765/overtourism-tourism-education-hugues-s%C3%A9raphin-anca-yallop?refId=982e78ac-e95f-4c05-a744-918eb28690 10&context=ubx

Macey, W. H., Schneider, B., Barbera, K. M., & Young, S. A. 2011. *Employee engagement: Tools for analysis, practice, and competitive advantage.* Hoboken, NJ: John Wiley & Sons.

MacLeod, D., & Clarke, N. 2009. *Engaging for success. Enhancing performance through employee engagement.* London: Office of Public Sector Information.

Milano, C., Cheer, J. M., & Novelli, M. 2019. *Overtourism: Excesses, discontents and measures in travel and tourism.* Wallingford, Oxfordshire and Boston, MA: CABI.

Miller, D., & Hartwick, J. 2002. Spotting management fads. *Harvard Business Review*, 80(10): 26–27.

Mintzberg, H. 1975. The manager's job: Folklore and fact. *Harvard Business Review.* July-August: 49–61.

Morrell, K., & Learmonth, M. (2015). Against evidence-based management, for management learning. *Academy of Management Learning and Education*, 14(4): 520–533.

Petticrew, M., & Roberts, H. 2003. Evidence, hierarchies, and typologies: Horses for courses. *Journal of Epidemiology & Community Health*, 57(7): 527–529.

Pfeffer, J. 2010. *Power: Why some people have it—and others don't.* New York: HarperBusiness.

Pfeffer, J., & Sutton, R. I. 2006. *Hard facts, dangerous half-truths, and total nonsense: Profiting from evidence-based management.* Cambridge, MA: Harvard Business Press.

Pohl, R. F. 2016. *Cognitive illusions: Intriguing phenomena in judgement, thinking and memory.* London: Psychology Press.

Rosenzweig, P. 2014. *The halo effect:… and the eight other business delusions that deceive managers.* New York, NY: Simon and Schuster.

Rousseau, D. M. 2006. Is there such a thing as "evidence-based management"? *Academy of Management Review*, 31(2): 256–269.

Sackett, D. L., Rosenberg, W. M. C., Gray, J. A. M., Haynes, R. B., & Richardson, W. S. 1996. Evidence based medicine: What it is and what it isn't. *BMJ*, 312(7023): 71–72.

Sackett, D. L., Straus, S. E., Richardson, W. S., Rosenberg, W., & Hayes, R. B. 2000. *Evidence-based medicine: How to practice and teach EBM* (2nd ed.). Edinburgh: Churchill Livingstone.

Stephens, J. C., Hernandez, M. E., Román, M., Graham, A. C., & Scholz, R. W. 2008. Higher education as a change agent for sustainability in different cultures and contexts. *International Journal of Sustainability in Higher Education*, 9(3): 317–338.

Tetlock, P. E., & Gardner, D. 2015. *Superforecasting: The art and science of prediction.* New York, NY: Crown: Random House.

Trinder, L., & Reynolds, S. 2000. *Evidence-based practice: A critical appraisal.* Oxford: Blackwell Science.

PART III
Innovative Practices in ME

9

TEACHING MANAGEMENT IN THE FOURTH INDUSTRIAL REVOLUTION

Cynthia V. Fukami, Douglas B. Allen, and Dennis P. Wittmer

Introduction

We have entered the Fourth Industrial Revolution (4IR), an era characterized by the adoption of advanced technologies including artificial intelligence (AI), robots, and machine learning, among others (Schwab, 2015). The workplace will be fundamentally altered and managers will be challenged to reconsider the way they design and organize work, as well as lead their teams of employees. The 4IR also challenges management educators to reconsider the fundamentals of their discipline. What in management education (ME) is obsolete? What remains relevant? And what must be added to a management curriculum to prepare managers for a dramatically different workplace? Each of the previous economic revolutions (the advent of agriculture, the harnessing of steam, electricity, and computing as economic drivers) also changed the way work was done and the way managers led their employees. However, the rate of change now underway promises to compress disruption that might have spanned generations in previous revolutions into the single career span of our current students. In this chapter, we aim to inspire awareness, purpose, optimism, but most of all desperately needed change in ME.

Beyond the technological impact the 4IR is having on the way work gets done, we believe that the 4IR will alter the relationship between management and workers in fundamental ways. Much of our work on understanding effective management is based on managers and workers engaging in face-to-face interaction. Now workers and their managers may no longer work in the same physical space or even in the same time zone. The "gig economy" has led to careers as independent contractors, providing new efficiencies for companies (Manyika & Bughin, 2016) but new challenges for managers supervising workers

DOI: 10.4324/9781003095903-12

who do not report directly to them. Will these efficiencies help connect workers and companies, or will these new capabilities sever the relationship between workers and employers almost entirely (Hartman & Karriker, 2020)? Some have responded by increasing the use of AI tools to micromanage and monitor employee behavior (Roose, 2019). Others, however, see an opportunity to use 4IR technologies to empower and engage employees. We see this as a fundamental question: to what extent will 4IR tools lead to greater monitoring and external control of workers, and to what extent will they lead to greater empowerment and reliance on workers controlling themselves? In this chapter, we argue that the 4IR represents an opportunity to finally put Theory X to bed and to strengthen our use of Theory Y approaches to management (McGregor, 1960).

Are management educators ready, willing, and able to boldly engage the 4IR? Doing so will require framing the issue from related but slightly different domains: the world of management itself, the world of higher education as an industry, the world of business education, and the world of ME. We argue that these domains work as a system. For example, there would be no ME without work, and there would be no business education without higher education. In short, while our primary focus is on management education, we must draw upon the other domains for insight, resources, and constraints.

Applying these ideas to the future of management education, we must look at both the content of *what* we teach as well as the process of *how* we teach: "Perhaps more than in most fields, in management *how* teachers teach and the tools we use closely mirror important aspects of *what* we teach about the nature and functioning of the phenomena" (Frost & Fukami, 1997: 1273). In other words, management as a discipline has the unique role of covering content about leadership, just as we educators are acting as leadership role models in the classroom. We truly have the opportunity *and* the responsibility to "practice what we preach." If it is our end goal to better prepare students to adapt to the 4IR, then educators must adapt as well.

The remainder of our chapter is organized into four sections. First, we briefly discuss the evolution of management thought. Second, we briefly look at predictions for the future of work and associated implications for the discipline of management. Third, we apply a critical eye to the particular future of ME as it responds to changes in higher education and business education in the context of the 4IR. We end with a discussion of ideas, frameworks, and models for thinking about and preparing for the future of a 4IR informed ME.

Foundations of Management Thought: Then and Now; What and How

The discipline of management and the basis of education in management started during the Second Industrial Revolution in the early 1900s, and it was called the "classical school of management" or "scientific management." According to

McGregor (1960), this era was characterized by "Theory X" approaches to managing others through tight control. Since then, the topics we teach, and the way we teach have embraced elements of a "Theory Y" approach, which assumes workers (and students) are capable of and interested in controlling themselves.

What We Teach

In the early days of management, the primary consideration was the efficient mass production of goods with economies of scale. The metaphors and metrics of "production" were extended to theories of managing people (Bowen & Greiner, 1986). It is interesting to note that scholars and practitioners of scientific management were primarily engineers, not behavioral scientists (Freedman, 1992). Additionally, the management literature was largely dominated by North American and Western European writers (Cummings, Bridgman, & Hassard, 2017). This rather narrow view of management became and remains the dominant paradigm in the field.

A shift in thinking occurred when respect for and appreciation of the complexity and importance of humans in organizations was recognized (e.g., with memorable research such as the Hawthorne Experiments by Elton Mayo and others in the 1920s). As this research began to influence management departments and business schools, a more humanistic approach to management was proposed with behavioral scientists providing different perspectives than engineers (see Akrivou et al. chapter in this volume). Managers still needed to make budgets and plan schedules, but now employees were regarded more as respected elements of the enterprise, demanding more careful and thoughtful strategies to achieve organizational goals.

Across the twentieth century and beyond, scholars of the so-called "human side of enterprise" (McGregor, 1960) argued that work satisfied intrinsic as well as extrinsic needs and that workers were capable of and interested in assuming a level of responsibility for their work in what came to be known originally as Theory Y (McGregor, 1960) and later as "high commitment management" (Beer, Spector, Lawrence, Mills, & Walton, 1984).

Theory X exemplifies bureaucratic, control-based practices where management assumes the "worst" of employees and is similar to what Hamel more recently referred to as Management 1.0 (Hamel, 2011; Hamel & Zanini, 2020). Today management educators are challenged to prepare students to build organizations characterized by agility, creativity, and innovation, capable of responding to a world characterized by the acronym VUCA: Volatile, Uncertain, Complex, and Ambiguous (Giles, 2018). While the objectives of stability and predictability through authoritarian control may have been useful in an era characterized by slower change, today these same qualities often represent organizational liabilities.

The 4IR provides tools for an enhanced ability for surveillance, control, and micromanagement – a chilling continuation of Theory X management style. Yet, the needs of the turbulent environment in which businesses operate cry out for Theory Y: trust, empowerment, transparency, ownership, meritocracy, and community, among others (Hamel & Zanini, 2020). These issues are not new, yet business has continued to revert to imposed control (Pfeffer, 1998).

We believe that the combination of the 4IR and the COVID-19 challenge could encourage managers to embrace a more human-centric approach to management and business. If so, how do we as educators intentionally assist our students in making the transition to this new state? What default assumptions about the world, capitalism, the role of business in society, human nature, competition/collaboration, to name a few, need to be fundamentally questioned as we transition to this future world? What will that future be, and how will technology affect work? A strong shift to a more "Theory Y" infused approach to ME could indeed represent a beneficial outcome from both the pandemic and the 4IR – and a powerful "future-proofing" for our students' careers as managers in the 4IR.

How We Teach

In the early twentieth century, business classes were taught by practitioners, until studies by the Ford Foundation (Gordon & Howell, 1959) and the Carnegie Corporation (Pierson, 1959) on US business schools in the late 1950s gave rise to research-based teaching. Business school faculty were selected for research skills and were rewarded and promoted for research output, while teaching was re-legated to second class status.[1] Students were lectured on "what the professor knows, but not how to think, write, or find their own paths" (Fukami, 2010: 48). The professor was the "font of all knowledge and the students are sponges who soak it up." (Fukami, 2010: 47).

Criticisms of this shift to research-based teaching eventually started to appear, and reforms were called for by several management scholars (Bennis & O'Toole, 2005; Boyatzis, Cowen, & Kolb, 1995; Mailick et al., 1998; Porter & McKibbin, 1988). Some began to think of the importance of students learning, and not just professors professing.

Groups of teacher-scholars in management started to form associations aimed toward the support and development of innovative teaching. In the 1970s, the Organizational Behavior Teaching Society (OBTS) was founded as one such organization. The OBTS (now Management and Organizational Behavior Teaching Society), held conferences for the presentation and discussion of teaching issues and produced a journal to carry these ideas into the written literature. From the informal, hand-typed newsletter, *Exchange*, to the current *Journal of Management Education,* there is a roughly 45-year history of the Scholarship of Teaching and Learning (SOTL) in management. Since then, the number of business education journals has grown tremendously (Currie & Pandher, 2013; Rynes & Brown, 2011), and many universities and colleges allocate significant staff and other resources to the support of effective teaching and learning. Disciplinary associations, such as the *Academy of Management*, now devote a substantial portion of meeting program time to the presentation and discussion of effective teaching. Currently, we see a long-overdue emergence of attention directed toward the development of teaching and learning in doctoral programs, suggesting the legitimacy of teaching within the academy (Trank & Brink, 2020).

Overall, the pendulum had swung from practitioner faculty to research-centered faculty, and now it seems to be seeking a new and yet-to-be-determined dynamic equilibrium. To be sure, the 4IR may require even more of an emphasis on student learning than today. The idea of the professor as the "font" and the student as the "sponge" may be history.

In the same way that the 4IR is forcing managers to move toward a more collaborative relationship with their employees, the challenges of the 4IR require that faculty model the way for Theory Y by adopting student-centered approaches (Hoidn, 2017; Hoidn & Klemencic, 2020). These approaches, sometimes referred to as "heutagogy," can help model Theory Y management practice and at the same time invite the use of 4IR tools to further empower students to own their learning.

The teaching support systems now in place in many institutions of higher education arrived just in time. During the pandemic they often played a crucial role in assisting faculty to adopt new technologies as colleges and universities across the globe were forced to go online. Through this experience, many, if not most, faculties have gained at least a basic familiarity with new technologies supporting online and hybrid classroom modalities. The combination of this hard-won experience with new forms of educational delivery and increased teaching support offers new opportunities for faculty and their institutions to adopt 4IR savvy teaching strategies. It occurs to us, however, that even as we are now in the process of updating our teaching strategies, management educators continue to teach outdated and less useful concepts to our students.

The Future of Work: We Have Been through This Before, or Have We?

Technological change has been part of human existence since well before the First Industrial Revolution. Those changes have almost always been greeted with the same anxiety many are now experiencing. In the early 1800s, for instance, Luddites[2] worried about the elimination of workers by machines, yet, in the long term, those fears proved to be largely misplaced as technological change resulted in new jobs. Unfortunately for the Luddites, the new jobs often came far too late to offset the job loss experienced by the Luddites themselves (Frey, 2019).

Susskind (2020) argues that in the 4IR, technology will not do everything, but it will do more, while humans will face an ever-shrinking set of traditional work activities. As Semuels (2020: 1) states: "Machines don't fall ill, they don't need to isolate to protect peers, they don't need to take time off work." Robots are now delivering room service in hotels, cleaning floors at the airport, guarding malls, using chatbots to serve customers, and taking fast-food orders (Semuels, 2020). What new skills will managers require to coordinate this work?

Traditional work will still exist, just not enough for everyone who seeks employment. Humans will quite possibly face new challenges about how they will spend their lives and how they will be supported financially. As outlined above, scholars of the Human Relations School first observed that work is not simply a means to a wage but a source of direction, meaning, and purpose. To illustrate, Jahoda, Lazarsfeld, and Zeisel (1933/1971) found that the loss of work during the Great Depression was upending for many workers. It resulted in growing apathy, loss of direction, and increased ill will toward others. Displaced workers borrowed fewer books from public libraries, dropped out of politics, and stopped attending cultural events. Similarly, there are concerns about the impact of the loss of work in the 4IR. Yuval Harari (2015) predicted that the widespread use of AI would lead to the rise of "economically useless" people in our current economic system. And, if there is not enough demand for the jobs and tasks that people are being educated to do, "...a world-class education will be of little help" (Susskind, 2020).

Others have questioned this pessimistic outlook for the future of the worker. For example, Hamel and Zanini (2020, Introduction: xviii) argue that:

> It is a thinking error to assume that the vast majority of jobs in an economy offer little scope for the application of the uniquely human capabilities that distinguish people from machines.... While there may be a finite number of routine tasks to be performed in the world, there's no limit on the number of worthwhile problems that are begging to be solved.... The threat that automation poses for employment depends mostly on whether or not we continue to treat employees like robots.

Which prediction is correct? What role will human work play in the 4IR economy? Given the competing predictions, what should managers' and by extension management educators' roles be in helping to achieve a smoother transition to the 4IR?

Perhaps there is a self-fulfilling prophecy at play here as suggested (long before the 4IR materialized) by McGregor (1960). Jobs currently being eliminated through automation involve predominantly repetitive low skill work often designed by managers through the lens of a Theory X mindset. The rather pessimistic view of human nature Theory X implies may inhibit the imagination required for a new approach to job creation that engages workers as creative partners in the enterprise. Unless future managers are educated to think differently and systematically introduced to a more collaborative management model, they may be inclined to look at the future through the all too familiar Theory X lens. As a result, they may not be fully capable of seeing the possibility of a new relationship between worker and manager. Yet the ability to reimagine the "job" may prove to be a key capacity of the 4IR manager.

We expect that future managers and leaders will require versatility in addressing these very issues, as will management educators in terms of deciding what and how to teach in the future. Perhaps it is not an overstatement to say that entirely new approaches to management and new theories to support those approaches will be required in the 4IR. These theories may build on the work of the human relations school, proponents of values-based leadership, and others but will almost certainly involve new applications that assist managers in making practical and ethical choices as they embrace the technologies of the 4IR.

The Future of Management Education: What *Should* We Teach and How?

The purpose of higher education as it relates to business has been a matter of discussion if not contentious debate (Bennis & O'Toole, 2005) about the proper balance between citizenship, professionalism, and job-related skills. Business schools, at least in part, seek to prepare students for their roles and responsibilities as managers even as they often emphasize a wider range of technical and interpersonal skills.

Pfeffer and Fong's (2002) seminal work questioned whether earning an MBA resulted in any tangible benefit, other than the credential itself. They argued that companies recruit at top MBA-granting institutions because it saves time and effort spent in evaluating job candidates. If a candidate was screened, accepted into, and graduated from an elite institution, there was no need for the company to screen job candidates. Almost 20 years later, some (e.g., Walsh, 2020) are drawing the same conclusion as Pfeffer and Fong: the only value of a college degree is credentialing. We believe higher education can and does achieve more than credentialing, and that we can do a better job of proving and delivering our value. More than that, in the current environment, we believe views of the credentials will change. As we argued previously, market shifts, along with technological change, are sending a strong signal that business schools must rethink their value proposition.

In the 4IR many alternative credentialing systems (some even offered free of charge) are appearing on the ME scene (Hommel & Vandenbempt, this volume).

Google offers free of charge credentialing in project management and other areas (Hess, 2020), and Quantic now advertises a free MBA program to qualified applicants (Quantic School of Business and Technology, 2020). Both claim to develop field-related skills while also certifying their graduates. Although the quality of these programs is yet to be determined, we must prepare for a world where these types of programs will fill at least some, if not most, of the traditional limited roles of ME. What is left for ME? What new demands will be placed on managers by their organizations in the 4IR that ME is well suited to address? What is ME's new value proposition?

Proponents of the power of these new technologies (e.g., Colvin, 2015; Friedman, 2016) already claim that AI can do many cognitive functions of management at least as well, if not better, than humans. Hearkening back to Harari (2015), AI will continue to develop capacity in understanding and knowing humans – in some cases better than humans themselves. AI management systems may also understand some aspects of employees better than their human managers. For instance, AI may be able to determine what may motivate employees, as well as how to encourage and coach them, in some sense supplementing or assisting the role of managers as emphasized by the Human Relations School. We already see this being implemented in some of IBM's advanced HR systems (Burrell, 2018) as well as the Apple Watch. As such technologies become widely adopted, what might be the new or remaining roles and functions of managers in 4IR? Even as we are on the cusp of designing human-like *machines,* we are confident we will learn that many human qualities cannot or should not be extended to machines. Even as we write, IBM has announced that it is pulling out of some AI-based technologies such as facial recognition because of the danger of algorithmic bias and other misuses (Allen, 2020).

Anticipating the impact of the 4IR, Harari addresses education and argues that schools should redirect their efforts toward:

> The four C's – critical thinking, communication, collaboration, and creativity. More broadly, they believe, schools should downplay technical skills and emphasize general-purpose life skills. Most important of all will be the ability to deal with change, learn new things, and preserve your mental balance in unfamiliar situations. To keep up with the world of 2050, you will need not merely to invent new ideas and products but above all to reinvent yourself again and again. (Harari, 2018: 266)

Preparing 4IR Managers

As we review our own experience and scan the literature, we conclude that there are at least four broad domains involved in the preparation of 4IR managers. Two of these are addressed at least to some degree in the traditional management curriculum (human and operational skills), and at least in the case of business schools, two represent rather uncharted territory (technological savvy and predictive capacity). We briefly address each below.

Human interactive skills

As mentioned above, Susskind (2020) identifies both character and competence as necessary requisites for success in managing in the 4IR. The relationship between manager and employee may evolve to the point that the very title of "manager" will require updating to conceptually capture a more collaborative relationship between worker and manager. As Hamel and Zanini (2020: xvii) write: "…an organization has little to fear from the future or its competitors when it's brimming with self-managing 'micropreneurs'." A Theory X approach to management will certainly not foster an environment conducive to micropreneurship!

The 4IR offers managers the opportunity to recognize and release, perhaps once and for all, the human potential of the workplace. Work that is demeaning or dehumanizing is work that can and should be relegated to robots and automation in short order. Ironically, this is what Herzberg suggested many years ago (Herzberg, Paul, & Robertson, 1969). What remains to be tapped in the 4IR is the true human value offered by employees at all levels. Managers will require skills and training to engage employees in the remaining work as the creative, wise, and responsible beings McGregor (1960) described. We believe that if managers of the future are exposed primarily to the technical side of business, they will likely default to Theory X. The ultimate value of ME may be seen as preparing students to manage the human side of business in a more productive and more humane Theory Y style. Management educators must adopt a learning mindset as they experiment with new approaches to achieve this goal.

Operational skills

At the same time, control and other technical tasks remain important factors for organizations but need revision in the 4IR. Many of the technical aspects of management are early candidates for automation. In the 4IR, managers will still require the capacity to plan, organize, etc. However, these activities will likely be enhanced by information aggregation and decision-assisting algorithms utilized in a more collaborative mode with workers at all levels.

Helping prepare future managers to work effectively with these technologies will be a crucial new dimension of ME. At the same time, educating managers to make wise and informed decisions about when to maintain control over these operational responsibilities and when to delegate responsibility to their employees will be critical as well. Managers will be called upon to build the capacity of their employees through training and coaching experiences on the one hand and to develop a two-way relationship of trustworthiness on the other. This will involve an increased interdependence between the human skillset and the operational skillset.

Technological savvy

This capability involves managing the human/technology interface. While managers will not be required to become engineers or computer scientists, they will need to have an applied understanding of technology and its impact on the workplace. Informed decisions regarding the adoption and ongoing management of technology will require the ability to collaborate with technology experts. During the 3IR and the advent of computers, technological savvy was often left to the CIO and their staff who served line managers as customers. The 4IR and its emphasis on smart technologies are pulling these domains together in new and unexpected ways. In some organizations, machines are badged as members of staff, and employees find themselves working side by side with "cobots" – collaborative robots designed to work with humans.

Advanced technologies of the 4IR are capable of taking on at least some managerial responsibilities. In a fascinating experiment at the University of Manitoba, researchers found that a human manager was obeyed by workers 86% of the time, which is hardly surprising. What *was* surprising was that a robot manager was obeyed 46% of the time. Even more surprising was that the human subjects responded to the robot as if it were a human (Young & Cormier, 2014). In the 4IR organization, understanding and responding to the promise and danger of these new technologies move into the forefront of a manager's responsibility and authority even as some of their work may well be assumed by those same technologies!

Predictive capacity

We exist today in a world that is uncertain, but not entirely unpredictable. Managers will be challenged to develop and maintain a modifiable viewpoint (Allen, Fukami, & Wittmer, 2020) as the 4IR unfolds. They will require a mental map of the state of the workplace and business, including the changing needs of employees, opportunities to adopt new technologies, and ways society is impacted by and responds to these changes. Managers will be called upon to explain and interpret these trends, changes, and challenges to their employees and a variety of stakeholders who will view these developments with vastly different perspectives, ranging from deep skepticism to enthusiastic acceptance.

We now develop some possible options for ME in this world of 4IR and suggest some possible frameworks and models for thinking about the "how" of the future of ME. We use the perspectives of four main protagonists or stakeholders in this system: students, faculty, educational institutions, and society.

Stakeholder Perspectives on the Future of Management Education

The Student Perspective

A model that seems especially suited to the velocity of change in the 4IR is heutagogy, or "student-determined" learning (Blaschke, 2012). Rather than putting the professor at the center of learning, heutagogy aims to create a learner-centered model in which students are empowered to take control over and responsibility for their learning (Blaschke, 2012) (see also the Rivers and Holland chapter in this volume). In doing so, students develop self-efficacy and skills to learn, hence preparing them to adapt to rapid changes in their futures and to engage in life-long learning. Heutagogy builds on a long history of active learning, which puts the learner on center stage and moves the educator to the role of mentor or guide (Hase & Kenyon, 2013).

We believe heutagogy is closely related to a concept we have touched on in our previous work: the need for practical wisdom to be developed through professional education (Wittmer & Fukami, 2016). From the writings of Aristotle, practical wisdom is essentially the virtue of knowing what to do in specific situations. We argued that students need to be actively engaged in problem-solving and to take responsibility for their learning and the learning of their peers. We have also argued that pedagogical choices involving active learning in its various forms can support the development of wisdom in students (Fukami, 2007) (see also the Arkivou et al. chapter, this volume).

It is apparent to us that current students in our classrooms (in person or online) are not the same students we used to "instruct." Today's students are less inclined to see us as experts (Nichols, 2017) who know all of the answers. Instead, they are more willing to co-create knowledge with their peers while being mentored by faculty. This synchronizes well with the requirements of the 4IR in that students will need to be self-directed, life-long learners who can rapidly adapt to changes in work and society.

The Faculty Perspective

While faculty in management departments are unlikely to become technical experts in AI, robotics, and related areas of automation, they will need to be sufficiently familiar with them to understand and discuss with students their potential impact on work, employees, and managers (Allen, 2020). They will be challenged to develop their viewpoints about how these technologies should and will be used, how these technologies will impact the careers of their students, and what students can do to prepare for this new world. While a focus on the 4IR might begin as an "elective" in management departments (for instance, our course, Robotics, AI, and the Future of Work [Allen, Fukami, & Wittmer, 2020]), it should be made front and center – infused into the curriculum of most or even every management course. The 4IR *is* the future of business and more generally the future of organizations, whether for-profit, not-for-profit, or public (governmental).

Just as business managers and leaders need to be accustomed to the change from "boss" to "coach" in high commitment work systems (Beer et al., 1984), so will faculty members need to adjust to a different role in classrooms and lecture halls. Instead of being experts who merely need to be listened to, faculty must embrace the role of guides and mentors. Faculty will be required to practice what we preach to future business leaders: empowerment, self-control, and co-creation. Of note, the adoption of heutagogy will allow faculty to share with students some of the responsibility for keeping up with changes to managerial work and organizations.

Some have argued that business faculty create and disseminate knowledge that is unrelated or irrelevant to the practice of management (Grey, 2004; Starkey & Madan, 2001). Ghoshal (2005) sparked controversy by arguing that bad management theories are destroying good management practices. In the world of 4IR, faculty will be required to be more knowledgeable of, attuned to, and responsive to what managers are doing. Reminiscent of the classic work by Mintzberg (1973) who researched what managers do, faculty are now and will continue to be well served to be in touch with the actual work and activities of managers in various industries, perhaps by partnering with informed practitioners and spending more time in the field themselves (Wittmer & Fukami, 2016). Ongoing research about managerial work could satisfy both the requirements of faculty research and better inform schools about the skills that will be of use now and in the future.

The Educational Institution Perspective

Management departments and business schools operate within the larger institution of higher education. Faculty, in consultation with their administrative leaders, will need to determine the optimal mix of online and in-person delivery. This implies that a typical course may require a "hybrid" teaching strategy with simultaneous consideration of the ability to educate, economies of scale, student-centered design, and student preference. In Figure 9.1, we demonstrate how this approach might help us to better understand the relationship between educational economies of scale and student centricity with sample illustrations in each box. We note that while this grid offers a start to understanding this interaction, it likely will become the norm that institutions and individuals will choose increasingly innovative combinations of approaches found across multiple boxes.

Additionally, there need to be institutional changes such as rethinking what constitutes the basic building blocks of credentialing and degrees. Could

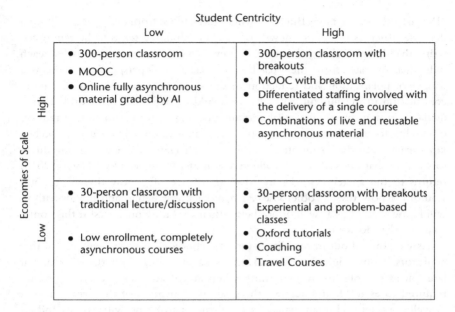

FIGURE 9.1   The relationship between economies of scale and student centricity in higher education

traditional four-year degrees be replaced by "stackable certificates," modular pieces that combined can be designed into a degree or stand on their own? Is the very notion of a "course" the best unit of program delivery, or should we think in terms of combinable "grinds," short one-day learning spaces that could combine into courses or certificates? These questions apply not only to the challenge of preparing students for work but also preparing students for life, including perhaps a life that interacts very differently with work than it does today.

The Societal Perspective

Harari (2018) argues that new technologies (AI) may be so powerful as to have the potential to "hack" human beings. This includes the capacity of AI to know one's preferences, patterns, and behaviors so well that humans become reliant on AI to select visual and audio stimuli. One simple and mundane example is how Spotify and other music apps can be relied upon to create a daily playlist for users. Algorithms are also already in use to help one select vacation locations, types of activities, retirement communities, or even spouses and partners. Still another example is the ability of Google to select search results that are tailored to our interests.

However, there is a downside to what at first seems to offer a wonderful efficiency and convenience. As is noted by Pariser (2011) in his TED Talk,

"Beware the Online Filter Bubble," when we all work from different and limited databases (such as sources of news), our current thinking tends to be reinforced rather than being challenged to think in new ways. At the same time, when each individual operates from their database of "facts" and perspectives, there is a danger of polarization and reduction in the ability to engage in full and frank consultation in meaningful ways. As the world of work and the world at large demand greater capacity for collaboration, reducing the ability to consult reduces our ability to engage in a collective process of innovation and creativity, likely a key capacity in 4IR organizations. How can managers and management educators ensure that the ability for productive consultation is retained? Harari (2018) returns to the ancient Greeks and the importance of "know thyself" (gnōthi seauton). Know thyself; otherwise, AI may hack our being, and the algorithms will know each of us as well, if not better than we know ourselves! If this comes to pass, what do we lose?

As we pointed out in our discussion of technological savvy, we believe that educators, technologists, policymakers, managers along with the citizenry at large need to collectively determine when and if advanced technologies are required to establish and achieve the goals and purposes of the organizations, as well as society. Human managers are already partnering with robots and AI in figuring out how to improve organizational effectiveness. Susskind (2020) notes that "…the challenge is to compete with computers *and* to cooperate with them." Management students will need to develop the capacity to determine how best to utilize AI and robots as assistants in the workplace. Managers will need to educate various stakeholders, including politicians, about these new production systems by helping promote a broader awareness of both the potential and the possible pitfalls involved with their implementation.

Additionally, government and policymakers will have to consider several issues related to the impact of the 4IR on society: regulation of advanced technologies, ownership of the technology, distribution of the financial benefits from the use of 4IR technologies (including options such as Universal Basic Income or UBI), and others.

Ideas for The Future of Management Education: Concluding Thoughts

Greater emphasis is now placed on "purpose-driven business" and "conscious business" (see also the Byrant et al chapter in this volume). Whether this is a real commitment or just a branding strategy, these businesses generally aspire toward some higher purpose beyond products, services, and profits. While human managers today can identify these higher purposes, we propose that partnerships with AI systems must be anchored in higher purposes related to societal well-being. We expect that an enhanced emphasis on higher purposes will attract and motivate humans. This suggests a fundamental reassessment of what organizations of the future will be *doing*. Certainly, businesses will continue to "make stuff," educate, entertain, and provide products and services. They may also exist to help humans be creative, socialize, and ultimately to find meaningful lives as they focus their work and their lives in a spirit of service to others. The question for the future of management, then, is what KSAPs (knowledge, skills, abilities, and perspectives) are to be taught in ME, and again we might look back to Harari's (2018) identification of the four Cs as a possible guide: critical thinking, communication, collaboration, and creativity applied in the context of supporting an engaged and empowered workforce.

Change is occurring so quickly that the world 30 years ahead is far too distant to predict with any degree of certainty. Perhaps the best way to future-proof our students and ourselves is to *adopt and encourage a mode of informed learning that embraces continuously updated perspectives as well as first-hand experience*. Our challenge is to closely couple these skills with the specific needs of future managers.

The world and human life have always been characterized by change. The Greek philosopher Heraclitus is remembered for his purported statement, "The only thing that is constant is change." Within one's lifetime, one is likely to experience major change(s), whether in technology, social mores, cultural practices, political institutions, health, and financial or economic shocks. Disruptors are ongoing and constant. Many (e.g., Frey, 2019; Harari, 2015, 2018; Susskind, 2020) argue that we are on the cusp of a different magnitude of shock when it comes to the 4IR. And those predictions were made before the COVID-19 pandemic, one of the greatest disruptors the world has seen in at least a century.

While the ultimate impact of the 4IR on work is far from determined, this is not a reason for management educators to pause or hesitate. It should be a call to action! We suggest that the current role for management educators is less about preparing our students for particular future outcomes of the 4IR but, much more urgently, about preparing our students to serve as managers, leaders, and guides as they assist organizations and employees in traversing a very turbulent period of change. Our current students face a career that extends 30 or more years into the future. It is likely that our students' careers will coincide much more closely with the process of the revolution and much less, if at all, with the outcome. The 4IR then should be viewed less as an event to be anticipated and more as a process to be influenced and shaped with the tools and values we might assist our students in acquiring. These navigators of this revolution in progress will be called upon to anticipate issues and challenges to be faced, to assist organizations and employees at all levels to survive and thrive in this journey, and to play their role in shaping our future state.

Our greatest hope is that the educational experience we create empowers our students with optimism and agency to be true shapers of 4IR organizations, thus taking full advantage of 4IR technologies to create organizations that are at once more effective and more human-centric. After all, AI, robots, and other technologies are merely tools that have not yet, and we believe never will completely replace the need for human workers and managers. What is desperately needed is wisdom on how and when to use the tools, leading us back to the importance of "practical wisdom," something the ancients understood before any industrial revolution. Some employees will be endowed with "episteme" (theoretical knowledge or understanding) on behavior and ethics, while other employees will specialize in "techne" (practical knowledge or "knowing how") to address the technical needs of the organization. Future managers will need to blend the two. It will be up to 4IR managers to assist the engineers of the Classical School of Management and other more recent attempts at optimization and the behavioral scientists of the human relations school work together to find the golden mean between those two extremes.

To us, there is no choice but to prepare students to navigate a real-time, emergent process of transformation that allows them to look toward 2050 and beyond with confidence and humility, on one hand, and with continued curiosity and optimism on the other. The preparation of our students for the *journey* to 2050 will be far more important than their preparation for the *destination*. To be sure, we teachers of management in higher education are facing the same VUCA world as our students. It's time to wake up, smell the coffee, and prepare for that world.

Notes

1 This may be more true in business schools in the United States than in other locations.
2 The term "Luddites" historically refers to a member of any of the bands of English workers who destroyed machinery, especially in cotton and woolen mills, that they believed was threatening their jobs (1811–1816). The term is now used to describe those who are reluctant to engage in technological change.

References

Allen, S. J. 2020. On the cutting edge or the chopping block? Fostering a digital mindset and tech literacy in business management education. *Journal of Management Education*, 44(3): 362–393.

Allen, D., Fukami, C., & Wittmer, D. 2020. A course on the future of work: Building the scaffold while standing on it. *Journal of Management Education*, in press. doi: https://doi.org/10.1177/1052562920983839.

Beer, M., Spector, B. A., Lawrence, P. R., Mills, D. Q., & Walton, R. E. 1984. *Managing human assets*. New York: The Free Press.

Bennis, W. G., & O'Toole, J. 2005. How business schools have lost their way. *Harvard Business Review*, 83(5): 96–104.

Blaschke, L. M. 2012. Heutagogy and lifelong learning: A review of heutagogical practice and self-determined learning. *The International Review of Research in Open and Distributed Learning*, 13(1): 56–71.

Bowen, D. E., & Greiner, L. E. 1986. Moving from production to service in human resources management. *Organizational Dynamics*, 15(1): 35–53.

Boyatzis, R. E., Cowen, S. S., & Kolb, D. A. 1995. A learning perspective on executive education. *Selections*, 11(3): 47–55.

Burrell, L. 2018. Co-creating the employee experience. *Harvard Business Review*, 96(2): 54–58.

Colvin, G. 2015. *Humans are underrated: What high achievers know that brilliant machines never will*. New York: Penguin Random House.

Cummings, S., Bridgman, T., & Hassard, J. 2017. *A new history of management*. Cambridge, England: Cambridge University Press.

Currie, R., & Pandher, G. 2013. Management education journals' rank and tier by active scholars. *Academy of Management Learning and Education*, 12(2): 194–218.

Frey, C. B. 2019. *The technology trap: Capital, labor, and power in the age of automation*. Princeton, NJ: Princeton University Press.

Freedman, D. 1992. Is management still a science? *Harvard Business Review*, November–December: 4–11.

Friedman, T. L. 2016. *Thank you for being late: An optimist's guide to thriving in the age of accelerations* (Version 2.0, with a new afterword). New York: Picador USA.

Frost, P. J., & Fukami, C. V. 1997. Teaching effectiveness in the organizational sciences: Recognizing and enhancing the scholarship of teaching. *Academy of Management Journal*, 40(6): 1271–1281.

Fukami, C. V. 2007. Can wisdom be taught? In E. H. Kessler & J. R. Bailey (Eds.), *Handbook of organizational and managerial wisdom*: 459–473. Newbury Park, CA: Sage.

Fukami, C. V. 2010. In search of enlightened business leaders. In D. Mayer & J. O'Toole (Eds.), *Good business*: 44–57. New York: Routledge.

Ghoshal, S. 2005. Bad management theories are destroying good management practices. *Academy of Management Learning and Education*, 4(1): 75–91.

Giles, S. 2018. How VUCA is reshaping the business environment, and what it means for innovation, *Forbes*. https://www.forbes.com/sites/sunniegiles/2018/05/09/how-vuca-is-reshaping-the-business-environment-and-what-it-means-for-innovation/

Gordon, R. A., & Howell, J. E. 1959. Higher education for business. *The Journal of Business Education*, 35(3): 115–117.

Grey, C. 2004. Re-inventing business schools: The contribution of critical management education. *Academy of Management Learning and Education*, 3(2): 178–186.

Hamel, G. 2011. First, let's fire all the managers. *Harvard Business Review*, 89(12): 48–60.

Hamel, G., & Zanini, M. 2020. *Humanocracy*. Cambridge, MA: Harvard Business Review Press.

Harari, Y. N. 2015. *Homo Deus: A brief history of tomorrow*. New York: Random House.

Harari, Y. N. 2018. *21 Lessons for the 21st century*. New York, NY: Random House.

Hartman, N., & Karriker, J. 2020. Preparing managers for a reconfigured world: management education's new gig. *Journal of Management Development*. 10.1108/JMD-05-2 020-0164.

Hase, S., & Kenyon, C. (Eds.). 2013. *Self-determined learning: Heutagogy in action*. London: Bloomsbury.

Herzberg, F., Paul, W. J., & Robertson, K. B. 1969. Job enrichment pays off. *Harvard Business Review*, 47(2): 61–78.

Hess, A. 2020. *Google announces 1,000,000 scholarships for online certificates in data analytics, project management and UX*. Accessed July 13, 2020, at https://www.cnbc.com/2020/07/13/google-announces-certificates-in-data-project-management-and-ux.html

Hoidn, S. 2017. *Student-centered learning environments in higher education classrooms*. London: Palgrave Macmillan US.

Hoidn, S., & Klemencic, M. 2020 *The Routledge international handbook of student-centered learning and teaching in higher education*. Abingdon, England: Routledge.

Jahoda, M., Lazarsfeld, P. F., & Zeisel, H. 1933. *Marienthal: The sociography of an unemployed community* (English translation, 1971). London: Tavistock Publications.

Mailick, S., Kfir, A., Stumpf, S. A., Grant, S., Stumpf, S., & Watson, M. A. 1998. *Learning theory in the practice of management development: Evolution and applications*. Boston, MA: Greenwood Publishing Group.

Manyika, J., & Bughin, J. 2016. *Independent work: Choice, necessity, and the gig economy*. Retrieved December 9, 2019, from https://www.mckinsey.com/featured-insights/employment-and-growth/independent-work-choice-necessity-and-the-gig-economy

McGregor, D. 1960. *The human side of enterprise*. New York: McGraw-Hill.

Mintzberg, H. 1973. *The nature of managerial work*. New York: Harpercollins.

Nichols, T. 2017. *The death of expertise: The campaign against established knowledge and why it matters*. New York: Oxford University Press.

Pariser, E. 2011. *Beware the online filter bubble*. TED Talk. https://www.ted.com/talks/eli_pariser_beware_online_filter_bubbles?language=en

Pfeffer, J. 1998. *The human equation: Building profits by putting people first*. Cambridge, MA: Harvard Business Press.

Pfeffer, J., & Fong, C. T. 2002. The end of business schools? Less success than meets the eye. *Academy of Management Learning and Education*, 1(1): 78–95.

Pierson, F. C. 1959. The education of American businessmen. *The Journal of Business Education*, 35(3): 114–117.

Porter, L. W., & McKibbin, L. E. 1988. *Management education and development: Drift or thrust into the 21st century?* Hightstown, NJ: McGraw-Hill Book Company.

Quantic School of Business and Technology. 2020. https://quantic.edu/

Roose, K. 2019. A machine may not take your job, but one could become your boss. *New York Times*, June 23.

Rynes, S., & Brown, K. 2011. Where are we in the "long march to legitimacy?" Assessing scholarship in management learning and education. *Academy of Management Learning and Education*, 10(4): 561–582.

Schwab, K. 2015, December 12. The Fourth Industrial Revolution: What it means and how to respond. *Foreign Affairs*. https://www.foreignaffairs.com/articles/2015-12-12/fourth-industrial-revolution

Semuels, A. 2020. Fewer jobs, more machines: In the pandemic economy humans are being left behind. *Time Magazine*, 196 (7/8): 64–71.

Starkey, K., & Madan, P. 2001. Bridging the relevance gap: Aligning stakeholders in the future of management research. *British Journal of Management*, 12: S3–S26.

Susskind, D. 2020. *A world without work: Technology, automation, and how we should respond*. London: Penguin UK.

Trank, C., & Brink, K. 2020. Teaching and learning in doctoral programs: An introduction to the themed section. *Journal of Management Education*, 44(4): 468–472.

Walsh, J. 2020, March 11. The coming disruption: Scott Galloway predicts a handful of elite cyborg universities will soon monopolize higher education. *New York Magazine*. https://nymag.com/intelligencer/2020/05/scott-galloway-future-of-college.html#:~:text=Scott%20Galloway%20predicts%20a%20handful,will%20soon%20monopolize

%20higher%20education.&text=The%20post%2Dpandemic%20future%2C%20he,the
%20world%20and%20elite%20universities

Wittmer, D. W., & Fukami, C. V. 2016. Educating future business leaders to be practically
wise. In Kupers, W. & O. Gunnlaugson (Eds.), *Wisdom learning: Perspectives on wising-up
business and management education*: 229–247. Abingdon, UK: Routledge.

Young, J., & Cormier, D. 2014, April 2. Can robots be managers, too? *Harvard Business
Review.* https://hbr.org/2014/04/can-robots-be-managers-too#:~:text=While%20we
%20do%20not%20yet,based%20on%20what%20is%20said

10

THE MANAGEMENT CLASSROOM OF THE FUTURE: MEGATRENDS AND GLOBAL CHALLENGES

John G. Cullen

Introduction

It is impossible to tell the future. History is the story of how societies and communities develop, but it is rarely shaped by our expectations of continuity. It is halted and redirected by unexpected events. Some of these are "shocks"; the impact of terrorist attacks, natural disasters, and pandemics, which change how we think of ourselves as groups of people in relation to others. Other events are "surprises"; diplomatic breakthroughs in long-standing conflicts, vaccines and treatments for long-standing illnesses, technological innovations that allow us to think about ourselves and our world in different ways. As management researchers and educators we often grapple with the "dark side" of organizations and their impact on society, but more often we focus on trying to assist our students to create and participate in businesses which create positive "surprises" that benefit society. Our management classrooms are full of models, ideas, and cases that present the thoughts and experiences of successful change-makers. However, predicting the future is much more difficult than presenting and discussing the past. The future will ask new questions of those who manage, and also of those who teach and learn about management.

Our recent experiences of how information technology has been used to connect people around the world (but also assisted the rise of dangerous extremist ideologies), the impact of the first global pandemic of the contemporary era, and the ever-growing urgency of addressing the Climate Emergency (Carrington, 2019) have all created a situation where management skills, knowledge, and capability are required more than ever before. At the same time, these experiences have also shown that the management classrooms of the future will likely

DOI: 10.4324/9781003095903-13

need to look very different from today's to enable management learners to develop the skillsets and mindsets that will enable them to succeed.

When sustainability and business ethics were once an occasional "elective" module in a management classroom that few showed interest in visiting (Bassiry, 1990), over the course of the last 30 years they have gradually become key to what is expected and required (see Bryant et al., this volume) to be taught and learned within business schools (Bagley, Sulkowski, Nelson, Waddock, & Shrivastava, 2020; Cullen, 2017; Gudic, Parkes, & Rosenbloom, 2016; Neal, 2017; Starik, Rands, Marcus, & Clark, 2010; Whiteman, Walker, & Perego, 2013; Yen-Chun Jim, Shihping, Lopin, & Wen-Hsiung, 2010).

This chapter will proceed by examining how large-scale social and technological challenges are likely to impact *what* is learned in the management classroom of the future, and *how* it will be taught. It will do this by firstly discussing megatrends currently encountered globally. Following this, technological trends and developments will be examined which are likely to impact the management classrooms of the future. The chapter will then discuss how management classrooms of the future must be more representative and inclusive of society in general, and how technology and pedagogy will combine to facilitate learning for all students.

Global Megatrends and Their Impact on Management Education

The United Nations Economist Network identified five global "megatrends" as the key challenges that must be addressed in order to obtain the prosperous, inclusive, and sustainable future envisioned by the 17 United Nations Sustainable Development Goals (United Nations, 2020). These are the climate emergency, the trend toward an ageing society, the growing tendency toward living in built-up urban environments, the proliferation of digital technology, and the persistence of inequality across the world. The report makes two important points about the nature of these trends. Firstly, they are inter-related, so solutions to challenges in one area may impact others. For example, the growth of urbanization contributes to ongoing environmental damage to a number of environmental and social systems, contributes to wealth concentrations which can influence inequality rates, and requires advanced levels of technological innovation. Secondly, these problems emerge from human decisions and actions; it implies that they can be solved by a shared resolve to address them. This has led to the naming of the current ecological epoch as "the Anthropocene" or an era where human activity (and the interests of some humans) has influenced the natural world and bio-systems more than any other on earth (Campbell, McHugh, & Ennis, 2019; Gasparin et al., 2020).

The 17 UN Sustainable Development Goals (SDGs) emphasize that meeting targets in relation to an individual SDG can also help others to be addressed.

The global systemic, inter-related nature of these megatrends means that management education (ME) is ideally placed to help address them. However, the individual student in the management classroom of the present may become overwhelmed at the enormity of the issues and come to believe that no single individual, profession, organization, or even country can do anything to address them. Aragon-Correa, Marcus, Rivera, and Kenworthy (2017) write that when sustainability is taught in the management classroom it must be done in a highly inter-disciplinary manner, which does not focus on environmental concerns alone but encompasses other social issues such as poverty, inequality, and economic development. They also stress that the outcome must be of a highly pragmatic, experiential nature and should aim at implementation of actions and evaluations of their success, while remaining respectful of the more traditional outcomes of ME (such as career and business success). Although the wicked problems so common in management practice are messy, difficult to define and are troubling in that we can never be sure of what their outcomes will be (Grint, 2005), the management classroom of the future must become a site where individuals encounter the realities of dealing with uncertainty, failure, and the complexity of systems (Fraher & Grint, 2018).

Many liberal democracies have experienced the aftermath of damage to social and political systems as a result of the utilization of new information technology and social media. Although this is a somewhat dark example, it highlights the importance of technology in enabling large-scale systemic change. The emergence of digital technologies is one of the five critical megatrends identified in the UN report mentioned at the outset of this section. In that report it is discussed as a change agent with the potential to radically change labor markets, work practices, efficiency as well as driving most of the UN SDGs.

Technology for Engagement and Learning in Management Classrooms of the Future

For many years, techno-educational evangelists have predicted how advances in information technology stand to disrupt the nature of ME (see also Lefevre & Caporarello, this volume). The global COVID-19 pandemic prompted many higher-level institutions to adopt a mode of online teaching and learning, and it is unlikely that student expectations with regard to this form of engagement will fully revert to previous models and expectations (see also Rivers & Holland, this volume). Many Colleagues in ME from around the world felt exhausted following the pivot to remote learning; not just because of the technological demands, need for new skills acquisition or even the development of new content, but also because of an emerging range of student issues and requirements on a scale not encountered before. Business schools face the excitement of larger, more diverse classes but the burden of this cannot be carried sustainably by overworking faculty.

Inferring that business schools were "forced" to implement online learning carries a negative connotation: that somehow online classes are substitutes for real classes. Goumaa, Anderson, & Zundel (2019) have demonstrated that online class discussions have the potential to create active understandings within Communities of Inquiry as learners work on problems together through dialogical exchanges (see Rivers & Holland, this volume). Although such community-based learning has long been a feature of management development and executive education, moving such activities "online" creates international perspectives where shared understandings can be crafted on a more global scale. This, of course, is not to say that the move to remote learning has been unproblematic for learning, engagement, and student development.

The mainstreaming of remote approaches to learning and assessment required by the technological pivot brought on by the pandemic, however, does not encapsulate the full extent of how technological trends are likely to impact the management classroom of the future. Another chapter in this collection considers ME from the perspective of educational technology and the emerging strategic options and challenges (Lefevre & Caporarello, this volume), and argues that the pandemic accelerated the evolution of the digital management classroom. Lefrevre and Caporarello highlight that ME tends to be far more "conservative" than management practice, but make a solid case that the business school of the future will be based on a genuinely hybrid approach where teaching and assessment will be heavily influenced by new technological realities (see also Fukami et al., this volume; Rivers & Holland, this volume).

These trends of technology deployment in education are not limited to the management classroom, or even higher-level educational institutions, but can be considered "megatrends" in how they will impact the IT sector and beyond. Microsoft CEO Satya Nadella has identified three technologies that will shape the global tech sector (and others) in the coming years: quantum computing, mixed reality, and artificial intelligence (Nadella, Shaw, Nichols, & Gates, 2017). *Quantum computing*, which promises to deliver exponentially more processing power than today's super computers, is likely to be the engine for increasing the speed at which complex problems can be solved (Frishberg, 2018). Quantum computing has the potential to underpin the development and widespread deployment of the other two trends mentioned by Nadella – mixed reality and artificial intelligence. As such, it is a facilitator of these technological trends which will impact on the introduction of mixed reality and artificial intelligence into future management classrooms, rather than a phenomenon that will directly impact teaching and learning. *Mixed (or augmented) reality* attempts to integrate our experience of the physical world with a digital vista that will enhance how we work, live, and create in ways that may not have been previously imagined.

These technologies might add an experiential dimension to the management classroom of the future. Experiential learning, "learning through experience and reflection" (Sanderson, 2021: 1), is a key pedagogy in ME and beyond.

Experiential learning, however, is not without emotional risk to students, which raises ethical issues when deployed in the management classroom (Allen, 2018; Clancy & Vince, 2019; Dean, Wright, & Forray, 2020; Russ, 1998). Interactive experiential approaches such as case studies and business simulations have been used for decades in an effort to introduce students to understanding the complex implications of strategic decisions. It is always difficult to incorporate the broadest possible range of stakeholders in such approaches, and impossible to anticipate the long-term impact of such decisions. Earle and Leyva-de la Hiz (2021) discuss the potential of using augmented and virtual reality to teach students about grand challenges and sustainability in a way that is more relevant to their lived experiences, and the ones that they will have in their management careers.

Artificial Intelligence is a technology that many can imagine in practice but very few actually understand, which has resulted in concerns about job losses and human obsolescence in professions previously thought unassailable (Haw, 2019; McCurry, 2017). Its very existence has meant that we are now faced with a scenario that the thought experiments, such as the infamous "trolley problem" (Cathcart, 2013; Edmonds, 2014), which are often used in introductory business ethics classes, are now the subject of real-world, high-stakes problems. In another chapter in this collection, River and Holland discuss how AI can be used to create personalized learning experiences for learners in the management classroom. While careful to discuss the benefits of AI in creating enhanced personalized learning experiences, Rivers and Holland (see this volume) give significant attention to the role of the human management educator and how their continued presence determines critical understandings of student satisfaction and feelings of membership of a learning community. With the predicted impact of AI on the jobs and workplaces of the future, they explored the evolution of how AI-driven management educators will impact business schools and those who will learn in them. It is interesting to note that they cite work on the large undergraduate management classroom of the past as a space where students could feel "unseen" in terms of their contribution and learning. Indeed, data on the growing numbers of students electing to study business at all levels is placing increased pressures on business schools to deliver rich forms of experiential education that are very labor-intensive and time-consuming for faculty to deliver (Cullen, Clancy, Hood, & McGuinness, 2019).

AI will not replace human educators but can assist them develop understandings of the variety of their students' learning needs. For example, one of AI's signature features is its capacity to learn, which means that it may also develop the capacity to understand and determine the unique learning needs of those who engage with it, in a way that assists the provision of individualized feedback to an increasingly diverse body of students (Graßmann & Schermuly, 2021). The management classroom of the future will increasingly be called on to be a space where all aspects of a student's identity will be recognized as key components in their experiences as learners. If the management classroom of the future contains a large class of students with diverse needs, AI can assist faculty meet these in ways that are respectful of the individual experience of students.

The challenges discussed in our diverse, inclusive classrooms are global, wicked, and messy. The management classroom of the future must be one where the potential of new forms of advanced technology (such as AI and AR) is exploited to engage with these problems "head-on."

The Inclusive Management Education Classroom of the Future

Demographic change is one of the megatrends impacting societies across the world. Fertility rates in developed economies are generally decreasing and migration rates are increasing. However, the changing profile of these populations has not resulted in equal representations or opportunities for all groups. This is reflected in the fact that three of the UN SDGs (Goal 4 "Quality Education," Goal 5 "Gender Equality," and Goal 10 "Reduced Inequalities") are concerned with ensuring equality of opportunity for all. As business operates within a global framework, there have been significant amounts of research, which attempts to try to understand the management classroom of the future through the lens of global virtual classrooms that provide learners with opportunities to create connections and develop understandings of learners in other parts of the world (see also Lefevre & Caporarello, this volume). Taras et al.'s (2013) in-depth longitudinal study uncovered a significant amount of activity and success in this area from experiential learning with others in different locations and from different cultures.

Management educators are concerned with teaching about the diversity in the world of business and organizations as well as with realizing that this diversity exists within our management classrooms itself (Trehan & Rigg, this volume). At its most fundamental level this diversity exists in relation to the various motivations that students bring to their learning (Cullen, 2011; Mingers, 2000), which can differ from what future employers require from new graduates, but the roots of the problem might be deeper than this. Writers such as McSweeney (2002), Ailon (2008), and Joy & Poonamallee (2013) demonstrate how the development of the management curriculum, and particularly the ways in which it approaches culture, has been conducted from a particular cultural perspective which does not take into account the heterogeneous nature of management classrooms around the world, or the learners who occupy them. This has resulted in management educators who are not from the dominant Western educational and cultural perspective having to do significant "identity work" in order to negotiate working in a functionalist paradigm in a specific locale (Kothiyal, Bell, & Clarke, 2018), or just even to make the curricular standards required from international accreditation bodies relevant to the reality that their students will enter into (Darley & Luethge, 2019). The management classroom of the future, in other words, will have to include critical discussions of the methods and rationales of the models that have been used to explain international business cultures, rather than the results from these studies themselves.

Prominent theories and research concepts, which have become prominent in the humanities and other areas of the social sciences, which have not been seen as "native" to management or business studies, are becoming increasingly relevant; not just because of trends in workplace equality and diversity legislation or human resources practice (Goldman, Gutek, Stein, & Lewis, 2006) but also due to more nuanced understandings of how unconscious bias or unintentional or indirect discrimination may impact on the learning experiences of ME students on the basis of their gender identity (Robinson, Van Esch, & Bilimoria, 2017), gender (Arevalo, 2020; González-Morales, 2019), language proficiency (Pudelko & Tenzer, 2019), nationality or race (Doyle Corner & Pio, 2017), or their experiences of ableism, ageism, or religious discrimination (Gebert, Boerner, Kearney, King, Zhang, & Song, 2013; Gebert, Buengeler, & Heinitz, 2017).

This does not mean that the management classroom of the future will involve a shift to a learner-centric design of courses and learning spaces, as this has been a key feature of many management classrooms for some time (Bain, 2004; Whetten, 2007). Rather it will facilitate the diversity that exists within our student populations not only in relation to who they are and what we teach them but also in how we engage with and understand them (Trehan & Rigg, this volume). There is now a general expectation that polymathic "super scholars" do not exist and every individual has a unique set of skills and competencies that are valuable to businesses and society. Despite this, educators are often expected to rate, rank, and grade student work often according to a single standard. Huge advances have been made in the field of universal instructional design (Holbrook, Moore, & Zoss, 2010), which attempts to create learning experiences that meet pre-stated learning outcomes, while simultaneously helping learners grow according to their interests and context.

This is not to say that the management educator of the future needs to meet the needs of multiple learners, rather there is a need for appreciating that every learner has multiple learning styles and potential futures, and this variety itself is required and must be leveraged to meet the grand challenges of the future. Technologies such as AI and augmented reality may assist the engaged teacher in the management classroom of the future to help meet the needs of the individual learner by providing personalized responsive learning (Rivers & Holland, this volume).

The Management Educator of the Future

In the *Varieties of Religious Experience* (1902), William James observed that although there were a growing number of religions in his environment that it would be a mistake to assume that these represented the totality of how people engaged with faith. In other words, if a person attended a Roman Catholic Church, it would be an error to assume that their inner world and values all aligned perfectly with the dogmas and creeds of that religious organization. Instead, James wrote, every person experiences religion in a variety of different ways in their lives. Sometimes the faith is strong and sometimes less so. Few are actually completely committed believers or non-believers.

Beyond the realm of religious psychology, this work has profound implications for every aspect of our lives; we also have a variety of learning experiences, and our inner lives are as diverse as any other aspect of our mind. The practically unlimited range of learning possibilities is required to not only solve the problems of the business and workplaces that managers of the future will work in but also the grand challenges faced by us all as humans on the planet. As perhaps one of the few places where complex economic, social, and (increasingly) environmental problems are engaged with, the management classroom of the future will increase in its impact within the university and beyond. As the wicked problems of today require advanced levels of systems thinking and an understanding of complexity, it is vital that the students in these classrooms be facilitated through deep learning experiences that require feedback and engagement and the re-commitment of faculty to teaching.

It must be noted that there is often a focus within academia on producing research for the purposes of promotion, rather than on improving teaching practice. This was recently emphasized in a broadside against current trends in business schools and how they impact the management classroom and is discussed in other chapters in this edition (see Ratle et al., this volume; Wood, this volume). Harley (2019) wrote that young business academics are told that to progress in their field they must publish their research relentlessly without stopping to consider whether this work is helpful or useful. The result is that many are told that teaching is somehow necessary, but far less valuable activity, in relation to their career development (see Ratle, Bristow, & Robinson this volume for further discussion of the experiences of early career academics in business schools). This means that many academics come to understand, directly or otherwise, that their energy should be directed away from the management classroom where they will teach, toward their own research projects.

The implications of this are massive: unhealthy and unsustainable practices such as workaholism and "gaming" the publications game become the norm, leading to the creation of classroom experiences that are divorced from the reality of working life or the needs of business and society. If the business school is to genuinely serve the "Public Good" (Kitchener & Delbridge, 2020) through developing management teaching, knowledge *and* practice (Dean et al., 2020; Nicolini, 2013) the management classroom of the future must be understood and viewed as the primary site where a successful student is more than an afterthought of academic endeavor (see Hommel & Vandenkemp, this volume).

And to the Future...

This chapter began with a statement about the impossibility to truly anticipating the future, despite the desire of classical scientific management theory to direct the future on the basis of how it measures the present. We can, however, anticipate the technologies, student populations and learning styles that will enter and *occupy* the classroom. By *occupy*, I mean inhabit both the curriculum and the minds of future management students. Our classrooms will not only be the places where we will apply technologies such as AI and augmented reality and develop new understandings of the benefits of an inclusive workplace but will also be learning sites which will be enhanced by them. When the management classroom of the past was initially established to apply scientific principles to business practice, the result was the creation of functional sub-disciplines which played down the need to develop management practice (Kelley & Nahser, 2014; Mintzberg, 2004). If the management classroom of the future is one where sustainability is a genuine *value* that is central to our teaching, and responsible management learning is its goal rather than some vague rhetorical obligation, we need to ask tough questions of how we can get to a destination that benefits all of our students and society in general.

This chapter focused on how some "meta-challenges" will impact management classrooms in the future and concludes that although we cannot predict with absolutely accuracy what is to come, we can develop a sense of what the management classroom could – and maybe should become. This idea, informed and supported by many of the specific explorations provided by other chapters in this book, may help us question current practices as well as emerging changes and responses to the volatile environment of ME (see Hommel & Vandenkempt, this volume; Wood, this volume). Actively engaging with this vision, which is built on recognizing the overarching importance of the UN SDGs and the pressing global megatrends they address, particularly the need to address the Climate Emergency, can help place these themes and the concomitant teaching and learning practices into the center of the management classroom of the future. Technological developments must be integrated into ME practice in ways that help address these megatrends, as well as serve the individual learning needs and objectives of the management learners of the future. A vision of the management classroom as a shared space for accessible, aware, inclusive, responsible, and responsive ME for all can provide the guiding light to steer our future in a more promising direction.

References

Ailon, G. 2008. Mirror, mirror on the wall: Culture's consequences in a value test of its own design. *Academy of Management Review*, 33(4): 885–904.

Allen, S. J. 2018. Yes! And … I'm so tired of experiential learning. *Journal of Management Education*, 42(2): 306–312.

Aragon-Correa, J. A., Marcus, A. A., Rivera, J. E., & Kenworthy, A. L. 2017. Sustainability management teaching resources and the challenge of balancing planet, people, and profits. *Academy of Management Learning & Education*, 16(3): 469–483.

Arevalo, J. A. 2020. Gendering sustainability in management education: Research and pedagogy as space for critical engagement. *Journal of Management Education*, 44(6): 852–886.

Bagley, C. E., Sulkowski, A. J., Nelson, J. S., Waddock, S., & Shrivastava, P. 2020. A path to developing more insightful business school graduates: A systems-based, experimental approach to integrating law, strategy, and sustainability. *Academy of Management Learning & Education*, 19(4): 541–568.

Bain, K. 2004. *What the best college teachers do*. Cambridge: Harvard University Press.

Bassiry, G. R. 1990. Ethics, education, and corporate leadership. *Journal of Business Ethics*, 9(10): 799–805.

Campbell, N., McHugh, G., & Ennis, P. 2019. Climate change is not a problem: Speculative realism at the end of organization. *Organization Studies*, 40(5): 725–744

Carrington, D. 2019. Why the Guardian is changing the language it uses about the environment. In *Guardian*. UK: Guardian Media Group.

Cathcart, T. 2013. *The trolley problem, or, would you throw the fat guy off the bridge?: A philosophical conundrum* (1st ed.). New York: Workman Publishing.

Clancy, A., & Vince, R. 2019. "If I want to feel my feelings, I'll see a bloody shrink": Learning from the shadow side of experiential learning. *Journal of Management Education*, 43(2): 174–184.

Cullen, J. G. 2011. The writing skills course as an introduction to critical practice for larger business undergraduate classes. *International Journal of Management Education*, 9(4): 25–37.

Cullen, J. G. 2017. Educating business students about sustainability: A bibliometric review of current trends and research needs. *Journal of Business Ethics*, 145(2): 429–439.

Cullen, J. G., Clancy, A., Hood, A., & McGuinness, C. 2019. Experiential learning in large classes. *Journal of Management Education*, 43(4): 471–476.

Darley, W. K., & Luethge, D. J. 2019. Management and business education in Africa: A post-colonial perspective of international accreditation. *Academy of Management Learning & Education*, 18(1): 99–111.

Dean, K. L., Wright, S., & Forray, J. M. 2020. Experiential learning and the moral duty of business schools. *Academy of Management Learning & Education*, 19(4): 569–583.

Doyle Corner, P., & Pio, E. 2017. Supervising international students' theses and dissertations. *Academy of Management Learning & Education*, 16(1): 23–38.

Earle, A. G., & Leyva-De La Hiz, D. I. 2021. The wicked problem of teaching about wicked problems: Design thinking and emerging technologies in sustainability education. *Management Learning*, 52(2): 581–603.

Edmonds, D. 2014. *Would you kill the fat man?: The trolley problem and what your answer tells us about right and wrong*. Princeton; Oxford: Princeton University Press.

Fraher, A., & Grint, K. 2018. Agonistic governance: The antinomies of decision-making in U.S. Navy SEALs. *Leadership*, 12(2): 220–239.

Frishberg, M. 2018. Quantum computing moves toward reality. *Research Technology Management*, 61(2): 3.

Gasparin, M., Brown, S. D., Green, W., Hugill, A., Lilley, S., Quinn, M., Schinckus, C., Williams, M., & Zalasiewicz, J. 2020. The business school in the Anthropocene: Parasite logic and pataphysical reasoning for a working earth. *Academy of Management Learning & Education*, 19(3): 385–405.

Gebert, D., Boerner, S., Kearney, E., King, J. E., Zhang, K., & Song, L. J. 2013. Expressing religious identities in the workplace: Analyzing a neglected diversity dimension. *Human Relations*, 67(5): 543–563.

Gebert, D., Buengeler, C., & Heinitz, K. 2017. Tolerance: A neglected dimension in diversity training? *Academy of Management Learning & Education*, 16(3): 415–438.

Goldman, B. M., Gutek, B. A., Stein, J. H., & Lewis, K. 2006. Employment discrimination in organizations: Antecedents and consequences. *Journal of Management*, 32(6): 786–830.

González-Morales, M. G. 2019. A more feminine scholarship: Relational practice for setting a good example. *Academy of Management Learning & Education*, 18(2): 302–305.

Goumaa, R., Anderson, L., & Zundel, M. 2019. What can managers learn online? Investigating possibilities for active understanding in the online MBA classroom. *Management Learning*, 50(2): 226–244.

Graßmann, C., & Schermuly, C. C. 2021. Coaching with artificial intelligence: Concepts and capabilities. *Human Resource Development Review*, 20(1): 106–126.

Grint, K. 2005. Problems, problems, problems: The social construction of 'leadership.' *Human Relations*, 58(11): 1467–1494.

Gudic, M., Parkes, C., & Rosenbloom, A. 2016. *Responsible management education and the challenge of poverty*. Sheffield: Greenleaf.

Harley, B. 2019. Confronting the crisis of confidence in management studies: Why senior scholars need to stop setting a bad example. *Academy of Management Learning & Education*, 18(2): 286–297.

Haw, M. 2019. Will AI replace university lecturers? Not if we make it clear why humans matter. *The Guardian*. Manchester: Guardian.

Holbrook, T., Moore, C., & Zoss, M. 2010. Equitable intent: Reflections on universal design in education as an ethic of care. *Reflective Practice*, 11(5): 681–692.

James, W. 1902. *The varieties of religious experience: A study in human nature*. London: Longman.

Joy, S., & Poonamallee, L. 2013. Cross-cultural teaching in globalized management classrooms: Time to move from functionalist to postcolonial approaches? *Academy of Management Learning & Education*, 12(3): 82–99.

Kelley, S., & Nahser, R. 2014. Developing sustainable strategies: Foundations, method, and pedagogy. *Journal of Business Ethics*, 123(4): 631–644.

Kitchener, M., & Delbridge, R. 2020. Lessons from creating a business school for public good: Obliquity, waysetting, and wayfinding in substantively rational change. *Academy of Management Learning & Education*, 19(3): 307–322.

Kothiyal, N., Bell, E., & Clarke, C. 2018. Moving beyond mimicry: Developing hybrid spaces in indian business schools. *Academy of Management Learning & Education*, 17(2): 137–154.

McCurry, J. 2017. Japanese company replaces office workers with artificial intelligence. *The Guardian*. London: Guardian Group.

McSweeney, B. 2002. Hofstede's model of national cultural differences and their consequences: A triumph of faith – a failure of analysis. *Human Relations*, 55(1): 89–118.

Mingers, J. 2000. What is it to be critical? *Management Learning*, 31(2): 219–237.

Mintzberg, H. 2004. *Managers not MBAs: A hard look at the soft practice of managing and management development*. New Jersey: Pearson Education.

Nadella, S., Shaw, G., Nichols, J. T., & Gates, B. 2017. *Hit refresh: The quest to rediscover Microsoft's soul and imagine a better future for everyone* (1st ed.). New York: Harper Business, an imprint of HarperCollinsPublishers.

Neal, M. 2017. Learning from poverty: Why business schools should address poverty, and how they can go about it. *Academy of Management Learning & Education*, 16(1): 54–69.

Nicolini, D. 2013. *Practice theory, work, and organization: An introduction* (1st ed.). Oxford: Oxford University Press.

Pudelko, M., & Tenzer, H. 2019. Boundaryless careers or career boundaries? The impact of language barriers on academic careers in international business schools. *Academy of Management Learning & Education*, 18(2): 213–240.

Robinson, M. J., Van Esch, C., & Bilimoria, D. 2017. Bringing transgender issues into management education: A call to action. *Academy of Management Learning & Education*, 16(2): 300–313.

Russ, V. 1998. Behind and beyond Kolb's learning cycle. *Journal of Management Education*, 22(3): 304–319.

Sanderson, K. 2021. Instilling competence: Emotional preparation for experiential learning. *Journal of Management Education*, 45(4): 652–672.

Starik, M., Rands, G., Marcus, A. A., & Clark, T. S. 2010. From the guest editors: In search of sustainability in management education. *Academy of Management Learning & Education*, 9(3): 377–383.

Taras, V., Bryla, P., Caprar, D. V., Ordenana, X., Rottig, D., Bode, A., Sarala, R. M., Schuster, A., Zakaria, N., Vaiginiene, E., Zhao, F., Froese, F. J., Jimenez, A., Bathula, H., Wankel, C., Yajnik, N., Lei, W. S., Baldegger, R., Minor, M. S., & Huang, V. Z. Y. 2013. A global classroom? Evaluating the effectiveness of global virtual collaboration as a teaching tool in management education. *Academy of Management Learning & Education*, 12(3): 100–121.

United Nations, 2020. Shaping the trends of our time: Report of the UN economist network for the UN 75th anniversary: 194. New York: United Nations.

Whetten, D. A. 2007. Principles of effective course design: What I wish I had known about learning-centered teaching 30 years ago. *Journal of Management Education*, 31(3): 339–357.

Whiteman, G., Walker, B., & Perego, P. 2013. Planetary boundaries: Ecological foundations for corporate sustainability. *Journal of Management Studies*, 50(2): 307–336.

Yen-Chun Jim, W. U., Shihping, H., Lopin, K. U. O., & Wen-Hsiung, W. U. 2010. Management education for sustainability: A web-based content analysis. *Academy of Management Learning & Education*, 9(3): 520–531.

11

MANAGEMENT EDUCATION AND ARTIFICIAL INTELLIGENCE: TOWARD PERSONALIZED LEARNING

Christine Rivers and Anna Holland

Introduction

At the heart of management education (ME), as a discipline and scholarly subject area, is a need for educational innovation and expressing an instructional entrepreneurial spirit in the classroom with and without technology (Rivers & Kinchin, 2019). ME is particularly well suited to continuously exploring new ways of enhancing learning and learner experience. Often characterized by a variety of management subjects, typically large class sizes and yet low risk (in comparison to medical and health sciences for instance) ME is involved in using and trailing different learning and teaching approaches and technologies, and thus offers an excellent playground for experimentation. In addition, most management subjects require a certain level of complexity thinking (Axley & McMahon, 2006) of individuals and in groups to manage and solve problems or make agile decisions (Druckman & Ebner, 2018; Nason, 2017) applicable to various business contexts. This includes the development of employability skills such as team working, critical thinking, resilience, and decision-making (Rivers & O'Brien, 2019). The ability to use technology to support the development of such skills transferrable across multiple business contexts (Hurrell, 2015) is a welcome opportunity.

While the COVID-19 pandemic has created many challenges for business schools, it has also created opportunities, and with its momentum, to accelerate technical solutions that enhance learning and drive conversations with various stakeholders, and particularly around massification versus personalized responsive learning (Amemado, 2020; Chartered Association of Business Schools CABS, 2019). In this chapter, we offer prospective thinking to consider how

DOI: 10.4324/9781003095903-14

this human-facilitated and technology-facilitated teaching and learning can be co-deployed to offer personalized responsive learning at scale.

The content of this chapter is particularly timely given the shift in paradigms to learning and teaching from on-campus and predominantly face-to-face delivery to blended, hybrid, and fully online learning and teaching, due to the global pandemic. It is important to recognize, however, that a myriad of terms are used in this context and a common definition to describe the range of teaching and learning that takes place both in person and online, either synchronously or asynchronously is hard to reach (Medina, 2018). Thus, for consistency the umbrella term "blended learning" is applied throughout. Blended learning, considered by many to be more effective than either classroom-based learning or online learning alone (Schneider & Preckel, 2017), is understood as combining face to face (either in person or virtually) and technology-mediated learning instruction (Medina, 2018; Saichaie, 2020).

While outside of the scope of this discussion, a wider part of the conversation surrounding teaching and learning in ME includes approaches to blended learning design. Learning design has been researched extensively and has commonly centered on the holistic balance and integration of face to face and online learning (Saichaie, 2020; Serrano et al., 2019). However, there is acknowledgement of a shift which recognizes the complexity of learning environments and the need to foster learner engagement to promote learning (Wasson & Kirschner, 2020). This chapter prioritizes the strategic, conceptual aspects of what and how personalized responsive learning can be delivered at scale in ME and leaves the operationalization of specific learning designs, informed by the presented discussions, as a subsequent consideration.

Rapid growth and a trend toward massification of learning witnessed in ME has resulted in perceived and real challenges for educators to maintain the quality of teaching and learning experience at scale (Ryan, French, & Kennedy, 2019). Proponents point to the diversification of the higher education sector, socioeconomic benefits, and increased access to higher education afforded by massification (Evans, Rees, Taylor, & Fox, 2020). However, Giannakis and Bullivant (2016) argue that this has often come at the cost of quality and the individualized experience (personalized responsive learning) so valued by learners and management educators alike. We draw on experiences from other industries that deploy Mass Customization based on technology-driven solutions (such as AI) to provide tailored products and services at scale to consider the possibilities and transferability of their experiences for ME.

We provide a framework for visualizing the relationships between learning and teaching formats in the Dimensions of Teaching and Learning in ME matrix figure (see Figure 11.1). The resulting four quadrants are explored to provide insight and identify opportunities for the future of ME. Each quadrant gives room to specific learning formats. Formats include:

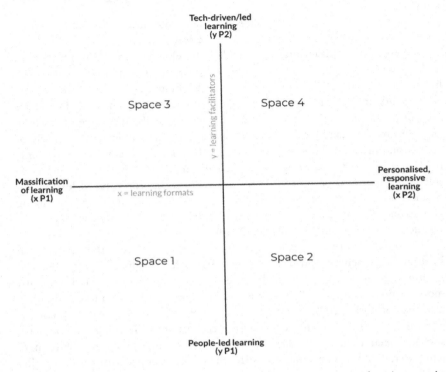

FIGURE 11.1 Dimensions of teaching and learning in management education matrix

- Traditional lectures, seminars, tutorials, MOOCs (García-Peñalvo, Fidalgo-Blanco, & Sein-Echaluce, 2018)
- On-demand pre-recorded content (Islam, Kim, & Kwon, 2020; Syynimaa, 2019)
- AI personalized learning journeys in highly sophisticated virtual learning environments (Messinger, Ge, Smirnov, Stroulia, & Lyons, 2019)
- The use of chatbots (Molnár & Szüts, 2018)
- learning-mediated, personalized and responsive interactions (Kokku, Sundararajan, Dey, Sindhgatta, Nitta, & Sengupta, 2018; Mansur, Yusof, & Basori, 2019).

Combining and exploring the interplay between learning formats and teaching formats within the matrix offers contrasting perspectives that provide the foundation on which to build further prospective thinking.

Receiving personalized feedback and experiencing responsiveness have been identified as two important aspects by both learners and educators to foster and support learning (Kokku et al., 2018; Mansur et al., 2019). Such a personalized and responsive approach is believed to support subject-specific learning, foster belonging and self-directed learning (Jones, 2019), and most importantly gives individuals the opportunity to perceive learning as a life-long endeavor that can help them develop and grow continuously. Personalized responsive learning is therefore understood as the ability to recognize learners' changing needs and to quickly adjust the dynamics in the facilitation of teaching and learning to respond to and meet these.

To contextualize and frame these dynamics, the principles relating to learner and teacher actions in three teaching philosophies are considered. In this context, we conceive of teaching philosophies as a generic term to describe pedagogy, andragogy, and heutagogy: fundamental approaches to teaching and learning characterized by the variance in direction of educator-learner relationship (Akyildiz, 2019). Teaching philosophies are an important consideration in the discussion of personalized responsive learning because to be responsive is to recognize and adapt to learner-led changes in dynamics at a point in time.

We begin the discussion by introducing the Dimensions of Management Education Matrix to identify gaps and opportunities for development. We include a review of various relevant concepts and terminology, which leads to a more in-depth conversation surrounding the purpose and value of human–human interaction (see also Akrivou, Fernandez Gonzalez, Scalzo, & Murcio Rodriguez, this volume) between the learner and the management educator in comparison to an AI management educator (AIME). The discussion will address issues of learning and teaching formats and approaches in ME as well as management learner needs at different levels. We also discuss the possibilities afforded by the Collaborative Model of Management Education, describing the changing dynamics between management learners, management educators, and AIMEs and therefore address some of the big challenges business schools face. More ambitiously, we consider if there is a way to exploit AI to assist and extend our human capacity instead of replicating or replacing humans (Cope, Kalantzis, & Searsmith, 2020), and attempt to answer the question: *How can management educators and technology be usefully combined to offer highly personalized, responsive learning experience at scale?*

The Dimensions of Teaching and Learning in Management Education Matrix

The Dimensions of Teaching and Learning in Management Education Matrix provides a visual representation of the opposing dimensions of learning formats and teaching formats utilized in management education (see Figure 11.1). The x-axis represents the spectrum of learning formats which shapes the experiences learners may encounter, from being one of many (massification) to individualized tailored approaches (personalized responsive learning). The y-axis by contrast represents the facilitators of teaching and learning; people or technology, and the level of interaction the learner experiences. Creating four quadrants (Q1–Q4) the matrix provides a framework to situate various teaching and learning formats (such as lectures, tutorials, MOCCs, etc.) contingent to the properties of the dimensions typically recognized in the format. It is recognized that there is objectivity in the categorization across the quadrants; however, the matrix supports the recognition of opportunities to leverage existing learning formats further or to identify new spaces for prospective thinking. Figure 11.1 shows the two dimensions and its four distinct quadrants.

Q1: Massification of Learning & People-Facilitated Teaching and Learning

Quadrant 1 focuses on teaching formats that are people-led, often aimed at large audiences such as traditional lectures. In ME, such lectures delivered face-to-face in large row-seated lecture halls were common practice pre-COVID-19. While some might contend that traditional lectures are not fit for purpose, scholars have argued in defense of the traditional lecture as a mode of learning (French & Kennedy, 2017; Fulford & Mahon, 2020). Fulford and Mahon (2020) refer to the traditional lecture as the voice of the lecturer modulated specifically for the hearing of the learner and emphasize the value of the lecture. Offstein and Chory (2019) identify a list of benefits for learners and educators to attend and deliver lectures. These include that management learners do not view lectures as passive, instead learners perceive lectures as actively processing information, which leads to long-term learning. The latter is often disputed and contradicted by the perspective that in live lectures, less information is successfully retained in comparison to flipped classroom approaches (Short & Martin, 2011; Thai, De Wever, & Valcke, 2017), and that they do not foster long-term learning. Proponents argue that lectures help learners develop information-processing skills and improve listening and critical thinking skills through the presentation of different perspectives. However, the traditional lecture, specifically in ME, provides learning for the masses, comparatively cost-effectively and resource-efficiently simultaneously addressing a large number of learners (Offstein & Chory, 2019). They do not however offer a personalized or a responsive learning experience.

Q2: Personalized Responsive Learning & People-Facilitated Teaching and Learning

The traditional seminar/tutorial aimed at small group interaction, situated in Quadrant 2, allows a greater level of personalized and responsive learning experience. Such approaches are traditionally people-led, although there may be some use of technology to support the learning experience.

Another format of more personalized responsive learning is supervision, which often takes place in a one-to-one or one-to-two setting. Traditional supervision is purely people-led and involves direct personal interaction and learning between the learner and management educator. The value of supervision is the direct and often highly personal attention and interaction, with typically very specific content shared and relevant for the particular learning challenges of the supervisee. Supervision facilitated by or mediated through technology can remain personal and responsive but can impact learners differently. While dos Santos and Cechinel (2019) report that the form of communication chosen for supervision online or face-to-face is perceived as equally valuable by both learners and supervisors, Bengtsen and Jensen (2015) outline various conditions under which this may change. They highlight that while online supervision can be more diverse and multimodal, specific features of the online platform used to enable supervision interactions can play an integral part in how learning from such dialogue is ultimately facilitated (Bengtsen & Jensen, 2015).

Q3:   Massification of Learning & Technology-Facilitated Teaching and Learning

In Quadrant 3 the facilitation of learning shifts from the human management educator toward technology. Learning in this quadrant is designed by the management educator creating content, determining the sequence of learning for learners and defining transmission routes for learning. Educators provide materials they believe are the sources of information and determine the incremental stages of learning by releasing what is adequate at a specific time (Rivers & Holland, 2020). The learner predominately engages with the teaching and learning via technology.

Massive Open Online Classes (MOOCs) are a learning format that relies on facilitation through technology and, in stark contrast to supervision, is delivered to many via a single platform. Therefore, MOOCs can be described as a format that fits neatly with conventional pedagogic didactic formats of delivery facilitated by technology. Developed in 2008, the first online MOOC aimed to facilitate autonomous learning, exploration and analysis and the generation of shared knowledge among participants to encourage learning (García-Peñalvo et al., 2018). MOOCs quickly gained momentum and popularity and were described as a disruptive innovation with the potential to open learning to the masses and create additional revenue streams for institutions (Reich & Ruipérez-Valiente, 2019). However, in recent years the traditional MOOC model has come under increasing scrutiny. Issues arising center on low completion rates, with less than 10% of participants progressing to completion and certification, and an underpinning requirement for learners' self-regulated learning (Reparaz, Aznárez-Sanado, & Mendoza, 2020). Vorbach, Poandl, and Korajman (2019) point out that MOOCs, while bridging the time and space challenge, do not support learner interaction. MOOCs are of more value for certain subjects and potentially more at the introductory level due to their reduced live interactive nature between peers and the educator (Hung & Chen, 2018).

Similarly, the swift move to blended or fully online learning due to the pandemic has shifted didactic delivery to pre-recorded video lectures as part of a wider blended learning offering. Empirical research conducted by Islam et al. (2020) revealed that business and management learners prefer smaller pre-recorded video lectures, accessed in their own time and at a pace that suits them, over live online lectures. Flexibility, convenience, and educational effectiveness are the main reasons for this preference. On the negative side engagement with pre-recorded materials depends on learners' motivation which can be a barrier and lead to learners binge-watching lecture material before exam periods thus resulting in stress and anxiety. However, using pre-recorded lectures has been found to have a statistically significant positive effect on grades and learner satisfaction (Syynimaa, 2019). Accessing content when it suits (e.g., on-demand) can be perceived as a more personalized approach, yet as the content is a one size fits all and the medium is non-responsive, learning is led through the technology.

Q4: Personalized Responsive Learning & Technology-Facilitated Teaching and Learning

Using AI-driven technology similar to algorithms used for behavioral targeting in online advertising (H. Li, 2019) is one solution to address the challenge of personalized learning in education (Vincent-Lancrin & Van der Vlies, 2020). However, such algorithms only follow a certain behavioral pattern and remain unresponsive despite appearing personalized.

Chat-bots, responsive voice or text-based chat applications powered by artificial intelligence (Molnár & Szüts, 2018), are one such example of how interactive technology has been applied to communicate with learners. Molnár and Szüts (2018) pointed out that learners are more likely to believe in information received from chat-bots rather than search engines as there is a more personalized component to the communication taking place. Most importantly, chatbots work well where learners spent a lot of time in a specific environment, such as a virtual learning environment (VLE). However, these authors emphasize that the error rate at which chat-bots work is high in the beginning and this approach works best with predefined topics. The more chatbots are used, the more appropriately responsive their algorithms become, and the error rate reduces overtime.

A successful example of using chat-bots in large classes, predominantly for pure online learning programs, is the case of Jill Watson, a virtual assistant developed by Georgia Tech to assist teaching staff with the facilitation of a busy discussion forum and less complex queries on an online master's in science program (Goel & Polepeddi, 2016). Utilizing increasing AI capabilities, Jill's broader application has been to make online learning scalable and personable with a strong focus on community building including giving social support and enhancing virtual collaboration among online learners. Although, positively perceived by learners, they were divided about its usefulness with regard to building communities and how information provided should be acted upon. The latter is particularly interesting as the level of responsiveness does not seem to have supported learners taking actions aligned with progressing their learning (Wang, Jing, Camacho, Joyner, & Goel, 2020).

In some way this is not surprising as research on virtual collaborations and teams has stressed the limitations of nonverbal communication for team effectiveness, motivation, and intersubjective understanding, among other aspects (Darics, 2020). Darics (2020) points out that the only way to overcome this issue at present is with more resource-intensive verbal feedback.

Exploring the relationship and interaction between learner, educator and virtual assistant is key in understanding the potential opportunities for AI in ME. This raises a series of questions that impact the way personalized responsive learning is perceived and delivered, therefore the next sections will consider: is this relationship between learner, management educator, and AI management educator equal at all times? And what value does the management educator have in facilitating personalized responsive learning if AIMEs have the capability to provide such learning at scale?

The Value of the Management Educator

Predictions have been made that by 2030 800 million jobs will have been taken over by machines (Stachowicz-Stanusch & Amann, 2020). AI is expected to reach human capacity in regard to complex and analytical decision-making but will remain unable to make decisions based on uncertainty and equivocality (Jarrahi, 2018). Understandably, this poses a threat to many professions including management educators. Calvo, Peters, Vold, and Ryan (2020) refer to the threats outlined above as innate concerns linked to three basic human needs: autonomy (e.g., machines are taking over), competency (e.g., machines replace our skills) and relatedness (e.g., machines reduce human–human interaction).

Garrison's (1989) *Community of Inquiry (CoI) framework* (within online environments) is one of the underlying concepts in the context of human–human interaction in learning referring to cognitive, social, and teaching presence. These elements refer to learners' meaning-making ability through reflection and discourse (*cognitive presence* – see Garrison, Anderson, & Archer, 1999: 89), the degree of participation and interaction of collaborative group members (*social presence* – see Kreijns, Van Acker, Vermeulen, & Van Buuren, 2014), and design and deployment of cognitive and social processes to facilitate meaningful and worthwhile learning outcomes (*teaching presence* – see Anderson, Rourke, Garrison, & Archer, 2001: 5). While all three elements have important roles to play, teaching presence is of particular importance here as it is "a significant determinant of learner satisfaction, perceived learning, and sense of community" (Garrison & Arbaugh, 2007: 163).

This claim has further been explored specifically in blended learning environments, which although previously popular are currently a vital mode of learning for business and management learners due to the impact of the COVID-19 pandemic (Saichaie, 2020). Hewett, Becker, and Bish (2019) compared the impact of physical, present human interaction versus absent human interaction within a blended learning environment and reported that the *presence of human interaction* led to more active behavioral engagement, higher cognitive engagement and stronger and more positive emotional engagement of learners. Law, Geng, and Li (2019) also found that social presence of the educator has a direct positive impact on cognitive and social presence of learners and an indirect positive impact on learning performance. Management educators are well positioned to respond to verbal and non-verbal ques and nuances in their interaction with learners. Learners value such interactions as developmental and supportive factors in their learning experience. Thus, the importance of the educator in being "present" either in a virtual or physical environment is crucial and technology can only extend the qualities and its existence.

Strongly linked to learner performance is *learning motivation* (Law et al., 2019). In blended learning or technology-enabled learning environments, intrinsic motivation is found to determine high performance levels. Thus, learners who have lower levels of intrinsic motivation might find it challenging to pursue self-study with a blended approach, which in turn could lead to poorer performance. The presence of an educator can act as a stimulus and activate motivation to learn leading to higher engagement as highlighted by Arbaugh (2007).

In addition, Arbaugh (2007) emphasizes that the presence of the management educator also fosters *belonging*. Diep, Zhu, Cocquyt, De Greef, Vo, and Vanwing (2019) refer to belonging as one of the adult learners' needs. Sense of belonging refers to the dimension of relatedness and is supported by educator facilitation and online peer interaction. Furthermore, Hsieh and Tsai (2012) and Asoodar, Vaezi, and Izanloo (2016) explain that educator facilitation in real-time does not just strengthen that sense of belonging but also enhances the quality of learning and learner interaction.

The presence of a management educator in a blended environment is a necessity to motivate learners, create a sense of belonging and facilitate inter-action. Thus, creating an effective learning community supporting cognitive, social and teaching presence online and offline requires the educator to re-cognize and respond to learner needs. Educators, as opposed to AI, possess the ability to develop and utilize emotional intelligence (EI). EI refers to an individuals' ability of recognizing, managing, understanding, and utilizing the emotions of themselves and others to enhance experience (Serrat, 2017). EI is a valuable skill of management educators but also crucial to be developed by learners, and management educators play a vital role in the development of EI as a graduate attribute (Rivers & O'Brien, 2019). EI can be of benefit when management educators facilitate negotiation between group members, espe-cially when group issues arise (Lee, Smith, & Sergueeva, 2016). Such nego-tiation relates to the human capacity which AI remains unable to perform as there is equivocality and uncertainty in decision-making (Jarrahi, 2018).

This raises the question of which or what behavior could be performed by AI-driven technology as an extension of the management educator that adds value to learner learning and experience?

The Value of the AI-Driven Management Educator (AIME)

The section above explored the value of the human management educator and specifically the aspects and needs the human management educator fulfills to enhance learning and learner experience. This section will look at the enhancement of the human management educator through an AI-driven management educator. The following section will then reflect on what other challenges business schools face that could be addressed with such technology including the delivery of management education at scale and personalized responsiveness.

The question of delivering personalization at scale, although relatively new to ME, has been the focus of many organizations. Mass Customization is defined as "the customization of products according to customer needs while simultaneously keeping efficiency as high as in traditional mass production" (Gassmann, Frankenberger, & Csik, 2014: 222). Mass customization leverages technology to enable customers to be personally involved in individualizing the product or service they seek, thus benefitting customer relationships through an increased sense of loyalty. Arguably, these beneficial factors are easily relatable to ME with the potential to increase learner engagement and motivation. Prentice and Nguyen (2020) mention that the value of AI in service organizations is to enhance operational efficiency and improve customer experience. Their study, while situated in industry and explored from a customer perspective, provides great insight into the value of human versus AI-interaction in terms of enhancing the user experience and thus appears relevant to the ME context. Prentice and Nguyen's (2020) results show that customers value interactions with human employees, and emotional intelligence plays a pivotal role in higher engagement and satisfaction. In particular, human empathetic responsiveness, including assurance, was found to be significant. However, it has been highlighted that customers also value the timely response of AI-driven tools but less so the standardized responses, especially if they are not helpful.

Another educational operational process technology has been found to be useful for is in identifying the level of engagement in terms of frequency and patterns (e.g., counting how often learners are present in a virtual space, engagement with materials and resources). This is certainly a task that can be performed much better and more efficiently by a technology-driven system. Similarly, AI can be effective in using data to create personalized learning paths for learners such as the addition of value-added training or extra learning opportunities to a standard learning plan (Somasundaram, Junaid, & Mangadu, 2020). Another way to assess the benefits of utilizing AI is to look at the "pains" of management educators, outsource what they do not want and keep what they find enjoyable and motivating. "Pains" might include repetitive tasks such as answering the same questions several times, marking quantities of assessments with the same content, bureaucratic administration work, and keeping track of the engagement and progress of individual learners and initiating action if problems are detected. Automation and learning analytics play a crucial role in addressing these issues but combined with AI would add real value to the management educator. Similarly, "actions to keep" might include engaging in live interactions with learners about subject specific dilemmas, supporting learners emotionally, solving complex problems, preparing learning materials that inform critical thinking and sharing research with learners to name a few. Most of those actions refer to Jarrahi's (2018) aspects that distinguish AI from human capabilities such as dealing with complexity, uncertainty and equivocality.

Advanced AI-driven technologies are not as well deployed in education as compared to other industries. One of the main reasons is because AI developers are not familiar with learning research. Any effective educational AI technology should be designed based on theories and research of learning. Luckin and Cukurova (2019) point out that AI algorithms are beneficial to analyze rich educational data at speed, which would help human management educators to support learners faster, and to provide more personalized scaffolding. This argument is in line with Calvo et al. (2020), who refer to design for human autonomy as opposed to machine autonomy and in turn allow responsible AI development, if AI is to genuinely benefit and advance humanity. Further emphasizing the need for responsible development of AI in education, Garrett, Beard, and Fiesler (2020), identify AI education ethics as at an embryonic stage of development.

Luckin and Cukurova (2019) suggest the use of a co-design framework to develop AI education technology, including AI developers, learning design specialists, and educators aligned to the need for AI education technology to be pedagogically and technically sound. So, what are the teaching philosophies one should consider including learning patterns and behaviours?

Teaching Philosophies Shaping AIME Development

In ME a mix of pedagogy, andragogy and heutagogy is evident (Rivers & Holland 2020; Stoten, 2020). Educators often apply approaches as deemed appropriate to learners at different educational levels of learning (e.g., undergraduate, postgraduate, or doctoral), which is an important consideration in this context. While the nature of these approaches as teaching philosophies is complex, we distinguish them for the purpose of our discussion according to three fundamental characteristics: learner role, educator role, and their respective levels of control for learning context and outcomes (Figure 11.2).

Pedagogy can in the broadest sense be referred to as "the art and science of teaching" (Beetham & Sharpe, 2007). The many perspectives on pedagogy indicate a lack of a conclusive and universally recognized definition and the contested nature of qualifying adjectives to describe variations between pedagogic

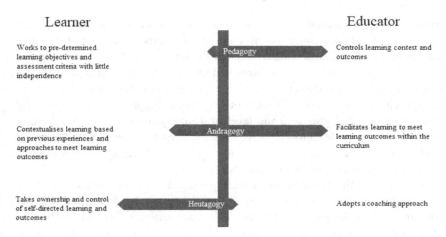

FIGURE 11.2 A summary of pedagogy, andragogy, and heutagogy

approaches (Black & Wiliam, 2018). To highlight the fundamental differences between the three philosophies discussed, we position pedagogy in its most traditional form; as a teacher-led philosophy which places control and agency for learning with educators as they decide content, transmission routes, and timing and thus determine what, how, and when learners are learning (Knowles, 1984).

Andragogy, in contrast, focuses on adult learning and advocates autonomous and self-directed learning. Learners are understood as independent individuals who decide for themselves what, how, when and most importantly why to learn. Motivation to learn comes from within. Educators have the role as facilitators beyond the transmission and transaction of learning. Knowles (1984) defines andragogy as a learner-centered teaching philosophy suitable for mature learners. In ME both pedagogy and andragogy are widely debated and practiced (e.g., Jones, Penaluna, & Penaluna, 2019; McNally, Piperopoulos, Welsh, Mengel, Tantawy, & Papageorgiadis, 2020; Muduli, Kaura, & Quazi, 2018) and are often joined by discussions around heutagogy.

Heutagogy builds on the above teaching philosophies and refers to learning as self-determined (Mann, Ker, Eden-Mann, & O'Brien, 2017). Learners are independent, proactive and have a great level of self-efficacy. While the educator still functions as facilitator, the educator is also a coach and mentor, enabling learning through the development of learners' capabilities. With such new capability, learners shape their own learning and take ownership and control in all aspects of their learning. Stoten (2020) specifically highlights that heutagogy is an attempt to personalize the curriculum particularly important in ME where learners need to develop capabilities for the management of technology and people.

All three of these teaching philosophies are approaches currently applied in ME and evident in curriculum and assessment design, although different ME contexts are characterized by different management learners (e.g., UG management courses at universities versus high-end executive education for senior managers) and have fundamentally different dominant models. These approaches reflect assumptions made by educators and learning designers as well as by the management learners themselves and reflect how they expect learners to learn and engage with educators and content. Stoten (2020) conceptualizes the proportion of each philosophy relative to the level of a management learner. Progressing from undergraduate level to executive level the need for teacher-led philosophy (pedagogy) decreases and the need for self-directed (andragogy) and self-determined (heutagogy) learning increases.

Referring to the Dimensions of Management Education Matrix, the three teaching *"philosophies"* are present in all four quadrants depending on how the educator designs the learning. The question that remains is how AI can be utilized to maximize personalized responsive learning and impact the relationship between learner, educator and virtual assistant.

The Collaborative Model of Management Education

The Collaborative Model of Management Education consists of three players: the learner, the management educator and the AIME. Figure 11.3 depicts the dynamics of the relationships among them in a simplified overview.

Interactions among the parties in the tripartite relationship between the educator, learner, and virtual assistant that combine human decision-making and AI capabilities can increase learner engagement and attainment (Kokku et al., 2018). To achieve this, content is created and provided by the management educator in a way that scaffolds learning and prompts engagement but also manages learner's expectations and participation around engagement and learning progress. The participation approaches for all partners, especially for the learners, need to be explicitly communicated in a clear and succinct way to encourage learning from the start. The management educator collaborates with AIME on a supply-demand relationship. The AIME provides learning analytics and more sophisticated reports to identify and highlight patterns of learning behavior individual learners portray within the blended learning environment. Based on their behavior the AIME can identify learning needs, learning preferences, awareness, motivation, and expectations in terms of progress.

Learning needs can be understood as the ways in which individual learners would benefit from receiving feedback. Some might need one-to-one sessions in face-to-face or online mode. Others might need feedback on draft outlines via email. Learning preferences refer to various learning formats (e.g., pre-recorded lectures, live lectures, small group seminars) to retrieve information, make sense of information and develop higher-order thinking skills. Learning awareness encompasses learning needs and preferences to some degree, but it also refers to learners' understanding about their strengths and limitations and their learning

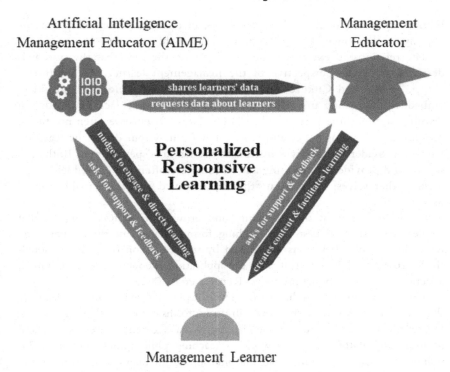

Artificial Intelligence
Management Educator (AIME)

Management
Educator

shares learners' data

requests data about learners

**Personalized
Responsive
Learning**

nudges to engage & directs learning

asks for support & feedback

asks for support & feedback

creates content & facilitates learning

Management Learner

FIGURE 11.3   A Collaborative Model of Management Education

motivation, driven variously by extrinsic or intrinsic factors or a combination of both. What motivates a learner to continue and engage is unique; identifying and leveraging this motivation can help the management educator to support individual learners in a way that suits each of them at that point in time. With motivation often come expectations and managing those expectations is integral to a positive experience which also further fuels learning motivation.

When learner-driven, the interaction between AIME and the learner also follows a supply and demand approach. In the first instance the learner is introduced to the system and the capabilities of AIME and how AIME can support learning. For instance, AIME can detect reduced engagement and nudge the learner to re-engage. Nudging can range from sending notifications to providing direction to specific content that has last been accessed or additional materials that would further learning based on request. This level of "intervention" provided by AIME is optimized for the learner in advance and can be adjusted along one's learning journey. Such optimization needs guidance from the management educator and a certain level of awareness and understanding of the learners' own needs, preferences, motivation and expectations for learning support. This is a great starting point to involve learners in a wider conversation about their future study goals. It supports learner's awareness of themselves as learners, gives them responsibility and autonomy for their own learning and progress and at the same time agency.

The relationship explained above is built on the idea that the system is designed from the perspective of the management learner. As mentioned above, Luckin and Cukurova (2019) argue that AI has not yet fully been embedded in learning and teaching because AI developers lack knowledge in learning and teaching theory and research. Thus, systems are often not fit for purpose as technology specialists look at it from system design or teaching content provider perspectives instead of the learners' perspective. Both, designers and providers of teaching and learning are often not embedded in the learning themselves, which means they are removed from the actual learning/ user experience.

Lessons learnt from the popularity and growth of MOOCs suggest that learners who succeed best in a teaching format that is mostly facilitated by technology display behaviors recognized by self-regulation of learning models (K. Li, 2019). Such behaviors include the application of cognitive, metacognitive, affective, and motivational processes (Reparaz et al., 2020).

These behaviors may influence the level of personalized responsive learning the management learner seeks, which in turn informs the level of either teacher-led, self-directed and self-determined learning a management learner requires and positions this within the framework of teaching philosophies. Stoten (2020) pointed out that of the three teaching philosophies, heutagogy seems to be the "best" way to educate management learners in the future, as it would allow management learners to develop critical future skill sets relevant for professional practice (e.g., reflection and metacognition).

However, we argue that to categorize teaching approach and learner position within the confines of either pedagogy, andragogy or heutagogy does neither recognize the complexity of teaching philosophies nor the impact of internal and external factors on an individual learner's learning context. For example, a learner studying a familiar topic may seek an enquiry-based approach and seek to control and problem solve in their own way (heutagogy). Conversely, the same learner undertaking learning in a completely new and unfamiliar topic may seek the reassurance of educator-controlled, passive learning (pedagogy). Thus, the Collaborative Model of Management Education becomes a mechanism for personalized responsive learning through the utilization of AI technologies which are used as a diagnostic device to ascertain what approach best supports student learning at a particular juncture. As demonstrated in Figure 11.3, the model can shift and pivot to visualize the relationship between the learner, educator, and AIME to reflect the locus of control within the relationship and adopt relevant aspects of the most suitable teaching philosophy.

Defining the level of teacher-led, self-directed, and self-determined learning a learner would most benefit from initially requires the management educator to interpret the data and reports provided by AIME. Depending on the outcome, the management educator can select from a range of strategies to support the learner, for example through providing more instructional learning materials with varied levels of support. In collaboration with AIME, the learning materials can be shared with the learner and form part of their learning experience. A first-year undergraduate learner, for instance, might have learned how to sit exams and developed techniques to quickly regurgitate information but struggles to answer essay-based questions that require higher-order critical thinking skills (e.g., formulating coherent critical arguments). The learner has set AIME to a low level of intervention (e.g., nudging only via notifications). Based on the data the management educator can also initiate further actions and dialogue with the learner around the progress in a sensitive and mindful way. This might include prompting the learner to increase the level of intervention to ensure better support. This is a good example of how the management educator can help develop awareness skills of the learner beyond providing content and instructional learning activities; however, in time a highly developed and capable AIME will be able to recognize and learn patterns from the management educators' actions and therefore generate responsive strategies itself.

Conclusion

In this chapter we addressed the issue of how management educators and technology can be usefully combined to offer highly personalized, responsive learning experiences at scale. Recognizing the momentum created by a rapid shift to an increased use of blended learning supported by technology as a response in ME to the COVID-19 pandemic, we considered how the future of ME could be shaped by combining the strengths of human management educators and technology (specifically AI) to build a Collaborative Model of Management Education. Rooted in the observed growth of massification in learning, and specifically in management and business education, the opportunity to offer a personalized responsive learning experience at scale has been explored through several perspectives; the role of the management educator, the role of an AIME and the utilization of teaching philosophies as a framework to recognize and address individual learner needs.

The potential application of the model across the many faces of ME is far-reaching and not constrained by curriculum, syllabus or assessment. Moreover, the opportunities presented by the relatively low risk implications of experimentation and testing in the ME environment suggests that further research to develop the Collaborative Model of Management Education is feasible. Drawing on the lessons learnt and successes of mass customization in other industries, a partnership approach should be forged to bring together management educators and learners with AI developers and learning designers to shape the future of personalized responsive learning at scale.

References

Akyildiz, S. T. 2019. Do 21st century teachers know about heutagogy or do they still adhere to traditional pedagogy and andragogy? *International Journal of Progressive Education*, 15(6): 151–169.

Amemado, D. 2020. COVID-19: An unexpected and unusual driver to online education. *International Higher Education*, 102: 12–14.

Anderson, T., Rourke, L., Garrison, D. R., & Archer, W. 2001. Assessing teaching presence in a computer conferencing context. *Journal of Asynchronous Learning Networks*, 5(2): 1–17.

Arbaugh, J. B. 2007. Introduction: Project management education: Emerging tools, techniques, and topics. *The Academy of Management Learning and Education*, 6(4): 568–569.

Asoodar, M., Vaezi, S., & Izanloo, B. 2016. Framework to improve e-learner satisfaction and further strengthen e-learning implementation. *Computers in Human Behavior*, 63: 704–716.

Axley, S. R., & McMahon, T. R. 2006. Complexity: A frontier for management education. *Journal of Management Education*, 30(2): 295–315.

Beetham, H., & Sharpe, R. 2007. An introduction to rethinking pedagogy for a digital age. In *Rethinking pedagogy for a digital age: designing and delivering e-learning*: 1–12. London: Routledge.

Bengtsen, S. S., & Jensen, G. S. 2015. Online supervision at the university: A comparative study of supervision on student assignments face-to-face and online. *Tidsskriftet Læring og Medier (LOM)*, 8(13). https://doi.org/10.7146/lom.v8i13.19381

Black, P., & Wiliam, D. 2018. Classroom assessment and pedagogy. *Assessment in Education: Principles, Policy & Practice*, 25(6): 551–575.

Calvo, R. A., Peters, D., Vold, K., & Ryan, R. 2020. Supporting human autonomy in AI systems: A framework for ethical enquiry. In C. Burr & L. Floridi (Eds.), *Ethics of digital well-being: A multidisciplinary approach*, vol. 140: 31–54. Cham, Switzerland: Springer.

Chartered Association of Business Schools (CABS). 2019. *The changing shape of business education provision.* Accessed December 23, 2020, at https://charteredabs.org/publications/the-changing-shape-of-business-education-provision/

Cope, B., Kalantzis, M., & Searsmith, D. 2020. Artificial intelligence for education: Knowledge and its assessment in AI-enabled learning ecologies. *Educational Philosophy and Theory*, 53(12): 1229–1245.

Darics, E. 2020. E-leadership or "How to be boss in instant messaging?" The role of nonverbal communication. *International Journal of Business Communication*, 57(1): 3–29.

Diep, A. N., Zhu, C., Cocquyt, C., De Greef, M., Vo, M. H., & Vanwing, T. 2019. Adult learners' needs in online and blended learning. *Australian Journal of Adult Learning*, 59(2): 223–253.

dos Santos, H. L., & Cechinel, C. 2019. The final year project supervision in online distance learning: Assessing students and faculty perceptions about communication tools. *Behaviour & Information Technology*, 38(1): 65–84.

Druckman, D., & Ebner, N. 2018. Discovery learning in management education: Design and case analysis. *Journal of Management Education*, 42 (3): 347–374.

Evans, C., Rees, G., Taylor, C., & Fox, S. 2020. A liberal higher education for all? The massification of higher education and its implications for graduates' participation in civil society. *Higher Education*, 81: 521–535.

French, S., & Kennedy, G. 2017. Reassessing the value of university lectures. *Teaching in Higher Education*, 22(6): 639–654.

Fulford, A., & Mahon, Á. 2020. A philosophical defence of the university lecture. *Oxford Review of Education*, 46(3): 363–374.

García-Peñalvo, F. J., Fidalgo-Blanco, Á., & Sein-Echaluce, M. L. 2018. An adaptive hybrid MOOC model: Disrupting the MOOC concept in higher education. *Telematics and Informatics*, 35(4): 1018–1030.

Garrett, N., Beard, N., & Fiesler, C. 2020. More than "If time allows": The role of ethics in AI education. *Proceedings of the AAAI/ACM Conference on AI, Ethics, and Society*: 272–278. Accessed October 13, 2020, at https://dl.acm.org/doi/10.1145/3375627.3375868

Garrison, D. R. 1989. *Understanding distance education: A framework for the future*. London: Routledge.

Garrison, D. R., Anderson, T., & Archer, W. 1999. Critical inquiry in a text-based environment: Computer conferencing in higher education. *The Internet and Higher Education*, 2(2-3): 87–105.

Garrison, D. R., & Arbaugh, J. B. 2007. Researching the community of inquiry framework: Review, issues, and future directions. *The Internet and Higher Education*, 10(3): 157–172.

Gassmann, O., Frankenberger, K., & Csik, M. 2014. *The business model navigator: 55 models that will revolutionise your business*. Harlow, UK: Pearson.

Giannakis, M., & Bullivant, N. 2016. The massification of higher education in the UK: Aspects of service quality. *Journal of Further and Higher Education*, 40(5): 630–648.

Goel, A. K., & Polepeddi, L. 2016. *Jill Watson: A virtual teaching assistant for online education*. Georgia Institute of Technology. Accessed February 6, 2021, at http://hdl.handle.net/1853/59104

Hewett, S., Becker, K., & Bish, A. 2019. Blended workplace learning: The value of human interaction. *Education + Training*, 61(1): 2–16.

Hsieh, Y. H., & Tsai, C. C. 2012. The effect of moderator's facilitative strategies on online synchronous discussions. *Computers in Human Behavior*, 28(5): 1708–1716.

Hung, I. C., & Chen, N. S. 2018. Embodied interactive video lectures for improving learning comprehension and retention. *Computers & Education*, 117: 116–131.

Hurrell, S. A. 2015. Rethinking the soft skills deficit blame game: Employers, skills withdrawal and the reporting of soft skills gaps. *Human Relations*, 69(3): 605–628.

Islam, M., Kim, D. A., & Kwon, M. 2020. A comparison of two forms of instruction: Pre-recorded video lectures vs. live ZOOM lectures for education in the business management field. *Sustainability*, 12(19): 8149.

Jarrahi, M. H. 2018. Artificial intelligence and the future of work: Human-AI symbiosis in organizational decision making. *Business Horizons*, 61(4): 577–586.

Jones, J. A. 2019. Scaffolding self-regulated learning through student-generated quizzes. *Active Learning in Higher Education*, 20(2): 115–126.

Jones, C., Penaluna, K., & Penaluna, A. 2019. The promise of andragogy, heutagogy and academagogy to enterprise and entrepreneurship education pedagogy. *Education + Training*, 61(9): 1170–1186.

Knowles, M. S. 1984. *Andragogy in action*. San Francisco: Jossey-Bass.

Kokku, R., Sundararajan, S., Dey, P., Sindhgatta, R., Nitta, S., & Sengupta, B. 2018. Augmenting classrooms with AI for personalized education. *2018 IEEE International Conference on Acoustics, Speech and Signal Processing (ICASSP)*: 6976–6980. Accessed December 21, 2020, at https://ieeexplore.ieee.org/abstract/document/8461812

Kreijns, K., Van Acker, F., Vermeulen, M., & Van Buuren, H. 2014. Community of inquiry: Social presence revisited. *E-learning and Digital Media*, 11(1): 5–18.

Law, K. M., Geng, S., & Li, T. 2019. Student enrolment, motivation and learning performance in a blended learning environment: The mediating effects of social, teaching, and cognitive presence. *Computers & Education*, 136: 1–12.

Lee, S. H., Smith, D., & Sergueeva, K. 2016. What do students think about group work in business education? An investigation into the benefits, challenges, and student-suggested solutions. *Journal of Education for Business*, 91(7): 380–386.

Li, H. 2019. Special section introduction: Artificial intelligence and advertising. *Journal of Advertising*, 48(4): 333–337.

Li, K. 2019. MOOC learners' demographics, self-regulated learning strategy, perceived learning and satisfaction: A structural equation modeling approach. *Computers & Education*, 132: 16–30.

Luckin, R., & Cukurova, M. 2019. Designing educational technologies in the age of AI: A learning sciences-driven approach. *British Journal of Educational Technology*, 50(6): 2824–2838.

Mann, S., Ker, G., Eden-Mann, P., & O'Brien, R. 2017. Designing for heutagogy: An independent learning pathway approach. *Capable–Scope: (Flexible Learning)*, 2: 59–70.

Mansur, A. B. F., Yusof, N., & Basori, A. H. 2019. Personalized learning model based on deep learning algorithm for student behaviour analytic. *Procedia Computer Science*, 163: 125–133.

McNally, J. J., Piperopoulos, P., Welsh, D. H., Mengel, T., Tantawy, M., & Papageorgiadis, N. 2020. From pedagogy to andragogy: Assessing the impact of social entrepreneurship course syllabi on the millennial learner. *Journal of Small Business Management*, 58(5): 871–892.

Medina, L. C. 2018. Blended learning: Deficits and prospects in higher education. *Australasian Journal of Educational Technology*, 34(1): 42–56

Messinger, P. R., Ge, X., Smirnov, K., Stroulia, E., & Lyons, K. 2019. Reflections of the extended self: Visual self-representation in avatar-mediated environments. *Journal of Business Research*, 100: 531–546.

Molnár, G., & Szüts, Z. 2018. The role of chatbots in formal education. *2018 IEEE 16th International Symposium on Intelligent Systems and Informatics (SISY)*: 197–202. Accessed August 22, 2020, at https://ieeexplore.ieee.org/abstract/document/8524609

Muduli, A., Kaura, V., & Quazi, A. 2018. Pedagogy or andragogy? Views of Indian postgraduate business students. *IIMB Management Review*, 30(2): 168–178.

Nason, R. 2017. *It's not complicated: The art and science of complexity in business*. Toronto: University of Toronto Press.

Offstein, E. H., & Chory, R. M. 2019. In defense of the lecture: Revisiting and re-assessing its place within management pedagogy. *Organization Management Journal*, 16(4): 350–362.

Prentice, C., & Nguyen, M. 2020. Engaging and retaining customers with AI and employee service. *Journal of Retailing and Consumer Services*, 56: 102186.

Reich, J., & Ruipérez-Valiente, J. A. 2019. The MOOC pivot. *Science*, 363(6423): 130–131.

Reparaz, C., Aznárez-Sanado, M., & Mendoza, G. 2020. Self-regulation of learning and MOOC retention. *Computers in Human Behavior*, 111: 106423.

Rivers, C., & Holland, A. 2020. *Does blended learning change what learning is?* Accessed December 23, 2020, at https://wonkhe.com/blogs/does-blended-learning-change-what-learning-is/

Rivers, C., & Kinchin, I. 2019. Dynamic learning: Designing a hidden pedagogy to enhance critical thinking skills development. *Management Teaching Review*, 4(2): 148–156.

Rivers, C., & O'Brien, J. 2019. Developing business-ready graduates: Teaching inside out. In H. T. M. Bui, H. T. M. Nguyen, & D. Cole (Eds.), *Innovate higher education to enhance graduate employability*: 83–94. London: Routledge.

Ryan, T., French, S., & Kennedy, G. 2019. Beyond the iron triangle: Improving the quality of teaching and learning at scale. *Studies in Higher Education*, 46(7): 1383–1394.

Saichaie, K. 2020. Blended, flipped, and hybrid learning: Definitions, developments, and directions. *New Directions for Teaching and Learning*, 2020(164): 95–104.

Schneider, M., & Preckel, F. 2017. Variables associated with achievement in higher education: A systematic review of meta-analyses. *Psychological Bulletin*, 143(6): 565–600.

Serrano, D. R., Dea-Ayuela, M. A., Gonzalez-Burgos, E., Serrano-Gil, A., & Lalatsa, A. 2019. Technology-enhanced learning in higher education: How to enhance student engagement through blended learning. *European Journal of Education*, 54(2): 273–286.

Serrat, O. 2017. Understanding and developing emotional intelligence. In *Knowledge solutions*. Singapore: Springer. Access October 8, 2020, at 10.1007/978-981-10-0983-9_37

Short, F., & Martin, J. 2011. Presentation vs. performance: Effects of lecturing style in higher education on student preference and student learning. *Psychology Teaching Review*, 17(2): 71–82.

Somasundaram, M., Junaid, K. M., & Mangadu, S. 2020. Artificial intelligence (AI) enabled intelligent quality management system (IQMS) for personalized learning path. *Procedia Computer Science*, 172: 438–442.

Stachowicz-Stanusch, A., & Amann, W. 2020. *Management and business education in the time of artificial intelligence: The need to rethink, retrain, and redesign*. Greenwich, United States: Information Age Publishing.

Stoten, D. W. 2020. Practical heutagogy: Promoting personalized learning in management education. *Adult Learning*, 31(4): 161–174

Syynimaa, N. 2019. Does replacing face-to-face lectures with pre-recorded video lectures affect learning outcomes? *International Conference on Computer Supported Education*, 2: 454–457.

Thai, N. T. T., De Wever, B., & Valcke, M. 2017. The impact of a flipped classroom design on learning performance in higher education: Looking for the best "blend" of lectures and guiding questions with feedback. *Computers & Education*, 107: 113–126.

Vincent-Lancrin, S., & Van der Vlies, R. 2020. *Trustworthy artificial intelligence (AI) in education: Promises and challenges.* Working paper, no. 218, OECD Education. Accessed November 21, 2020, at 10.1787/19939019

Vorbach, S., Poandl, E., & Korajman, I. 2019. Digital entrepreneurship education: The role of MOOCs. *International Journal of Engineering Pedagogy (IJEP)*, 9(3): 99–111.

Wang, Q., Jing, S., Camacho, I., Joyner, D., & Goel, A. 2020. Jill Watson SA: Design and evaluation of a virtual agent to build communities among online learners. *Extended Abstracts of the 2020 CHI Conference on Human Factors in Computing Systems*: 1–8. Accessed October 16, 2020, at https://dl.acm.org/doi/abs/10.1145/3334480.3382878

Wasson, B., & Kirschner, P. A. 2020. Learning design: European approaches. *TechTrends*, 64, 815–827.

PART IV

Dynamics of Accreditation and Regulation of ME

12

BEYOND THE "SCHOOL" AS THE OBJECT OF ASSESSMENT: SECTOR DISRUPTION AND THE CHANGING NATURE OF BUSINESS SCHOOL ACCREDITATION

Ulrich Hommel and Koen Vandenbempt

Introduction

The management education (ME) sector is currently exposed to a multitude of disruptive forces that will impact and fundamentally alter the role of business school accreditation in relation to reputation formation and competitive positioning (Hommel & Lejeune, 2013; Hommel & Thomas, 2014; Kaplan, 2018; Peters, Smith, & Thomas, 2018b). Accreditation traditionally acts as a resolver of the asymmetries between business schools and their stakeholders. But how can it continue to play this role if business schools are fundamentally transformed?

In this chapter, we use the changing object of accreditation as a starting point of our analysis. Accreditation agencies delineate the "school" as the institutional object for quality assurance and assessment (either in its own right or as a quality assurance umbrella for degree and non-degree programs). We posit that the provision of ME is undergoing a process of de-institutionalization and will become predominantly network-based or possibly even ecosystem-based, modular, learner-centered and produced through "unbundled faculty systems" of different types of education professionals. As a consequence, education modules will replace programs as units of production, value chains will become more fluid and quality will increasingly be shaped by multiple institutional contexts. While deliberate (effectively deterministic) strategizing, bureaucratic rituals and historical track records are currently key formative forces for successful accreditation, they will matter much less (and possibly in a different way) in an environment where business school boundaries are becoming porous, display a high degree of plasticity and where hierarchical direction is replaced by network coordination and collaboration among multiple entities and actors.

DOI: 10.4324/9781003095903-16

It is conjectured that the current system of external validation of quality will evolve into a contested field with (1) established accreditors being forced to change their approach in response to the emergence of new business models and (2) new and alternative means of quality validation emerging at the same time. With disruptive forces changing the higher education industry, the key question is how accreditation can continue to fulfill its role in providing credible quality signals to business school stakeholders (see also Blackmur, 2004). The chapter builds on a long-standing debate that started with Julian & Ofori-Dankwa (2006) and Zammuto (2008) of whether accreditation helps or hinders the business schools' adjustment to disruptive change.

The chapter is structured as follows: the second section clarifies how the concept of the "school" is used in international accreditation and how it has evolved over time. The third section introduces the theoretical grounding of this study using the Theory of Fields (Fligstein & McAdam, 2012). The conceptual frame helps to clarify the role of accreditors in maintaining order in the field or, as claimed by Spender (1989), as a dominant industry recipe of university-level ME. The fourth section then describes the forces of de-institutionalization that are eroding the "school" as a unit of quality assessment and are upsetting the "field of accreditation." In particular, we explain how unbundling (and re-bundling) leads to network-based provision of business school services and ultimately to institutional boundaries becoming even less deterministic within ecosystems. It will enable further reflections on the future role of business school accreditation in the fifth section. This future role is characterized as a choice that accreditors need to make; they can act as a barrier to change which in our view will expose them to existential risks, or they can evolve pro-actively and claim the role as architect of the future. The sixth section offers some final reflections.

The "School" as the Object of Accreditation

The ME industry is going through a period of change and disruption. The emergence of game-changing technologies, deregulation, demographic change, changing learner preferences and, on top, COVID-19 as a change catalyst of it all, are ending a long era of relative stability in this industry. In the fourth section we highlight and illustrate how the forces of unbundling and re-bundling are creating a new competitive landscape. The section lays the groundwork by clarifying the role of the "school" as the focus of international accreditation. First, the discussion focuses on how the AACSB (Association to Advance Collegiate Schools of Business) and EQUIS (offered by EFMD Global) systems bracket the boundaries of the "school" as part of their accreditation processes. We initially explain how the "school" is defined in each system to then highlight the ways in which the current forces of unbundling will be moving institutional realities away from these definitions. We conclude this section by explaining how quality assurance activities of (accredited) schools are morphing into a multi-layered process that requires a different accreditation approach.

Boundaries of the "School": AACSB versus EQUIS Perspective

The "school" is seen by the accreditation agencies as the institutional object for quality assurance and assessment. AACSB for instance states:

> The fundamental purpose of AACSB accreditation is to encourage business schools to hold themselves accountable for improving business practice through a commitment to strategic management, learner success, and impactful thought leadership. AACSB achieves this purpose by defining a set of criteria and standards, coordinating peer review and consultation, and recognizing high-quality business schools that meet the standards and actively engage in the process. (AACSB International, 2020: 9)

The default case is the accreditation of the applicant institution plus any business-related programs offered by a degree-granting parent university. Activities beyond the boundaries of the applicant can be excluded if they are sufficiently differentiated from the applicant's offerings in terms of branding and market perception.

EQUIS follows a similar approach by expecting reasonable autonomy as well as clearly identifiable boundaries to other units within the wider institutional structure (EFMD Global, 2020). It differs by not allowing the option of accrediting business-related programs offered by other units of the parent university (two units can however apply jointly if a management structure is in place that connects them in terms of strategizing and operations). In addition, EQUIS imposes constraints regarding an applicant's activity portfolio by limiting non-business activities within the applicant institution (they either support business-related activities and these are then accredited or are otherwise excluded from accreditation). Hence, while AACSB operates a mushroom model with the stem sitting in the applicant institution, EQUIS employs a cookie approach that under certain circumstances may look like a doughnut.

Key for the purposes of the discussion is that the concept of the "school" is based on the notion of comprehensiveness. EQUIS for instance requires that the applicant covers at least two areas for educational provision (bachelor, master, MBA, PhD, or executive education), though most cover at least three out of five, engages in research, has academic staff covering the principal management disciplines (which may lock out specialist providers) and can look back at a history of at least ten years (EFMD Global, 2020). These regulations and especially the notion of "comprehensiveness" appear at odds with the "school" evolving into a fragmented construct. In some respects, it may become a platform that external assets plug into (as an outgrowth of "unbundling"). In other respects, it may be in purely collaborative mode or contribute to value chains sitting on external platforms (as an example of "re-bundling"). The notion of "comprehensiveness" is likely to become even more important from a student perspective (in term of creating value-added in learning), but it is likely to lose its significance as an institutional currency as traditionally defined by accreditation agencies.

Quality Assurance as a Multi-Layered Process

The "school" as the owner or delegated holder of degree-awarding powers is responsible for the quality of degree provision which puts quality assurance and also external validation of quality in focus. Traditionally, actors at the top of the organizational hierarchy possess most of the knowledge and are the drivers of action. This is necessarily changing if knowledge is becoming more dispersed and hierarchies are disintegrating. Birkinshaw's concept of "hierarchy" (hierarchy of position, hierarchy of knowledge and hierarchy of action) can be applied to better understand how sector dynamics are impacting quality (Birkinshaw, 2010). Quality assurance can be seen as a multi-layered process with three intertwined and overlapping elements: the *nature of the process* (when is the process executed), the *knowledge centralization of the process* (where resides the knowledge to execute the process) and the *action element* (who can execute the process).

Quality assurance and assessment is so far characterized by discreteness. It follows the rhythm of degree delivery (e.g., courses and modules) and the structure of the academic year (e.g., semesters and semester blocks), both potentially arbitrary metrics in a de-institutionalized world of ME. Knowledge currently resides inside the "school" and is used to demonstrate performance against external accreditation standards. In the future, in contrast, self-reported information may become less relevant in comparison to crowd-based measures that allow for reliable inter-school benchmarking (Hommel & Osbaldeston, 2017). And, on top, externally sourced knowledge and expertise are likely to become embedded in the value chain of program design and delivery (e.g., via advanced forms of action/workplace learning).

Emerging delivery models are changing all layers of the quality assurance process. Stackable programs are for instance delivered in scattered time blocks and with a multitude of actors involved beyond the scope of one school (or even beyond the scope of academia). Given that every student may choose a different progression pattern, much greater continuity is required in assuring the quality of provision. Knowledge will no longer be concentrated within the "school", but dispersed in a wider network, which implies that many more actors must be enabled to take action and coordinated/deployed appropriately to safeguard quality.

Quality assurance work will change in the process. Educational value chains will be co-owned by a multitude of actors rather than just one business school. Hierarchical coordination (based on authority arising from the property rights of the entity) will need to be replaced with network or market coordination which means that the number of participating entities increases and the nature of value creation is less "controllable." Collaboration may take on many forms from joint venturing and networks to arm's length dealing, which will impact what quality assurance can be deployed and how. The challenge for business schools is to adjust to this new reality organically and by still living up to their responsibilities as degree-awarding institutions (whatever the shape or form these degrees may take on in the future). The implications for accreditations will likely to be massive. What will for instance be the future value of legacy measurements (e.g., institutional track record of academic publications and PhD production) when delivery of programs is becoming more disconnected from a business school's intellectual production system (see further below)?

Accreditation agencies need to adjust to this new reality as well (see, e.g., Hommel & Osbaldeston, 2017). They will liaison with accreditation offices that will be set up differently; they will need to reach out beyond institutional boundaries to assess quality and may need to develop new proxy metrics. In reference to Rindova, Williamson, Petkova, & Sever (2005), accreditors will face novel challenges in their effort to minimize the discrepancy between "Being Good" and "Being Known." Before digging deeper into the future role of accreditation agencies, we first introduce a theoretical lens to better understand the role these agencies will play and have played in the past.

Understanding the Role of Accreditation by Employing the Theory of Fields

Over the past two decades, "international" accreditation has assumed a key role in structuring the competitive contest between business schools globally. It has moved from the periphery of the sector to the very center and now acts as a "credible" signpost for proxying quality in a still very fragmented market (thereby often outshining national accreditations). To support sense-making of the role of accreditation, we do several things in this section. First, we introduce a theoretical lens by referencing the concept of Strategic Action Fields (Fligstein & McAdam, 2012). Next, we offer a typology of business schools as key actors in this "field" and their disposition toward accreditation. Finally, we look at how external forces are influencing the field stability.

Management Education as a Strategic Action Field

We conceptualize the role of accreditation agencies using Fligstein and McAdam's concept of Strategic Action Fields (Fligstein & McAdam, 2012) which differs from organizational fields in general (see Wooten & Hoffman, 2017) by allowing actors to engage in collective strategic action within a well-defined social space. Strategic action fields represent meso-level social orders that define purpose, relationships between actors as well as field governance. Business schools belong to a multitude of such fields with partially overlapping sets of actors and each field can even be disaggregated into nested subfields. Strategic action fields are established, reproduced, changed or dismantled as a result of collective action. In our context, this relates to the evolution and acceptance of accreditation standards regarding quality; it also captures the rivalry between alternative quality improvement frameworks, and the emergence and adoption of new ones.

Field actors are stakeholders with respect to the quality improvement agenda linked to business school accreditation. Next to the business schools themselves, this includes the school's stakeholders, accreditation agencies, and ranking providers as well as oversight bodies representing society at large. Actors socially construct these strategic action fields (e.g. Jepperson, 1991) and their ultimate influence is determined by the social power they wield (e.g., Bourdieu & Wacquant, 1992).

International accreditation systems are best understood as compliance frameworks that lay down behavioral norms and define minimum standards in terms of resource inputs, processes and outcomes. They, in effect, represent rules that align actors via each other. Their field-wide acceptance and enforcement is enabled by a shared understanding among all actors of what benefits are associated with accreditation.

Field stability does not require that accreditation standards remain static. In fact, accreditors are generally member-based organizations that organize a participatory process of reviewing and adjusting the "rules of the game" periodically. The accreditors themselves (and more specifically the teams charged with managing the systems) play a pivotal role as overseers of compliance and as facilitators of system reproduction. They act as internal governance units of the strategic action field that enable business schools to access resource rewards following a test of economic and social fitness (Alajoutsijärvi, Kettunen, & Sohlo, 2018; DiMaggio & Powell, 1983) and, hence, have a defining role in shaping the institutional infrastructure (Hinings, Logue, & Zietsma, 2017).

Typology of Business Schools within the Accreditation Field

The *accreditation field* is an arena of tension and contest with each business school vying for advantage. Some schools are more powerful than others, not the least because of superior resource endowments. Following Hommel & Woods (2018), we differentiate between three kinds of ME providers (see also Foster & Hibbert in this volume). *Elite incumbents* are lead business schools that are characterized by over-compliance and resource abundance (see also Khurana, 2007: 292–293). They can be found in the group of triple-accredited institutions and in the top layer of international rankings. Elite schools benefit from stakeholder perceptions of high reputation and institutional prominence. Over-fulfillment of accreditation standards enables these institutions to challenge the rules of the game and bring innovation to the sector (Corley & Gioia, 2000).

While elite incumbents exercise a disproportionate influence on the organization of the accreditation field, they require the group of *general incumbents* to help legitimize rule-consistent patterns of behavior. The latter are accredited institutions that utilize the normative pressures of accreditation as the way to compete (Granovetter, 1985) and as the dominant intra-school discourse (see Hardy & Maguire, 2010). General incumbents derive their identity from the pursuit and maintenance of international quality labels. They are likely to resist change in accreditation standards and processes if it increases the shadow value of resource constraints (as a representation of their tightness). At the same time, general incumbents have limited means to do so and will therefore be most under siege as conventional business models of business schools are becoming unbundled (Peters & Thomas, 2020).

Finally, the third group providers are *challengers* that occupy a peripheral space of the accreditation field (or no space at all). These institutions have no stake in the status quo and are not bound by the customs of inherited social order. As long as the accreditation field maintains stability, challengers remain restricted to their niche role. They are capable of conceiving new rules and are ready to support the resource-rich elite to alter field topography in their favor. In contrast to Fligstein and McAdam, field stability is not simply the reproduction of the status quo, it is the maintenance of a stable trajectory that reflects the current power structure and nature of contest (Cavico & Mujtaba, 2010; Fligstein & McAdam, 2012: 96).

The group of challengers is a diverse group. It includes maverick business schools with ambitions to join the elite on their own terms (e.g., achieved by Hult International Business School) as well as non-academic organizations interested in extending their business model to education (e.g., Google), in partnership with elite incumbents or on their own.

How the Strategic Action Field Changes

During "normal" times, change is affected by building up pressure on accrediting agencies as they act as the internal governance units of the field. Through their legitimization, routinization, and structuring activities, accreditors enforce compliance with the rules and norms of accreditation (Hommel & Woods, 2018), thereby furnishing audiences with reductionist means of comparing and judging business schools (Espeland & Stevens, 1998). Their normal modus operandi focuses on the reproduction of the status quo which positions them as a conservative (preserving) influence (see Pfeffer & Fong, 2002) and, in doing so, they "reinforce the dominant perspective and guard the interests of incumbents" (Fligstein & McAdam, 2012: 14). Historically, this helps address the question why there is "such startling homogeneity of organizational forms and practices" (practically explained by Datar, Garvin, & Cullen, 2010; DiMaggio & Powell, 1983) that invites iso-morphism and global mimicry (Wilson & McKiernan, 2011). At this point in time, the industry has embraced a dominant "recipe" of conducting its business (Matthyssens, Vandenbempt, & Berghman, 2006; Spender, 1989). Thomas, Billsberry, Ambrosini, & Barton (2014) therefore conclude that "whilst accred-itation is a necessary precursor for international competition, it is no longer a form of competitive advantage" (Thomas et al., 2014: 305).

The increasingly volatile and dynamic nature of the ME industry (Starkey & Tiratsoo, 2007) explains why no consensual logic exists that represents the interests of all actors. Whilst reproducing and adhering to the normative patterns that maintain the social arena of accreditations, business schools deploy resources and skill to challenge existing hierarchies. It creates a "jittery" equilibrium of sorts that can easily be perturbed by shocks.

A multitude of transformational dynamics are making the accreditation field more brittle (see next section). These include unbundling of business school services (e.g., academic degrees), institutional disintermediation (facilitated by technology platforms), changing inter-field resource dependencies (e.g., funding models) and macro-events (e.g., COVID-19). Individually, they can lead to chronic, low-intensity episodes of contention. In totality, they can represent compounding destabilizing influences with rapid increases in "speed of onset" and institutional vulnerability. It explains why accrediting agencies are facing a bifurcation going forward where they will either be barriers to change or ar-chitects of the future. The next section will take a closer look at the different stages of de-institutionalization, what the driving forces are and how this will affect accreditation on an operational level.

From Unbundling to Network Provision of Management Education to Ecosystems

This section focuses on the microprocesses driving de-institutionalization: unbundling traditional forms of organizing student learning which leads to novel forms of provision of ME through the collaboration of many partners (a "network") and/or even through ecosystems. We first discuss the process of unbundling in general and draw analogies to other industries. Next, we describe how re-bundling can take place, thereby shifting the focal point of analysis of an "institutional" to a "student-centered" view.

Unbundling and Re-bundling as Generic Change Processes

Unbundling and re-bundling of service offerings are common features in the evolution of industries. Technological breakthrough and heightening competi-tion can for instance push companies to rethink their market offer and allow new entrants to cream-skim the market. The de-construction of universal banking and the emergence of a multi-faceted, highly fragmented fintech sector serve as an illustration (Basole & Patel, 2018). Similar unbundling and re-bundling have reshaped and disrupted the printed media and music industry. Also, very traditional industries such as auction houses are experiencing unbundling, driven by actions of the big commercial galleries. The same can be said for real estate markets and the diminishing role of licensed realtors. Unbundling can also be triggered by the desire to enhance the customer experience, for instance by granting access to parts of service bundles with a high maximum willingness to pay.

Levine (2000) already discussed the unbundling of research and teaching in faculty work to explain the rising salary gap between research and mostly-teaching universities (see also Ehrenberg, 2011). Seers (2007) refers to the unbundling of programs in the context of creating market distinctiveness (developing flagship programs versus traditional bachelor programs) while McCowan (2017) relates the discussion to "product" unbundling and argues that "unnecessary" services can be stripped away from the core educational offer.

Unbundling is often followed by re-bundling, which in simplistic terms can be understood as the deconstruction of a Lego structure and using the blocks to build something new. Matthyssens & Vandenbempt (2008) illustrate in a B2B context that companies are re-bundling their offerings to seek further integration into the business and technical processes of their customers. Similar patterns can be observed in the electricity sector, digital services (e.g., music), financial services and, going forward, probably also in tertiary education.

The higher education sector is currently challenged to absorb a string of new technologies and meet heightened expectations of students that are now dispersed around the globe. It has already kicked into motion sector dynamics that have prompted the introduction of topically unique programs and the deployment of non-traditional delivery modes (Hanappi-Egger, 2020). This stands in contrast to conventional wisdom that questions the ability of business schools (and universities more generally) to adapt to changing circumstances (Wildavsky, Kelly, & Carey, 2011).

Part of the explanation resides in the "de facto" market imperfections and information asymmetries that are linked to the degree granting powers of the higher education industry. This license to operate focuses the higher education industry more on the advancement of its own profession than on the absorption of technological and societal changes. Back in 2007, Seers for instance argued that "[I]f management academics are going to have to adapt to market competition as knowledge suppliers, they will have to calibrate what they supply to market demand just the same as any other seller of goods or services" (Seers, 2007: 560). He pinpointed that "[T]he functions of teaching and research were derived in the preindustrial economy and are among the few career activities people still do in the mode of traditional craft work, in which the individual craft worker largely controls the design and implementation of the specific methods to be employed [...]" (Seers, 2007: 561). DeMillo (2011), Bowen (2013), and others put forward similar arguments, which has led Wildavsky (2010) to predict a shift of the sector ecology toward for-profit providers (similar issues arise when considering management and higher education as professions where the license to practice creates asymmetries of power and economic rents).

The dominant institutional logic nowadays positions business schools as surplus seekers (de facto mimicking for-profit behavior); they are trying to keep their "de facto" advantage (associated with the license to operate) by ensuring the value of their degrees. In this context, creating "student value" (in analogy with creating "customer value" for business organizations) has become a central pillar driving organizational change as well as the move toward network and ecosystem provision. The main visible effect of unbundling is the disaggregation of the design and the delivery of ME as well as knowledge and expertise beyond the boundaries of the business school. As a consequence, traditional partnerships based on student exchange are evolving into novel forms of alliances among business schools that enable the sharing of discipline knowledge, expertise and infrastructure access. Students enrolled in one institution can augment their learning journey by accessing specialized courses and additional reputational benefits offered by alliance partners. In other words, student learning is becoming more network-based. COVID-related efforts of establishing distributed business schools based on sets of bilateral student hosting agreements exemplify this development.

On top of this, the establishment of hybrid learning systems creates an amalgam of online delivery and traditional face-to-face formats of instruction that will open up avenues for experimental learning extending beyond the boundaries of a business school. A student's alma mater may eventually be reduced to serving as an entry and exit point of the learning experience while educational delivery takes place within a network of partner schools (and possibly also non-academic organizations). Stackable degree qualifications (Kofman, 2018) and micro-credentialing (Milligan & Kennedy, 2017) are likely to further unbundle the management curriculum across institutions, geography and also time.

Sector development is not likely to stop there and eventually move on to educational provision within ecosystems. Ecosystems are already reshaping many other industries and are best understood as a fluid network with value chains evolving opportunistically (see also Straub, 2019). Following De Meyer & Williamson (2020b), they offer novel sources of stakeholder value (in particular for students), access diverse capabilities of academic and non-academic partners and realize network economies in the process. Ecosystems furthermore excel with customization and functionality of service as the nodes within the network recombine more readily to achieve higher value-added (De Meyer & Williamson, 2020a). And applying the platform logic of Cusumano, Yoffie, & Gawer (2020), ecosystems of third-party firms, organizations and even individual contractors may allow business schools to bypass the traditional supply chain and labor pools (read: "own" faculty) required by conventional accreditation, thus for example allowing schools to insource capabilities that support the institutional impact/relevance agenda more effectively (see also the debate on the casualization of the HE workforce, e.g., Hommel & Hommel, 2020).

The transition from integrated provision of ME to production and delivery within ecosystems will lead to a looser coupling of institutional research activities and program delivery, which will raise the relative importance of non-faculty staff involved in relational work within the ecosystem (see also Matthyssens & Vandenbempt, 2008). It will furthermore force adjustments of internal processes in response to the increasingly outward orientation of (student) value creation.

The transformation of the ME sector will not be a discontinuous jump process, even with COVID, but rather an incremental change process through unbundling and re-bundling. Business schools are already moving forward in trial-and-error mode that will eventually transform experimental action into practices of greater permanence. The common denominator is the increased focus on creating value for student learners. The business school ecology will become more diverse in the process with general incumbents being especially subjected to pressures to depart from their "raison d'être."

All the above processes make the strategic action field more brittle and are (unintentionally) eroding the strength of the dominant industry recipe. We now turn our attention to how these forces can impact the future role of accreditation agencies.

Accreditation Agencies – Barriers to Change or Architects of the Future?

The heading of this section indicates that a wide range of scenarios can be envisioned when thinking about the future role of accreditation (and incumbent accreditors). Rather than predicting outcomes, the discussion highlights some of the dynamics that are likely to redefine the role of accreditors as internal governance units. We do this in two main steps. First, we reflect on what we label the "time-lag bias" in accreditation processes to then take stock of the drawbacks of these processes related to the above-mentioned changes in the ME sector and how international accreditation agencies can respond to these changes.

Time-Lag Biases in Accreditation Processes

International accreditation focuses on the past to appreciate the present and both combined is supposed to facilitate an understanding of the likely future. By design, the work of an accreditor relies heavily on the "rear mirror" view and uses institutional "track record" as a source of credibility (e.g., to assess program design and delivery). Innovation remains an untested idea until it has proven its effectiveness in an operational context. As a consequence, accreditors operate with a blurred vision in relation to current sector developments. We refer to it as the *first-order time-lag bias*.

Accreditors revise processes and standards periodically. Small changes (e.g., closing of loopholes, clarifications) may be implemented during annual review cycles. More fundamental adjustments happen less frequently and are embedded in formalized redesign rituals. Change processes are normally initiated following the operational observation of quality shortfalls (e.g., excessive risk taking, later followed up by a new standard for risk management) or the spread of innovative practices that have the potential of becoming state of the art (e.g., aspects of technology-enhancement of educational provision). Accreditors never front-run sector developments; they rather wait until a sector consensus emerges that is then codified with the involvement of their business school members. We call this the *second-order time-lag bias*.

In normal times, built-in time lags and membership participation are key ingredients for safeguarding the accreditors' role as internal governance units. They foster framework stability and prevent the drifting of standards in response to fashion and fads. In times of disruption, this combination however works against them. The conjectured transition from the "brick-and-mortar" business school to the ecosystem-based provision of ME is pushed forward by a multitude of "Gray Rhino" risks (Wucker, 2017) related to demographic shifts, technological change, changing educational needs of degree students and practitioners as well as geopolitical developments. "Gray Rhino" is used as a metaphor to describe a "clear and present danger" that is mostly ignored by decision-makers. Slow "speed of onset" and inaction by other business schools (herd behavior) are typically used as justifications for the delay in dealing with these threats (Hommel, 2020).

COVID-19 is a pandemic of historical proportions that is challenging the economic DNA of higher education in many respects. Technically, it is a "high impact, low probability (HILP)" event (see also Taleb, 2008) that, in addition to its own short-term consequences, interacts with the Gray Rhinos risks making them charge at business schools all of a sudden at much higher speed (see also Krishnamurthy, 2020). The combination promises to exert a catalytic influence on the emergence of credible network- and ecosystem-based business models for the provision of ME. As explained by McGrath (2019), once critical inflection points for the adoption of new industry practices have been reached (signaling market acceptance and economic viability), then elite incumbents together with challengers will push forward and contest existing field norms (Hommel & Woods, 2018). As a consequence, first-order as well as second-order time-lag biases of accreditation will widen which is likely to infringe on the acceptance of accreditors as internal governance units. Furthermore, as traditional business schools will be struggling to remain viable in the face of COVID-19 and other disruptions, the typical normative pressure of accreditation agencies will weaken in order to accommodate the struggle for institutional viability (or even survival). On the positive side, all these events will create scope for experimentation and renewal. As explained by Hommel, Kjellander, & Thouary (2021), exposure to revenue risk fosters a culture of ambidexterity in this context while a protective regulatory umbrella can cultivate the view that there is an identity between pre- and post-crisis worlds.

Pathways for Accreditation Agencies

What can accreditation agencies do to alleviate some of the pressures they are facing? For one, they can choose the *path of least resistance* that emerges organically and "sub-intentionally" by continuing to respect the current modus operandi. By choosing this route, accreditors create institutionalized tolerance for decoupling (Boxenbaum & Johnsson, 2017). Applying the logic of DiMaggio & Powell (1983), if mimetic pressures of isomorphism are pulling business schools in a different direction than the normative pressures exercised by quality assessment, then accreditors can loosen the coupling between the business schools' reported performance relative to the accreditation standards and actual behavior. This may occur in a latent fashion as accreditation standards are often framed as questions with peers charged to interpret whether school claims of compliance and excellence can actually be accepted.

By contextualizing the assessment, the interpretation of standards may gradually cast a wider net so that business schools stay compliant. Rasche & Gilbert (2015) make a similar argument when analyzing why business schools "never walk the talk" in relation to the implementation of responsible ME principles. Applying their logic, the push toward decoupling will occur and intensify if business schools have to cope with competing institutional pressures, are confronted with overt or covert resistance to change by accreditors and have to deal with a rising ambiguity with how standards are applied in practice. The resulting decoupling exposure can then causally lead to weakening of existing norms (Hensel & Guérard, 2020).

Although operating this valve can release short-term pressure, it risks degrading the accreditors' credibility in the longer term as the share of "false-negatives" in the pool of accredited schools will rise. It can ultimately lead to a "New Kodak Moment" for an accrediting agency, i.e., the realization that client preferences have changed so dramatically that it is too late to adjust and reform.

The alternative pathway is more fundamental and involves the *renewal of accreditation frameworks* (see also the contribution of Bryant et al. in this volume). What can be termed Accreditation 2.0 must grapple with the de-institutionalized nature of program design and delivery with no clear playbook available. Using the insights of Reeves, Levin, & Ueda (2016), accreditation agencies can undertake several actions. First, they may choose to "complicate" themselves by allowing more heterogeneity into their organizations, even at the fringes. Key questions we can put forward in this context are: Are accreditation agencies experimenting enough and are they willing to challenge their own business-as-usual (that still rewards individualistic academic production over a team-based approach)? Are they acting as enablers of 'business model' innovation on the part of their members? Peters, Smith, & Thomas (2018a) for instance envision the provision of ME on the basis of a multitude of different approaches, possibly employed side by side: a membership model, a subscription service model, as a combination of free base services and premium for-money offers, an eBay-like network orchestrator model or as a share-economy-like crowdsourcing model, and so forth.

Second, accreditors could develop more effective feedback loops and adaptive mechanisms to understand and appreciate new practices developed by business schools, especially those facing pressures for survival. The key questions are: How well are accreditation agencies set up to learn from the "market," especially at the periphery of the business school sector (where tangible disruption is often felt first)? How is informational dissonance treated in practice, is it explained away or utilized as an impetus for change? Accreditation work can invite behavioral hubris due to the combination of executive, legislative, and judicative roles. It is the antonym of maintaining relevance as internal governance units and must therefore be kept in check with ongoing review of how accreditors are governing themselves.

Finally, accreditation agencies can (and should) play a key role in strengthening trust and reciprocity within the wider ME ecosystem. The embeddedness of business schools in a network of diverse stakeholder organizations can help buffer disruption and change is a formative force of organizational resilience. One needs to ask: Are accreditors effective in acting as integrators of business schools and their stakeholders? Are they providing platforms to initiate dialogue in relation to how cooperative approaches within the ecosystem can help business schools to travel through difficult times? The current scorecard is mixed and leaves room for improvement, for instance evidenced by businesses and graduates being largely unaware of the quality-enhancing role of accreditors or missing links between accrediting agencies and professional associations delegating certification tasks to business schools. International accreditors face the added challenge of how to align their supra-national or even global outlook with the more regional or even local nature of resilience-enhancing ecosystems of business schools.

Conclusion and Outlook

International accreditors play an important role in legitimizing business schools, by associating their quality awards to excellence in service provision and a continuous quality improvement agenda. We started this chapter with a pressing question: how can accreditation (and accreditors) continue to fulfill this function in the future? Providing credible quality signals to business school stakeholders will remain key, but changes in (and of) the accreditation field makes this less straightforward. Based on our analysis, international accreditors have the opportunity to position themselves pro-actively as architects of the future and thereby support business schools in their efforts of successfully digesting disruptive change.

We posit that the role of accreditors is under threat because of the uncomfortable sandwich position they are in (commonly referred to as accreditation fatigue). On the one hand, their traditional role as internal governance units of the accreditation field is being diminished as the sector is moving toward ecosystem-based provision of ME. It will go hand-in-hand with the growing importance of market-based indicators (e.g., external rating of placement ability and facilitation of career progression) that describe the rate of return more accurately and timely than periodic accreditation reviews. On the other hand, new offers are challenging the accreditors' traditional role as arbitrators between academic and commercial interests in business schools reflecting a general push toward alternative, crowd-sourced proxies measuring academic reputation (e.g., using social media data to evaluate a school's brand awareness and competitive positioning). While accreditation has a future role to play, it will surely be different than current practice. The conjectures developed in this chapter will hopefully serve as general planks to understand that future better.

References

AACSB International. 2020. *2020 Interpretive guidance for AACSB business accreditation.* Tampa, FL: AACSB International.

Alajoutsijärvi, K., Kettunen, K., & Sohlo, S. 2018. Shaking the status quo: Business accreditation and positional competition. *Academic of Management Learning & Education,* 17(2): 203–225.

Basole, R. C., & Patel, S. S. 2018. Transformation through unbundling: Visualizing the global FinTech ecosystem. *Service Science,* 10(4): 1–18.

Birkinshaw, J. 2010. *Reinventing management: Smarter choices for getting work done.* Chichester, West Sussex: Jossey-Bass.

Blackmur, D. 2004. Issues in higher education quality assurance. *Australian Journal of Public Administration,* 63(2): 105–116.

Bourdieu, P., & Wacquant, L. J. D. 1992. *An invitation to reflexive sociology.* Chicago, IL: University of Chicago Press.

Bowen, W. G. 2013. *Higher education in the digital age.* Princeton, NJ: Princeton University Press.

Boxenbaum, E., & Johnsson, S. 2017. Isomorphism, diffusion and decoupling: Concept evolution and theoretical challenges. In R. Greenwood, C. Oliver, T. B. Lawrence, & R. E. Meyer (Eds.), *The Sage handbook of organizational institutionalism,* 2nd ed.: 77–101. London: Sage.

Cavico, F. J., & Mujtaba, B. G. 2010. The state of business schools, business education, and business ethics. *Journal of Academic and Business Ethics,* 2: 1–18.

Corley, K., & Gioia, D. 2000. The rankings game: Managing business school reputation. *Corporate Reputation Review*, 3(4): 319–333.

Cusumano, M. A., Yoffie, D. B., & Gawer, A. 2020. The future of platforms. *MIT Sloan Management Review*, 61(3): 46–54.

Datar, S. M., Garvin, D. A., & Cullen, P. G. 2010. *Rethinking the MBA: Business education at a crossroads*. Cambridge, MA: Harvard University Press.

De Meyer, A., & Williamson, P. J. 2020a. Building new ecosystems to create customer solutions. *Global Focus*, 14(1): 6–9.

De Meyer, A., & Williamson, P. J. 2020b. *Ecosystem edge: Sustaining competitiveness in the face of disruption*. Stanford, CA: Stanford Business Books.

DeMillo, R. A. 2011. *Abelard to Apple: The fate of American colleges and universities*. Cambridge, MA: The MIT Press.

DiMaggio, P. T., & Powell, W. W. 1983. The iron cage revisited: Institutional isomorphism and collective rationality in organizational fields. *American Sociological Review*, 48(2): 147–160.

EFMD Global. 2020. *The 2020 EFMD quality improvement system (EQUIS) process manual*. Brussels: EFMD Global.

Ehrenberg, R. G. 2011. Rethinking the professoriate. In B. Wildavsky, A. P. Kelly, & K. Carey (Eds.), *Reinventing higher education: The promise of innovation*: 101–128. Cambridge, MA: Harvard Education Press.

Espeland, W. N., & Stevens, M. L. 1998. Commensuration as a social process. *Annual Review of Sociology*, 24(1): 313–343.

Fligstein, N., & McAdam, D. 2012. *A theory of fields*. Oxford: Oxford University Press.

Granovetter, M. 1985. Economic action and social structure: The problem of embeddedness. *American Journal of Sociology*, 91(3): 481–510.

Hanappi-Egger, E. 2020. What digitalisation means for universities. *Global Focus*, 14(1): 14–19.

Hardy, C., & Maguire, S. 2010. Discourse, field-configuring events, and change in organizations and institutional fields: Narratives of DDT and the Stockholm Convention. *Academy of Management Journal*, 53(6): 29.

Hensel, P. G., & Guérard, S. P. 2020. The institutional consequences of decoupling exposure. *Strategic Organization*, 18(3): 407–426.

Hinings, C. R., Logue, D., & Zietsma, C. 2017. Fields, institutional infrastructure and governance. In R. Greenwood, C. Oliver, T. B. Lawrence, & R. E. Meyer (Eds.), *The Sage handbook of organizational institutionalism*, 2nd ed.: 163–188. London: Sage.

Hommel, M. J., & Hommel, U. 2020. Casualisation in HE is good for business: Get over it. *University World News*, December 12. https://www.universityworldnews.com/post.php?story=20201211110620766

Hommel, U. 2020. Universities need to prepare better for high risk crises. *University World News*, March 7, 2020. https://www.universityworldnews.com/post.php?story=20200302103912399

Hommel, U., Kjellander, B., & Thouary, C. 2021. Ambidexterity strengthens quality management during COVID-19. *Global Focus*, 15(1) (Forthcoming).

Hommel, U., & Lejeune, C. 2013. Major disruption ahead! *Global Focus*, 7(2): 10–13.

Hommel, U., & Osbaldeston, M. 2017. Maintaining the gold standard: Building on 20 years of EQUIS success. *Global Focus*, 11(3): 6–13.

Hommel, U., & Thomas, H. 2014. Research on business schools: Themes, conjectures and future directions. In A. Pettigrew, U. Hommel, & E. Cornuel (Eds.), *The Institutional Development of Business Schools*: 6–35. Oxford: Oxford University Press.

Hommel, U., & Woods, B. 2018. Squeezing the middle: The consequences of quality oversight in management education. *Journal of the Knowledge Economy*, 10.1007/s13132-018-0559-4

Jepperson, R. L. 1991. Institutions, institutional effects, and institutionalization. In W. W. Powell, & P. J. DiMaggio (Eds.), *The New Institutionalism in Organizational Analysis*: 143–163. Chicago: University of Chicago Press.

Julian, S. D., & Ofori-Dankwa, J. C. 2006. Is accreditation good for the strategic decision-making of traditional business schools? *Academy of Management Learning and Education*, 5(2): 225–233.

Kaplan, A. 2018. A school is "A building that has four walls... with tomorrow inside": Toward the reinvention of the business school. *Business Horizons*, 61(4): 599–608.

Khurana, R. 2007. *From higher aims to hired hands: The social transformation of American business schools and the unfulfilled promise of management as a profession*. Princeton, NJ: Princeton University Press.

Kofman, P. 2018. Stacking the odds. *Global Focus*, 12(2): 30–33.

Krishnamurthy, S. 2020. The future of business education: A commentary in the shadow of the Covid-19 pandemic. *Journal of Business Research*, 117 (September, Special Issue: COVID-19 Impact on Business and Research): 1–5.

Levine, A. E. 2000. The future of colleges: nine inevitable changes. *The Chronicle of Higher Education 47*, vol. 9(Oct 27, 2000): B10–12.

Matthyssens, P., & Vandenbempt, K. 2008. Moving from basic offerings to value-added solutions: Strategies, barriers and alignment. *Industrial Marketing Management*, 37(3): 316–328.

Matthyssens, P., Vandenbempt, K., & Berghman, L. 2006. Value innovation in business markets: Breaking the industry recipe. *Industrial Marketing Management*, 36(6): 751–761.

McCowan, T. 2017. Higher education, unbundling, and the end of the university as we know It. *Oxford Review of Education*, 43(6): 733–748.

McGrath, R. 2019. *Seeing around corners: How to spot inflection points in business before they happen*. Boston & New York: Houghton Mifflin Harcourt.

Milligan, S. M., & Kennedy, G. 2017. To what degree? Alternative micro-credentialing in a digital age In R. James, S. French, & P. Kelly (Eds.), *Visions for Australian Tertiary Education*: 41–53. Melbourne, VIC: The University of Melbourne: Melbourne Center for the Study of Higher Education.

Peters, K., Smith, R. R., & Thomas, H. 2018a. *Rethinking the business models of business schools*. Bingley: Emerald.

Peters, K., Smith, R. R., & Thomas, H. 2018b. *Rethinking the business models of business schools: A critical review and change agenda for the future*. Bingley: Emerald.

Peters, K., & Thomas, H. 2020. The complexity of business schools. *Global Focus*, 14(2): 20–25.

Pfeffer, J., & Fong, C. T. 2002. The end of business schools? Less success than meets the eye. *Academy of Management Learning & Education*, 1(1): 78–95.

Rasche, A., & Gilbert, D. U. 2015. Decoupling responsible management education: Why business schools may not walk their talk. *Journal of Management Inquiry*, 24(3): 239–252.

Reeves, M., Levin, S., & Ueda, D. 2016. The biology of corporate survival: Natural ecosystems hold surprising lessons for business. *Harvard Business Review*, 2016 (January–February): 47–55.

Rindova, V. P., Williamson, I. O., Petkova, A. P., & Sever, J. M. 2005. Being good or being known: An empirical examination of the dimensions, antecedents, and consequences of organizational reputation. *Academy of Management Journal*, 48(6): 1033–1049.

Seers, A. 2007. Management education in the emerging knowledge economy: Going beyond "Those who can, do; Those who can't, teach." *Academy of Management Learning & Education*, 6(4): 558–567.

Spender, J. C. 1989. *Industry recipes: The nature and sources of managerial judgement*. Oxford, UK: Basil Blackwell.

Starkey, K., & Tiratsoo, N. 2007. *The business school and the bottom line*. Cambridge: Cambridge University Press.

Straub, R. 2019. The power of ecosystems. *Global Focus*, 13(2): 28–32.

Taleb, N. N. 2008. *The black swan: The impact of the highly improbable*. London: Penguin Books.

Thomas, L., Billsberry, J., Ambrosini, V., & Barton, H. 2014. Convergence and divergence dynamics in British and French business schools: How will the pressure for accreditation influence these dynamics? *British Journal of Management*, 25(2): 305–319.

Wildavsky, B. 2010. *The great brain race: How global universities are reshaping the world*. Princeton, NJ: Princeton University Press.

Wildavsky, B., Kelly, A. P., & Carey, K. (Eds.). 2011. *Reinventing higher education: The promise of innovation*. Cambridge, MA: Harvard Education Press.

Wilson, D., & McKiernan, P. 2011. Global mimicry: Putting strategic choice back on the business school agenda. *British Journal of Management*, 22(3): 457–469.

Wooten, M., & Hoffman, A. J. 2017. Organizational fields: Past, present and future. In R. Greenwood, C. Oliver, T. B. Lawrence, & R. E. Meyer (Eds.), *The Sage handbook of organizational institutionalism*, 2nd ed.: 55–74. London: Sage.

Wucker, M. 2017. *The gray rhino: How to recognize and act on the obvious dangers we ignore*. New York: St. Martin's Press.

Zammuto, R. F. 2008. Accreditation and the globalization of business. *Academy of Management Learning and Education*, 7(2): 256–268.

13

A VISON FOR MANAGEMENT EDUCATION: THE AACSB PERSPECTIVE

Stephanie M. Bryant, Patrick G. Cullen, and Juliane E. Iannarelli

Introduction

Business schools are facing profound challenges that present an imperative to change. As professional schools located in universities, or in some cases as stand-alone entities, business schools are subject to the expectations and requirements of multiple stakeholders, including the academic community, business practitioners, a broad range of learners, governments, accreditors, and society at large. Yet these audiences often have different priorities, which create a tension that runs through every aspect of business education. Consequently, the value of business education to multiple audiences has been a subject of much debate throughout the history of business schools, with the current era seeing a wave of criticisms focusing on a broad range of topics from curricular content to questions about the values instilled through the culture of business schools (Datar, Garvin, & Cullen, 2010; Graduate Management Admission Council GMAC, 2013; Khurana, 2007). As the world's largest accreditor of business schools, AACSB is committed to helping business schools add value to all of its audiences. In this chapter, we focus on business education as a broad umbrella under which management education is a subset. Our interest is in advancing business, and consequently management, education to provide a positive impact on society.

Recognizing an opportunity, a variety of competitors to a traditional college degree, including corporate universities, online program managers, competency management systems and even employers have entered the space with programs marketed as more directly relevant to practice, more flexible, and in some cases, more cost-effective. These competitors derive profit by disaggregating what is currently delivered by business schools as a comprehensive business degree. These disaggregated components include design and development of curriculum

DOI: 10.4324/9781003095903-17

content, delivery of online instruction (including provision of the platform and maintenance and support thereof), delivery of single and bundled skills-based micro-credentials, provision of learner support services, and recruitment tailored to attract learners consistent with the provider's strategic initiatives. Such un-bundling by competitors directly threatens the model of holistic delivery of a business degree credentialed through a college or university (see also Hommel & Vandenbempt, this volume).

In response to criticisms and competition, many business schools have de-monstrated creativity and adaptability as they innovate in response to the chan-ging demands of their audiences. Yet fundamental questions remain about business education's value proposition for individual learners, organizations, and society. If business schools are to survive and thrive, they must recognize and address the need to simultaneously provide value to multiple stakeholders, in-cluding a whole spectrum of learners, a variety of organizations, and society as a whole.

The purpose of this chapter, therefore, is threefold: (1) to detail the challenges of providing value to multiple stakeholders, (2) to present three critical actions a business school can employ as a foundation for enhanced relevance and impact, and (3) to discuss how the 2020 AACSB Business Accreditation Standards can serve as a roadmap for actions by schools to begin to close the value gap perceived by some external stakeholders. The framework for this chapter is depicted in Figure 13.1.

What Learners Want

Learners have many reasons for undertaking business education. Increasingly, they are seeking this education at multiple stages of their lives. At the same time, strong criticism has emerged of the value propositions of business education as learners consider the wide range of options available to them (e.g., Parker, 2018). The pandemic has further sharpened the view of what learners want from their academic experience. Some of the major business school value propositions for learners are outlined below.

Business Knowledge and Skills

Learners expect business school programs to provide the knowledge – facts, frameworks, and theories – for each subject they study. They must also learn essential skills – competencies and capabilities and techniques that are critical for effective practice. Beyond this, there is an increasing expectation that schools will address values, attitudes, and beliefs.

Business schools are recognized as providing a strong foundation in business knowledge and a solid training in the skills required for practice – especially given their increasing emphasis on experiential and project-based learning. Yet one of

What Multiple Stakeholders Want	• Learners • Organizations • Society
Call to Action: A Collective Vision for Business Education	• Connect with other disciplines • Cultivate a position at the intersection of academia and practice • Be a driver of innovation in higher education
Roadmap Solution: 2020 Business Accreditation Standards	• Strategic Management and Innovation (Standards 1-3) • Learner Success (Standards 4-7) • Thought Leadership, Engagement, and Societal Impact (Standards 8-9)

FIGURE 13.1   A Path to increased value

the significant challenges for business schools is keeping their curricula and their faculty current – particularly for technology-based subjects such as data analytics, blockchain, robotics, and artificial intelligence applications within a business context. This concern raises serious questions about both the short-term and long-term value of business degrees in comparison with the value provided by more nimble competitors who respond to changing market demands for skills more quickly.

Economic Benefits, Relationships, and Career Advancement

There is evidence of substantial return on investment for graduates of business degrees (Association to Advance Collegiate Schools of Business AACSB, 2018–2019; Graduate Management Admission Council GMAC, 2018). In addition, the career advancement benefits of graduate business degrees are widely recognized. Both the knowledge and skills gained in degree programs, plus the social capital and expanded networks, provide significant benefits for graduates throughout their career. However, major concerns are often raised about the extent of the return on investment and how this return compares to those from alternative providers of business education (Altonji & Zhong, 2020).

Contributions to Building a Better Society

Learners are leading the call for the value of business degrees to be viewed more broadly than has traditionally been the case. Many learners across every generation conceive of return on investment as a balance between personal returns and social and environmental concerns as they focus on having a positive impact on society. As we look to the future, we must be aware of the influence of

"Generation Z" – generally defined as those learners who were born between 1996 and 2009 (Sladek & Miller, 2018). This group, representing some 57 million learners in the United States alone, is the most diverse generation of learners in history. They hold a broad view of value in which intrinsic happiness is central to their commitment, as is the desire to create, lead, learn, and make the world a better place in which to live – all of which informs their expectations of business education (Sladek & Miller, 2018). The question is, are colleges and universities meeting this need that not only Generation Z, but other learners as well, are clearly seeking?

What Organizations Want

Organizations in a wide range of business sectors have long depended on business schools to develop their future leaders, managers, and functional specialists. Despite the benefits to organizations of business education, significant and long-standing criticisms remain.

Workforce-Ready Graduates

One line of criticism claims that employers believe business school programs fall short in preparing graduates for the workforce. This is attributed in part to a lack of curricular currency and partly to the skills valued by employers not being taught or being taught ineffectively. This is often referred to as a "skills gap" – a criticism that results in organizations questioning the value of a business school degree. For example, QS Quacquarelli Symonds' annual *Global Employer Survey* of more than 11,000 employers around the world has provided consistent evidence over the past three years of a skills gap between employer's satisfaction with graduate hires and key employability skills (QS Quacquarelli Symonds, 2020). Problem-solving, communication, resilience, and flexibility are top areas where such skills gaps persist (QS Quacquarelli Symonds, 2020) according to this data.

This persistent skills gap is perhaps the most serious threat to business schools. There are clear signs that organizations that once heavily relied on business schools for their talent pool are either developing their own talent through in-house training or are seeking talent from alternative providers. For example, in response to the economic and resulting unemployment crisis precipitated by COVID-19, Google recently announced a new suite of Google Career Certificates with a stated purpose of "[helping] Americans get qualifications in high-paying high-growth job fields—no college degree required" (Walker, 2020). Similarly, the IBM Professional Certification Program (http://ibm.com/certify) aims to certify and validate a host of technology-related skills that do not require a college degree as a prerequisite.

The skills gap problem is a consistent theme in assessments of business degree curricula at both the undergraduate level and – especially – the graduate level

(Datar et al., 2010; Graduate Management Admission Council GMAC, 2013). In addition to the QS annual global survey of employers, other employer surveys provide further evidence of skills gaps that require judgment more than analysis, including leadership skills, critical and integrative thinking skills, communication skills, creative problem-solving skills, and the ability to work collaboratively in teams (National Association of Colleges and Employers NACE, 2019; Society for Human Resource Management SHRM, 2019). In addition, the need for technology competence is a priority. This is exemplified by the growing need for data analysts and the ability to understand the digital impact on business and society.

Relevant and Impactful Research

Another prominent criticism focuses on research produced by academics. Practitioners, students, and some faculty members argue that research produced by business school faculty has limited relevance to practice, and even less impact on the decisions made by practitioners. These arguments are often framed as the "rigor and relevance" debate (Bennis & O'Toole, 2004; Rubin & Dierdorff, 2009).

It is widely accepted in the business education community that both academic rigor *and* practical relevance are essential for effective research and teaching; however, as business schools adopted the practices of academic disciplines in the years following two influential reports sponsored in 1959 by the Ford Foundation and the Carnegie Foundation (Gordon & Howell, 1959; Pierson, 1959), research increasingly prioritized theory development and methodological rigor, which drives the choice of research topics. Faculties are also heavily influenced by the incentives of tenure models that often place greater weight on academic publications than books or articles written for practitioners. Recognizing these pressures, many schools have created incentives for faculty to develop research that has a positive impact on practice. AACSB has undertaken initiatives to encourage research with impact (Association to Advance Collegiate Schools of Business AACSB, 2012), and the Responsible Research in Business & Management movement (RRBM.net) was born out of the desire to foster business school research that is both practical and relevant. However, much work remains to be done, and calls persists to promote research that is published by academia and solves practical problems (Shapiro & Kirkman, 2018).

What Society Wants

At the societal level, business education is expected to contribute social and economic benefits that exceed those accruing to individuals (Fethke & Policano, 2012). Business education does play an important role in creating a well-educated citizenry, as well as helping to build the successful organizations – both for-profit and not-for profit – required to achieve prosperity. Yet many of the criticisms of business education contend that business schools are failing to meet many of their obligations to society at large (Conn, 2019; Khurana, 2007).

Purpose-Driven, Ethical Leaders Who Value Social Responsibility

While society at large expects business schools to develop purpose-driven and ethical leaders, one major stream of criticism argues that the culture and curricula of business schools have fostered a mindset that promotes short-term and selfish attitudes (Conn, 2019; McDonald, 2017). Recognizing the importance of purpose-driven and ethical leaders, AACSB is enabling and encouraging business schools to nurture these attributes in all learners (Association to Advance Collegiate Schools of Business AACSB, 2020). Ethical and socially responsible leaders are expected to foster and promote these values to ensure socially responsible employees.

Commitment To Resolving Major Societal Challenges

One of the strongest criticisms accuses business schools of neglecting society's biggest and most pressing challenges such as poverty, access to food and clean water, climate change, and the responsible use of natural resources among others. While other academic disciplines, such as engineering, have issued grand challenges to develop solutions to some of the world's most urgent environmental and social problems, business schools, collectively speaking, have been slow to address such broad societal challenges.

Responses to Criticisms

Business schools have responded to the wide-ranging criticisms emanating from many sources, including learners, governments, journalists, social movements, and faculty from many fields including business. At both the undergraduate and graduate levels, new courses have been developed and traditional courses have been revised to help learners think carefully about the role and purpose of business, including consideration of diversity, equity, and inclusion. These changes often focus on the concept of responsibility to the full range of an organization's stakeholders – customers, employees, and society at large in addition to shareholders.

Despite these countermeasures, the role of business school research in providing value to society is under scrutiny. Facing strong critiques such as the narrow focus of much research that targets scholars in the same sub-field, business school faculty are responding with both calls for action and new initiatives, including more attention to broad societal issues in journals. One prominent example of this action is the work of scholars in the Responsible

Research for Business and Management community that is "dedicated to in-spiring, encouraging, and supporting credible and useful research in the business and management disciplines." (Responsible Research in Business and Management (RRBM), 2017). Today there are some 1,200 endorsers, over 65 institutional partners, and seven pioneer schools who embrace the tenets of creating research that matters.

To summarize, what learners want are the knowledge, skills, abilities, and relationships on which they can build a solid career that establishes economic security for them while also engaging in purposeful work that gives their lives meaning. Organizations want to employ people who have technical, behavioral and critical thinking skills, while also partnering with business schools to pro-vide research that helps solve the practical problems they are facing every day. Society, broadly speaking, wants business school learners and academics to help take on solving some of society's grand challenges, while continuing to prepare learners for productive careers that advance the common good. For business education to meet all these needs, a multi-pronged approach is needed to frame the discussion. AACSB's *Collective Vision for Business Education* (2016) provides just such an approach.

A Call to Action: Strategies for Enhanced Value

The theoretical underpinnings of an overall direction were articulated in 2016 as AACSB's *Collective Vision for Business Education*. Five broadly framed direc-tions for business schools emerged from comprehensive reviews of literature and extensive listening to stakeholders within and outside business schools. These five roles, as shown in Figure 13.2, together offer business schools a series of positions that provide direct value to learners, organizations, and society. At the same time, they are sufficiently broad to offer business schools considerable flexibility to implement approaches that align with their specific missions and stakeholders.

The five roles and the specific actions envisioned within each have been covered extensively in the 2016 *Collective Vision* report and reinforced across subsequent work by AACSB. They have generated self-reflection, attention, and new strategic actions across the business school landscape. Moreover, they have influenced reflection on the ways in which the 2020 Business Accreditation Standards could ultimately accelerate the future envisioned by that framework.

The *Collective Vision*, however, specified three enablers of progress that have yet to be fully explored as connectors to an action plan that any business school could create to address the perceived gap in value by some stakeholders (see Figure 13.1). In this section, we highlight these three enablers of progress to provide a call to action, as follows: (1) connect with other disciplines, (2) cultivate a position at the intersection of academia and practice, and (3) be a

FIGURE 13.2 The Collective Vision for Business Education (Association to Advance Collegiate Schools of Business AACSB, 2016)

driver of innovation in higher education. Embraced strategically, these approaches offer access to new kinds of resources, new operating models, and ultimately new possibilities for achieving value. Further, they position business schools as trusted partners for other disciplines, organizations, and higher education as a whole.

Connect With Other Disciplines

AACSB's *Collective Vision* (2016: 15) calls for business schools to "seize opportunities to reinforce the complementarities between business education and other fields, including science, engineering, healthcare, and education. This collaboration will require expanding the models and incentives that support interdisciplinary research and the structures to facilitate interdisciplinary learning." In this chapter, we use the word "interdisciplinary" to apply to a range of multiple disciplinary approaches, including also multidisciplinary or transdisciplinary approaches. In practice, business schools will differ in their approaches depending on the knowledge objectives being pursued. In any case, despite the systemic institutional pressures that motivate and sometimes incentivize disciplinary independence across aspects of academia, both interdisciplinary education and interdisciplinary research can offer considerable opportunities for broadening the application of business knowledge across learners, organizations, and society.

Interdisciplinary Education

A greater involvement in interdisciplinary education is one way that business schools will evolve to meet the needs of learners and organizations. One common model is to offer formal interdisciplinary degree programs (e.g., engineering management or healthcare management), or formal degree pairings (e.g., JD/ MBA). Interdisciplinary coursework requirements for degree-seekers can also offer opportunities for breadth. Extra-curricular or co-curricular learning engagements may involve teams representing multiple colleges working on a business plan, or to solve a real-world problem for a local business or non-profit through application of expertise from multiple disciplines.

It is a worthwhile challenge for business schools to consider how to complement the learning of students in business degree programs with other non-business disciplinary lenses. It is another challenge entirely to consider how business education could be a relevant complement to learners pursuing non-business degrees. Leadership, management, and knowledge of the foundations of organizational operations are relevant categories of knowledge and skill across organizational roles traditionally filled by graduates with backgrounds ranging from STEM fields to the liberal arts, for entrepreneurs seeking to bring a product to market, or for a range of individuals in businesses traditionally operated as sole proprietorships.

Reaching those individuals requires creative solutions that extend access to business education beyond learners majoring in business. It requires the nurturing of trust-based relationships within and between universities, including with standalone business schools, a recognition that interdisciplinary initiatives must address the interests of all parties involved, and an openness to shared ownership of the model. Such interdisciplinary initiatives also require the stamina to work creatively through logistical issues (e.g., calendars and credits), to push for transparency on related revenue models, and to ensure that faculty contributions are valued and rewarded.

Interdisciplinary Research

As noted earlier, arguments that research produced by business school faculty has limited relevance are often rooted in the complexity and interdisciplinarity of the challenges facing organizations and society. These challenges are driving emerging fields of study and practice that draw from multiple traditional disciplines, such as artificial intelligence, business analytics, business ethics, and many more.

The need for research to have more practical relevance does not mean that scientific specialization is unimportant or does not contribute value. Deep, specialized knowledge is necessary for innovation and must continue to be nurtured. But business schools also must find ways to enable, support, and encourage the combining of different types of expertise through research initiatives, even when not compatible with the focus of prestigious journals. Doing so requires a willingness to revisit the appropriateness of traditional expectations for research methods, outputs, and measures of impact. That acceptance must be followed up by actual support. Faculty will engage in research centers and interdisciplinary initiatives when they feel that effort will be recognized and rewarded, rather than a costly career distraction.

Cultivate a Position at the Intersection of Academia and Practice

AACSB's *Collective Vision* (2016: 15) further reinforces the need for business schools and organizations "to engage each other more closely to co-educate and develop managerial talent, to co-create new ideas and understanding, and to innovate and establish new business." Business schools must continue to reposition their roles from *suppliers* of talent and research insights to *trusted partners*, as outlined below, in pursuit of talent empowerment and agility, the co-creation of knowledge, and idea exchange. This repositioning requires rethinking the nature of relationships with organizations, and the cultivation of meaningful engagements among them.

Talent Empowerment and Agility

Higher education providers and employers share a common interest in broadening and diversifying the pool of talent, as well as ensuring access to new knowledge and skills required for evolving careers and organizational needs (Association to Advance Collegiate Schools of Business AACSB & Chief Learning Officer Magazine, 2018). Yet as noted earlier, claims persist of a skills gap among graduates of business programs. Business schools must continue to work with organizational leaders to thoughtfully research the gaps employers are experiencing, and to quickly pivot their offerings to support those needs. Organizational and business school leaders both benefit from creative models for integrating practitioners within business education, embedding academics within organizational operations, and collaborating – not competing – to meet general and organization-specific needs for business talent. These models entail more than simply seeking to solve for a temporary staffing issue by either party; rather they are designed and executed in ways that are additive and complementary to the knowledge and perspectives otherwise available to the hosting organization and the individual.

In pursuit of those goals, higher education providers and employers also share questions about methods, i.e., how to scale personalized learning, identify appropriate competency combinations and learning pathways as preparation for different roles, and implement effective measures to assess learning gains.

Research focused on effective learning methods and tools benefits both. Collaborations with corporate talent development teams – with their access to data on job performance and career growth – provide opportunities for expanding analysis to longer term impacts and real-world applications.

Co-creation of Knowledge

The relevance of business research can be strengthened, and its reach amplified, through relationships between academics and practitioners. Co-creation of knowledge refers to a collaborative approach to defining and prioritizing research questions, testing hypotheses, and interpreting relevant insights for real-world contexts. This co-creation creates value through insights and understanding about how to effectively organize and motivate people, how to build sustainable organizations, and how to create value for stakeholders as well as shareholders. Co-creation is notably distinct from consulting practices or commissioned research in that true co-creation pursues impartial and objective insights to a question, rather than being conducted explicitly for the benefit of a particular organization.

In fact, as with many of the recommendations in this chapter, these relationships should not be limited to just one business school. Research networks involving academics from different institutions and representatives across industries or sectors bring diverse lenses to research challenges, and also enable important contextualization of management and leadership insights according to different contexts. The insights gained through these exchanges in turn become important inputs into the continued evolution of curricula and learning experiences.

Idea Exchange

Through their power to convene, business schools enhance societal value by facilitating the exchange and curation of information and ideas, ultimately leading to knowledge transfer and implementation. The opportunities for networking with individuals from diverse backgrounds are often sought in graduate and executive education, in particular. Incubators and accelerators provide valuable opportunities for entrepreneurs to learn from one another and experts among the school's faculty and practitioner community. Centers and special initiatives focused on particular industries, sectors, or specific societal challenges offer similar opportunities to seek solutions working with peers and experts.

Business schools similarly should consider how their networks enable them to crowd-source data, research subjects, data analysis, and reactions to findings. Or how they might leverage technology and content platforms to define a valued role as curator or disseminator of relevant insights.

Be a Driver of Innovation in Higher Education

Business schools must also seek to be trusted partners, innovators, and thought leaders within the higher education sector. The final intersection from AACSB's *Collective Vision* (2016: 15) encourages business schools to actively shape the evolution of higher education, serving as "active participants and leaders in the creation of the new systems, standards, and traditions within which they will operate and compete." In pursuit of value to learners, organizations, and society, business schools can be drivers and partners in support of innovation in educational models, faculty and staffing models, and operational models that drive added value.

Educational Models

Educational models include the identification of learning pathways, the development and delivery of learning experiences, the assessment of learning, and awarding of credentials that are external signals of competencies and capabilities. Within each of these elements, innovation is being driven by an emerging body of knowledge and rapidly evolving technological capabilities. As discussed earlier, disaggregation of this value chain is paralleling the emergence of new entrants narrowly focused on one or more elements. However, business schools have an opportunity here. Rather than view these developments as a threat, business schools should look for ways to learn with and engage with these alternative providers in ways that strengthen the overall business education ecosystem, and the role of business schools within it.

Fortunately, as the landscape of providers for different elements in the value chain broadens, the needs of learners (and their employing organizations) for business education also are broadening beyond business schools' traditionally narrow focus of degree-based education. Experimentation with micro- and stackable credentials – in complement to, or as an alternative to, degrees – is one way business schools are seeking to offer value through credential transparency and portability. Another is through broadening the definition of education – and learners – to incorporate a variety of formal and informal learning engagements aimed at individuals at all stages of their careers.

Faculty and Staffing Models

Interdisciplinary collaborations and academic-industry partnerships create new opportunities for business schools to leverage diverse expertise. These shifts also create space for new roles to emerge among faculty and the staff that work alongside them. For example, a greater reliance on partnerships and customized value creation puts greater emphasis on skills for managing client and partner relations. Increased emphasis on virtual and experiential learning opportunities may benefit from investments in instructional design talent, and the need for agility may require project leaders who excel at overseeing change initiatives. Talent-sharing such as through executive-in-residence or scholar-in-residence models, visiting faculty, and more may become more the norm.

Some of these shifts in collective knowledge and skills will occur through a paradigm of lifelong learning aimed at faculty and staff. Others will be supported through cultural shifts, such as toward valuing institution-wide contributions in addition to individualized actions. These shifts can feed evolution of how faculty expectations are defined – sometimes in customized ways – and their subsequent contributions measured and rewarded. A culture of training, support, and aligned recognition systems can be empowering in helping to create career agility and growth for faculty and staff as well.

Operational Models

Innovation in educational and staffing models requires parallel shifts in the op-erational models that underpin them. Financial structures and budgets will evolve to accommodate new methods of revenue generation and funding sources. Organizational leaders and governing boards will face new sets of questions about how to allocate financial resources in support of critical objectives and needed experimentation. Governance models must be adapted to support quick yet informed decision-making and more rapid product launches and pivots.

Operational partnerships, including reliance on carefully vetted partners for technology supporting a variety of activities, may become more commonplace, and should be when they free up institutional resources to focus on their primary added value, or augment that reach and value. Community partnerships offer opportunities to more closely link centers, research initiatives, and educational programming to specific needs among the business school's stakeholders. Across the university, it is within the business school where expertise about organiza-tional strategy and operating models is especially strong, and that means business schools can play a leadership role in incorporating these principles across their own operations, and more broadly in higher education.

The foundation, then, and road ahead is clear. To achieve a multi-pronged approach to providing value to learners, organizations, and society is to (1) connect with other disciplines; (2) cultivate a relationship at the intersection of academia and practice; and (3) be drivers of innovation in higher education. In the next section, we articulate a roadmap for implementing this model.

A Roadmap for Increased Value for Learners, Organizations, and Society: AACSB 2020 Business Accreditation Standards

Following the release of the *Collective Vision for Business Education* in 2016, AACSB began its work in 2017 on the operationalization of the theoretical model expressed therein. The Business Accreditation Task Force (hereafter "BATF") was formed and charged by the AACSB Board of Directors to hear the voice of our membership as to how to realize the *Collective Vision* through futuristic, innovative, and globally inclusive business accreditation standards. The task force consisted of 16 highly respected deans who traversed the world listening to our members and gathering and distilling input.

In July 2020, AACSB's Accreditation Council approved the AACSB *2020 Business Accreditation Standards*. These standards were the culmination of thousands of hours of work over two years by the BATF. The result is a remarkable set of standards for AACSB-accredited business schools unlike any standards we have passed in our over century of existence as an accrediting body. In essence, these standards are the operationalization of our *Collective Vision*, which provides the roadmap to how AACSB can be catalysts for change. This section examines the 2020 standards in the context of how they can help business schools bring enhanced value to learners, organizations, and society as well as meet their varying expectations.

The 2020 standards are organized around three constructs: strategic management and innovation; learner success; and thought leadership, engagement, and societal impact. We view these constructs as a process flow, as depicted in Figure 13.3.

The standards shift away from a purely compliance, rules-based mindset to a principles-based mindset. In the process, the standards "give permission" for business schools to be more nimble, experiment with new programs without fear of whether a program will work or not, utilize high-quality faculty staffing models that don't unnecessarily constrain business school leaders, and engage in partnerships within the university and organizations outside the university. By breaking down these barriers, we allow for real innovation to occur. Herein is how business schools can bring enhanced value to learners, organizations, and society at large.

Strategic Management and Innovation (Standards 1–3)

The first three standards relate to how a school manages its *strategic planning process* and importantly, requires input from all major stakeholders of the school,

Strategic Management and Innovation	Learner Success	Thought Leadership, Engagement, and Society Impact
1. Strategic Planning	4. Curriculum	8. Impact of Scholarship
2. Physical, Virtual, and Financial Resources	5. Assurance of Learning	9. Engagement and Societal Impact
3. Teaching Effectiveness and Impact	6. Learner Progression	
	7. Teaching Effectiveness and Impact	

FIGURE 13.3   Three constructs of AACSB 2020 Business Accreditation Standards

including faculty, learners, administration, advisory councils, and organizations with whom the business school is regularly engaged. This requirement is intended to ensure that in fact the business school is meeting the expectations of learners, organizations, and society, as framed in this chapter. Gaps in expectations can be identified and filled prior to the plan being formalized. The plan must also be regularly assessed with progress against goals tracked. Further, the strategic plan must state how the school intends to make a positive impact on society. This is a major new addition to the standards, and the societal impact provision in threated throughout the standards, starting in standard 1. It is not enough for an AACSB-accredited school to engage in activities that result in positive societal impact. Rather, the accredited school must commit to and communicate within their strategic plan how they intend to make such impact and connect this to their mission and planning activities.

While strategic management is the foundation for such societal impact, how the school uses its resource – both human and non-human – are paramount to demonstrate that commitment. This shows up in standards 2 and 3, with standard 2 focused on how the school allocates financial resources, manages its budget and ongoing operations, and maintains physical and virtual spaces to carry out their mission and demonstrate their societal impact. An example of managing these resources was clearly on display during the pandemic, as schools pivoted quickly to online teaching to continue providing high-quality education. Schools invested heavily in technology and training needed to support faculty and learners so that effective high-quality teaching was maintained. The need to continue to manage this complex learning environment will continue for years to come and new models of teaching and interacting with learners will emerge.

The standards also recognize that new staffing and operational models are needed to provide space for innovation in both teaching and research. While faculty who are highly qualified in their field of expertise are a cornerstone of AACSB accreditation, the new standards recognize that deployment of qualified faculty across degree programs is a strategic choice best made by the school. The focus now shifts away from inputs and outputs to successful learner outcomes. That is, staffing models and operating processes should produce observable and verifiable outcomes that demonstrate learners meet key competencies established by the program and that learners are successful with meeting post-university goals such as attending graduate school, gaining employment in the desired area, starting a business, working for a nonprofit, or other learner-specific goals.

Learner Success (Standards 4–7)

In this version of the standards, it is notable that we pivot away from the term "students" and instead refer to "learners." This change is aligned with our shift to recognizing that the learning journey is a lifelong pursuit. Learning does not stop when one matriculates from college. Successful professionals continue to upskill and reskill, particularly with respect to technology. Schools are also recognizing this shift, and executive education, stackable credentials, certificates, and micro-credentialing are now commonly found in the business school, with AACSB recognizing these as important lifelong learning experiences.

Standards 4–7 focus on quality of curriculum, assurance of learning, learning, learner progress, and teaching effectiveness. Within these standards, we intend to close the skills gap between what employers' value and the competencies of the graduates of our schools, to provide rich experiential learning that promotes critical thinking and the ability to synthesize information to solve practical problems both within industry and for society at large. Curriculum is now recognized as more competency-based, with an emphasis on the knowledge, skills, abilities, and behaviors that one would expect of a graduate of an AACSB-accredited business school. Curriculum is required to be regularly reviewed, including by external stakeholders such as advisory councils, for relevance and currency. Faculty and staff alike are expected to be agile with current and emerging technology and schools are required to demonstrate a commitment to the professional development of faculty and staff. Additionally, the standards place an emphasis on experiential learning, providing hands-on experiences that augment classroom learning. These standards, then, are aimed at promoting innovation, and meeting learner expectations that they are prepared for success upon entry into their professional lives.

Of particular note is the requirement that the school's strategy for making a positive societal impact be evident within the school's curriculum. That is, whatever area a school identifies in its strategic plan for this purpose should have corresponding coursework within the curriculum to support their intended strategies for societal impact. This is often where the experiential learning will also come into play. This answers both the learner desire to engage in meaningful and impactful learning experiences, and for organizations and society to likewise benefit.

Thought Leadership, Engagement, and Societal Impact (Standards 8–9)

The final section of the 2020 standards are focused on meeting expectations that business schools make a positive impact on society through both their research and the additional activities apart from scholarship sponsored by the business school. This emphasis on societal impact is threaded throughout the standards, and in fact, "Societal Impact" is one of the ten "Guiding Principles" of the standards. The standards reflect AACSB's vision that business education is seen as a force for good in society and makes a meaningful positive contribution to society, as identified in the school's mission and strategic plan. This includes an expectation that the school explicates its intended strategies to affect a positive impact on society, that the school's curriculum contains some components relating to societal impact, that the school's intellectual contributions portfolio contains some contributions focused on societal impact, and that the school is fostering and promoting curriculum and/or curricular activities that seek to make a positive societal impact. As is readily apparent, this guiding principle speaks to the value of societal impact to both learners and organizations.

Also contained within this set of standards is the reinforced and elevated focus in the 2020 standards toward the production of research that matters to society that was begun with the 2013 standards. This elevated focus is intended to drive toward the production of responsible research that creates bridges between business practitioners and academia. Further, the new standards require that AACSB-accredited schools maintain within the portfolio exemplars of research that have a positive impact on society. The 2020 standards are not prescriptive in how or in what area a school chooses to make its contributions, but instead require the school to identify where the school intends to make a positive impact on society.

These standards, thus, directly cultivate a position at the intersection of academia and practice, encourage connections with other disciplines, and the co-creation of knowledge. Partnerships between academia, governments, not-for-profits, and business practitioners are a major goal of these standards. Only through the collective power of our academic community and partnerships can our vision of business education as a force for good be realized. Further, learners – no matter where they are in their learning journey – can engage in meaningful work that improves society and moves us toward solving some of society's grand challenges.

What the Future Holds for Business Education

In this chapter we have made the case for why business education must change now and provided a model that lays the foundation for that change. We have also introduced the AACSB 2020 accreditation standards that serve as a roadmap that operationalizes the model. Where do we go from here? What does the future hold for business education?

While we do not have a proverbial crystal ball, here is what we see on the horizon. We believe business schools can and will rise to meet the expectations of learners, organizations, and society. Indeed, competitors to the traditional business degree, the increase in career paths that do not require a degree as a prerequisite credential to employment, and the technological forces that are disrupting how we have delivered education for hundreds of years will force change.

The path we have charted with AACSB's *Collective Vision for Business Education* and the standards that operationalize it provide a blueprint for how business schools can work together to achieve our vision of business as a force for good in society. We will do that by connecting with other disciplines to foster interdisciplinary research that answers important questions and by recognizing that it is the impact of intellectual contributions that matters and not the simple count of publications that is the imprimatur of quality research. We will cultivate a position at the intersection of academia and practice by working with governments, not-for-profits, and business practitioners to work together to solve some of society's grand challenges. And we will be drivers of innovation in both business education and research, not followers.

Through these efforts, we will both ensure that learners are well-prepared to begin their professional journey, and organizations will reap the benefits of a highly skilled, technology-agile workforce. Now is the time for a new vision for business education – a vision of being connected for a higher and better purpose. AACSB believes business education can lead change in the world, and we intend to do just that – change the world.

Acknowledgements

The authors wish to thank the AACSB Innovation Committee, Business Accreditation Task Force, and the AACSB membership at large who influenced the thoughts in this chapter.

References

Altonji, J., & Zhong, L. 2020. The labor market returns to advanced degrees. *NBER working paper no. 26959.*

Association to Advance Collegiate Schools of Business (AACSB). 2012. *Impact of research: A guide for business schools.* AACSB.

Association to Advance Collegiate Schools of Business (AACSB). 2016. *A collective vision for business education.* AACSB.

Association to Advance Collegiate Schools of Business (AACSB) & Chief Learning Officer Magazine. 2018. *To empower learning over a lifetime.* AACSB.

Association to Advance Collegiate Schools of Business (AACSB). 2018-19. *Employment module.* AACSB.

Association to Advance Collegiate Schools of Business (AACSB). 2020. *Societal impact starts here: Turn passion into action with business education.* AACSB.

Bennis, W., & O'Toole, J. 2004. How business schools lost their way. *Harvard Business Review*, 82(3): 96.

Conn, S. 2019. *Nothing succeeds like failure: The sad history of American business schools.* Ithaca, NY: Cornell University Press.

Datar, S., Garvin, D., & Cullen, P. 2010. *Rethinking the MBA: Business education at a crossroads.* Boston, MA: Harvard Business Press.

Fethke, G., & Policano, A. 2012. *Public no more: A new path to excellence for America's public universities.* Stanford, CA: Stanford University Press.

Gordon, R., & Howell, J. 1959. *Higher education for business.* New York: Columbia University Press.

Graduate Management Admission Council (GMAC) 2013. *Disrupt or be disrupted: A blueprint for change in management education.* San Francisco, CA: Jossey-Bass.

Graduate Management Admission Council (GMAC). 2018. *Corporate recruiters survey report 2018.* https://www.gmac.com/~/media/Files/gmac/Research/employment-outlook/gmac-2018-corporate-recruiters-survey-report.pdf

Khurana, R. 2007. *From higher aims to hired hands: The social transformation of American business schools and the unfulfilled promise of management as a profession.* Princeton, NJ: Princeton University Press.

McDonald, D. 2017. *The golden passport: Harvard Business School, the limits of capitalism, and the moral failure of the MBA elite.* New York: HarperCollins.

National Association of Colleges and Employers (NACE). 2019. *The four career competencies employers value most.* https://www.naceweb.org/career-readiness/competencies/the-four-career-competencies-employers-value-most/.

Parker, M. 2018. *Shut down the business school: What's wrong with management education.* London, UK: Pluto Press.

Pierson, F. 1959. *The education of American businessmen: A study of university-college programs in business administration.* New York: McGraw-Hill.

QS Quacquarelli Symonds. 2020. *Employer insights report 2020.* London, UK: QS Quacquarelli Symonds. Accessed at http://www.qs.com/qs-industry-reports/.

Responsible Research in Business and Management (RRBM). 2017, revised 2020. *A vision for responsible research in business and management: Striving for useful and credible knowledge.* Accessed at: http://www.rrbm.network

Rubin, R., & Dierdorff, E. 2009. How relevant is the MBA? Assessing the alignment of required MBA curricula and required managerial competencies. *Academy of Management Learning and Education,* 8(2): 208.

Shapiro, D. & Kirkman, B. 2018. *It's time to make business school research more relevant.* Boston, MA: Harvard Business Review.

Sladek, S., & Miller, J. 2018. Ready or not – here comes z. *XYZ University Research Paper.* http://www.xyzuniversity.com

Society for Human Resource Management (SHRM). 2019. *The global skills shortage: Bridging the talent gap with education, training, and sourcing.* Alexandria, VA: Society for Human Resource Management (SHRM). https://www.shrm.org/about-shrm/Documents/SHRM%20State%20of%20Workplace_Bridging%20the%20Talent%20Gap.pdf

Walker, K. 2020. *A digital jobs program to help America's economic recovery.* https://blog.google/outreach-initiatives/grow-with-google/digital-jobs-program-help-americas-economic-recovery/?utm_source=li&utm_medium=social&utm_campaign=og&utm_content=

PART V
Conclusion

14

QUO VADIS? RECONSIDERING THE FUTURE OF MANAGEMENT EDUCATION

Sabine Hoidn, Mairead Brady, and Martin R. Fellenz

This edited volume provides a timely discussion of current challenges and an exploration of future trends of management education (ME) from different angles: context, evolving perspectives and content, teaching and technology and internal/external regulation of ME. By ME we mean all forms of institutions providing educational and training services in the field of management and business at the tertiary level (see also Durand & Dameron, 2017). Grounded in comprehensive and critical considerations of the current state of ME, this book's core objective is to submit a well-argued outlook on the future genesis of ME informed by an educational perspective that is also mindful of the concerns of the individuals and institutions involved. The contributions in this book aim to provide thought-leadership in charting the likely – or at least possible – future of ME.

Current trends such as increasingly global, volatile, and competitive markets, the entry of non-traditional educational players, technological advances regarding human-computer interaction and technology deployment accelerated by the COVID-19 crisis, increasingly diverse faculty and student bodies, and the evolving skill requirements for responsible future leaders, all place huge demands on business schools as central players in ME. Many business schools are forced to reconsider their value proposition, engage differently with existing and novel stakeholders, and re-examine their educational approaches and the nature and quality of learning experiences they provide to their students to prepare them for their future roles. ME is at a crossroads: the future of ME will be shaped in significant part by business schools' capacity to anticipate, recognize and respond to an ever more complex and constantly changing global and digitalized environment.

DOI: 10.4324/9781003095903-19

The relevance of and demand for ME at Bachelors, MSc, MBA, DBA and executive education levels, while changing, remain generally high. These ME segments are differentially affected by macro-economic conditions (Wood, this volume) in a global market where for many countries ME has become a major export industry (Fellenz, Brady & Hoidn, this volume) and business schools will continue to face complex challenges coupled with opportunities for change in the years to come as they are confronted with new and emerging markets, competitors, scholars, students, accreditors, and regulators. Challenges that are likely to substantially determine the future development of ME include:

Fierce competition is thereon a crowded global stage with a variety of players as well as *alternative business models* at the intersection of education, business, and society. Micro-credentialing and stackable degree qualifications acquired across institutions, geography and time are on the rise (see Hommel & Vandenbemp, this volume). Market influence strategies diverge in that some business schools try to keep and extend their global market influence, brand and talent pool (attracting foreign students; hiring international faculty; developing inter-institutional partnerships; offering international tracks; double degrees; etc.) while others remain mainly embedded in the local, regional, or national institutional and business context they cater for (see Cullen, this volume; Wood, this volume). These market shifts, along with technological change, are sending a strong signal that business schools must rethink their value proposition: higher education, and thus, business schools, can and does offer benefits beyond credentialing by focusing more on creating value for their students (see Fukami et al., this volume).

Accreditation and rankings by different external parties (e.g., AACSB, EFMD-EQUIS, AMBA, Financial Times, Shanghai ranking) seem to push the governance, research and teaching agendas of business schools toward homogeneity rather than diversity. Accrediting agencies' normal modus operandi tends to preserve the status quo, although they can also become a force for change (Bryant et al., this volume). Continuing to convey a globalized and research-focused view of Western key success factors and quality markers of business schools evaluated by external accreditation bodies and aimed at making progress in international rankings does not seem to be the best way forward (see Hommel & Vandenbemp, this volume). Such a hazardous "one-size-fits-all" or "all-in-one" approach creates a limiting and impoverished environment for ME since it neglects the historical, socio-cultural and contextual embeddedness of business schools that try to differentiate by building on and foregrounding known strengths and local/national affordances (Abreu-Pederzini & Suárez-Barraza, 2020; Hibbert & Foster, this volume).

Technological advances such as robotics and artificial intelligence, and transformations to online, blended and hybrid teaching, accelerated through COVID-19, rapidly facilitate schools' outreach to disseminate knowledge to an increasingly diverse – and possibly dispersed – student body. Volatility in the global student market has emerged due to COVID era travel restrictions. The often poor national contingency planning and international coordination and cooperation during the COVID-19 pandemic, however, have produced additional political hurdles when it comes to international staff and student mobility and exchange. This has led to abrupt changes and "on the fly" implementations of educational responses under pressure that have had negative effects on teaching quality and learning outcomes (see Wood, this volume). Yet the promise of technologies such as AI and augmented reality to facilitate the co-deployment of human-facilitated and technology-facilitated learning and teaching may help to better meet the needs of individual learners and business schools alike by providing personalized responsive learning at scale (Rivers & Holland, this volume). And transitioning to become a "hybrid business school" offering "global virtual classrooms" that allow students to connect with learners and businesses in other parts of the world seems to have become a real option rather than a far-away aspiration (Lefevre & Caporarello, this volume).

The disconnect between research focus (to attract funding, high-quality academic staff and gain reputation) *and management practice* (real-world problems, what "real" managers or leaders do) leads to ME becoming increasingly irrelevant with business schools being seemingly out of touch with the priority issues identified by business and society (e.g., Bennis & O'Toole, 2005; Burke-Smalley, 2014; Datar, Garvin, & Cullen, 2010; Hoidn & Hawk, 2020; Khurana, 2007; Parker, 2018; Pfeffer & Fong, 2002). Management classroom experiences too often are divorced from the reality of working life and the needs of business and society with experiential education seeming to be too labor-intensive and time-consuming for faculty to deliver (Cullen, this volume). Particularly early career academics might be tempted to religiously follow the "publish or perish" game (while teaching falls short since it is perceived as less valuable and rather unimportant when it comes to advancing one's career) to get published in highly-ranked – all too often American – journals – without considering whether their work is useful (Ratle et al., this volume). To address shifting societal expectations and changing individual learners needs, humanistic approaches to management and issues of accountability, ethics, sustainability, and social responsibility gain increasing attention in business school programs and as accreditation criteria (Akrivou et al., this volume).

Traditional teacher-centered curricula and pedagogies emphasize the concerns of shareholders over those of stakeholders by focusing mostly (or "merely") on organizations in the private sector, sidelining interests in non-profit, volunteer, cooperative, governmental and religious organizations, for example. Thereby ME underperforms in educating future managers and leaders who can act responsibly in a volatile environment or, as Parker (2018) put it, "get things done" and literally leaves them with a "distorted view of management" (Ghoshal, 2005; Mintzberg, 2004). The current shock to the system due to COVID-19, which recognizes the Scholarship of Teaching and Learning as "mission-critical," provides an opportunity for business schools to "reinterpret their traditional teaching-oriented research and scholarship to give it a more central place in their narrative" (see Hibbert & Foster 43, this volume). Disciplinary associations (e.g., AOM), higher education institutions, doctoral programs, and management scholars alike give more attention to effective learning and teaching with evidence-based management education and experiential learning gaining ground (Briner et al., this volume; Cullen, this volume; Fukami et al., this volume).

Working with *diversity* (e.g., gender, race, ethnic) in ME in general and in the management classroom in particular continues to be a challenge. The nurturing of diversity requires more inclusive pedagogical approaches in terms of purpose, design, content and process, i.e., what is being taught and how it is being taught – and why. Thereby the pedagogical process is as important as the content for management learners. So far, ME seems to have largely ignored varying cultural perspectives (due to its focus on Western educational and cultural perspectives [Abreu-Pederzini & Suárez-Barraza, 2020]) as well as differences that surface in the classroom (see Trehan & Rigg, this volume). The excessive push toward strategic convergence faced by business schools seems to neglect their core purposes of educating a diverse group of responsible and innovative (future) managers and leaders and to better engage with society (e.g., Bryant et al., this volume; Fukami et al., this volume).

Many of the challenges identified and discussed in this volume are not new and have been identified before (e.g., Bennis & O'Toole, 2005; Khurana, 2007; Parker, 2018; Pfeffer & Fong, 2002; Thomas, Lee, Thomas & Wilson, 2014). The impact of the recent pandemic has brought about profound changes to ME, some of them previously almost unthinkable. In light of its ability to successfully pivot and address the suddenly changed realities with often profound transformations, the persistent failure of ME over years and decades to address long-standing challenges and long-ignored calls for change (Ghoshal, 2005; Khurana, 2007; Parker, 2018; Pfeffer & Fong, 2002) comprehensively and successfully is a distinct failure. The status quo does not seem to remain an option for ME because changes in market demands and the evolving nature of competition among established and new ME providers will punish those who are too wedded to traditional models no longer fit for purpose. It is therefore vital for business schools and the wider ME sector to face longstanding criticism and address these traditional and emerging new challenges.

What does the future of ME hold? How can ME be crafted in the future? Where to go from here? What is a reasonable (or likely) way forward? What kinds of managers and leaders do we need in the future? What should be taught and learnt in ME and how? These are some of the burning questions ME faces moving forward. Will there be a "shakeout" in the world of business schools and ME providers? Will business schools manage to renew themselves and adapt to the rapidly changing environment or will they rather (continue to) muddle through for survival as some suggest (e.g., Thomas, Lee, & Wilson, 2014)?

Most business schools are a part of universities and thus subject to the regulations, funding models, and performance indicators associated with the higher education system. At the same time, they serve business and society and have to find ways to successfully reposition themselves in terms of their identity, mission, and educational offerings to address the real needs of their stakeholders such as students, employers, faculty, and society at large. Today's management educators are required "to prepare students to build organizations characterized by agility, creativity, and innovation, capable of responding to a world characterized by the acronym VUCA: Volatile, Uncertain, Complex, and Ambiguous" (Giles, 2018) (Fukami et al., this volume).

These challenges to the purpose and traditional hegemony of business schools will not be successfully met by charting a single course for all business schools. Rather, the key to success for business schools lies in responding in flexible and differentiated ways to the changing and complex environment they face by finding specific market niches they can serve well, be they local, regional, national, or international. Strategic differentiation (e.g., internationalization, specialization) and strategic partnerships (e.g., alliances) will be key for business schools to distinguish and successfully reposition themselves and carve out and sustainably leverage their competitive advantage while facing an uncertain future (Durand & Dameron, 2017). By exploring and exploiting each school's history and traditions, for example, business schools can develop their strategic advantage to address the interests and concerns of their specific key stakeholders (Hibbert & Foster, this volume). Technology will play an increasingly central role in this and some business schools might transition to become "hybrid" with changing organizational structures and roles, a reconfigured virtual and physical campus, and an extensive external network of partners (Lefevre & Caporarello, this volume). Hybrid learning systems can open up avenues for experimental learning extending beyond the boundaries of a business school with educational delivery taking place within a network of partner schools (and possibly also non-academic organizations) (Hommel et al., this volume). For some segments technology may be deployed in a supporting rather than starring role, but its presence will be felt more and more in all aspects of ME.

A key ingredient necessary for success in virtually all of these differentiated ways of offering ME will be the recognition that ME must explicitly address the role it has for the wider social, economic and ecological environments in which it operates, and for which it shares responsibility. Management is not a profession (Khurana & Nohria, 2008), and unlike established professions such as medicine, law or psychology, management does not have the benefit of formal protection of professional practice or of the educational pathways leading to recognised and protected professional qualifications in return for offering services at high technical and ethical standards to address a recognised social need. Yet despite this, ME's purpose must be central to developing and delivering educational services that address societal and human needs in effective and sustainable ways because it educates those moving into – and already in – positions that magnify their impact on the social and physical world (Bennis & O'Toole, 2005; Ghoshal, 2005; Khurana, 2007; Parker, 2018; see also Kreber, 2019; Walker & McLean, 2013). In light of such possibilities and the social expectations it validly creates and amplifies, lip service to these societal obligations will not suffice as legitimacy based on tradition, or on mimicry and isomorphism, will no longer be an option, especially as traditional barriers to entry will be partially obliterated by technology. In the near future greater emphasis might be placed on "purpose-driven business" (Bryant et al., this volume) with businesses "aspiring toward some higher purpose beyond products, services, and profits" related to social well-being (Fukami et al., this volume). Business schools will need to earn their legitimacy anew and renew it with their ongoing actions and contributions – pretenders and imposters need not apply.

For individual management learners of the future, the value proposition of ME must go far beyond the reputational transfer through a business school brand or the cachet of a degree because market transparency will increase and employers are increasingly sophisticated in selecting applicants based on actual skill. Future managers will need critical thinking skills, emotional intelligence, interactive skills, technological skills, and "practical wisdom," that is theoretical knowledge as well as practical knowledge to create more effective and human-centric organizations (Roos, 2014). Again, technology will play a large role in this, as do the changes to ranking and accreditation approaches as well as the increasing popularity of skill-based micro-credentialing. These technological trends and the COVID-19 challenge might propel a more human-centric approach to management and business (education) which AI remains unable to perform (e.g., Fukami et al., this volume).

Moreover, management learners may well demand ME offerings that match their individual learning needs, preferences and interests. Thus, the diversity of learning needs will have to be matched by commensurate variety in ME offerings that will be created either by the flexibility and customizability of offerings from individual business schools and other providers, or by the range of ME services available from different providers in the market. This might entail a shift toward humanistic personalist approaches to management and ME placing the person as a human being at the center with future managers and leaders being oriented toward the service of the whole person and society at large (e.g., Akrivou et al., this volume). And while technology can be used in ME to provide more per-sonalized learning experiences (at scale), it will not replace human educators. It can, however, assist them in identifying and better understanding the variety of their students' learning needs to provide individualized feedback and learning support to an increasingly diverse body of students (Graßmann & Schermuly, 2021; Rivers et al., this volume).

Finally, a major challenge for the future success of ME is the role of research informing not just the content of ME, but also co-determining the processes of teaching and learning. Despite ME's popularity among academic subjects and its importance for society, there is a curious absence of a distinct ME philosophy and a body of ME specific educational theory. Recognizing its distinctive nature, and more fully theorizing and comprehensively researching it, will provide a significant contribution to educational value creation and will provide a source for differentiation and competitive success for business schools and other ME providers. In this regard, business schools have a responsibility to equip students with the knowledge, skills and attitudes to make informed decisions since the decisions managers make can have profound implications not only for the organizations in which they work but in society more broadly. Current developments surrounding the COVID-19 pandemic highlight the need for a generation of managers who can make well-informed decisions based on data and different sources of evidence. (Briner et al., this volume) In this context, educational innovation that deploys and actively leverages rather than simply follows technology will be a key differentiator of successful ME provision into the future. Nevertheless, the management educator being "present" either in a virtual or physical environment remains crucial due to their capacity for social interaction, emotional intelligence and empathetic responses which seem pivotal for higher engagement and satisfaction (Hewett, Becker & Bish, 2019; Prentice & Nguyen, 2020; Rivers & Holland, this volume).

In conclusion, ME as a sector has shown by its response to the pandemic that started in 2020 that it can respond quickly and – despite many shortcomings and problems – largely successfully to urgent pressures for change. Yet such change to *urgent* challenges cannot make up for the slow response to *important* demands for change to ME that have been verbalized repeatedly – and apparently largely ignored – for over 60 years (e.g., Bennis & O'Toole, 2005; Ghoshal, 2005; Khurana, 2007; Mintzberg, 2004; Parker, 2018; Porter & McKibbin, 1988; Roos, 2014) going back to the influential Carnegie and Ford Foundation reports published in 1959 (Gordon & Howell, 1959; Pierson, 1959; see also Spender, 2016a; 2016b). Once again, the analyses and discussion contained in this book highlight that business schools and the sector as a whole are at a cross-roads where decision-makers across the many business schools, emerging alternative ME providers, and other ME stakeholders can choose to actively and constructively respond to the large scale shifts and developments identified above, or – to use the words of Porter and McKibbin (1988) – "drift reactively" in light of these changes.

The future of ME is not written in stone. Rather, it will be created by the individuals and institutions that offer, accredit, regulate, support, use, and challenge ME now and in the time to come. Our hope is that – individually and collectively – we will create a vibrant range of ME that matches the ambitions, needs and diversity of current and future management learners. Ideally, this future ME will earn its legitimacy not based on tradition but by meeting its current and emerging educational, social, environmental, and sustainability responsibilities while contributing positively to the development and practice of management in society.

References

Abreu-Pederzini, G. D., & Suárez-Barraza, M. F. 2020. Just let us be: Domination, the postcolonial condition, and the global field of business schools. *Academy of Management Learning & Education*, 19(1): 40–58.

Bennis, W. G., & O'Toole, J. 2005. How business schools have lost their way. *Harvard Business Review*, 83(5): 96–104.

Burke-Smalley, L. R. 2014. Evidenced-based management education. *Journal of Management Education*, 38(5): 764–767.

CABS. 2017. *The impact of executive education: A review of current practice & trends*. London: Chartered Association of Business Schools.

Datar, S. M., Garvin, D. A., & Cullen, P. G. 2010. *Rethinking the MBA: Business education at a crossroads*. Boston, MA: Harvard Business School Press.

Durand, T., & Dameron, S. 2017. Trends and challenges in management education around the world. In. S. Dameron & T. Durand (eds.), *The Future of Management Education. Challenges facing business schools around the world*, vol. 1. UK: Palgrave Macmillan.

Ghoshal, S. 2005. Bad management theories are destroying good management practices. *Academy of Management Learning and Education*, 4(1), 75–91.

Giles, S. 2018. How VUCA is reshaping the business environment, and what it means for innovation. *Forbes*. https://www.forbes.com/sites/sunniegiles/2018/05/09/how-vuca-is-reshaping-the-business-environment-and-what-it-means-for-innovation/

Gordon, R. A., & Howell, J. E. 1959. *Higher education for business*. New York: Columbia University Press.

Graßmann, C., & Schermuly, C. C. 2021. Coaching with artificial intelligence: Concepts and capabilities. *Human Resource Development Review*, 20(1): 106–126.

Hewett, S., Becker, K., & Bish, A. 2019. Blended workplace learning: The value of human interaction. *Education + Training*, 61: 2–16.

Hoidn, S., & Hawk, T. 2020. Towards a more holistic approach to competence development: The case for student-centered management and business education. Paper presented at the *80th Annual Meeting of the Academy of Management*, Vancouver, British Columbia, Canada.

Khurana, R. 2007. *From higher aims to hired hands: The social transformation of American business schools and the unfulfilled promise of management as a profession*. Princeton: Princeton University Press.

Khurana, R., & Nohria, N. 2008. It's time to make management a true profession. *Harvard Business Review*, 86(10): 70–77.

Kreber, C. 2019. The idea of a 'decent profession': Implications for professional education. *Studies in Higher Education*, 44(4): 696–707. 10.1080/03075079.2017.1395405

Mintzberg, H. 2004. *Managers not MBAs. A hard look at the soft practice of managing and management development*. San Francisco, CA: Berrett-Koehler Publishers, Inc.

Parker, M. 2018. *Shut down the business school. What's wrong with management education*. London, UK: Pluto Press.

Pfeffer, J., & Fong, C. 2002. The end of business schools? Less success than meets the eye. *Academy of Management Learning and Education*, 1(1): 78–95.

Pierson, F. C. (1959). *The education of American businessmen*. New York: McGraw-Hill.

Porter, L. W., & McKibbin, L. E. 1988. *Management education and development: Drift or thrust into the 21st century?*. Hightstown, NJ: McGraw-Hill.

Prentice, C., & Nguyen, M. (2020). Engaging and retaining customers with AI and employee service. *Journal of Retailing and Consumer Services*. 10.1016/j.jretconser.2020. 102186

Roos, J. 2014. The Renaissance we need in business education. *Harvard Business Review*. Accessed May 2, 2021, at https://hbr.org/2014/07/the-renaissance-we-need-in-business-education

Sawhney, M. 2021. Reimagining executive education: What program delivery should look like post-pandemic. *Harvard Business Publishing*. Accessed May 4, 2021, at https://hbsp.harvard.edu/inspiring-minds/reimagining-executive-education

Spender, J. C. 2016a. How management education's past shapes its present. *BizEd*. Accessed April 2, 2021, at https://bized.aacsb.edu/articles/2016/03/how-management-education-past-shapes-present

Spender, J. C. 2016b. A brief and non-academic history of management education. *BizEd*. Accessed April 2, 2021, at https://bized.aacsb.edu/articles/2016/03/brief-non-academic-history-management-education

Thomas, H., Lee, M., Thomas, L., & Wilson, A. 2014. *Securing the future of management education: Competitive destruction or constructive innovation?* Bingley, UK: Emerald.

Thomas, H., Lee, M. P., & Wilson, A. 2014. Future scenarios for management education. *Journal of Management Development*, 33(5): 503–519.

Walker, M., & McLean, M. 2013. *Professional education, capabilities and contributions to the public good: The role of universities in promoting human development.* London, UK: Routledge.

INDEX

Printed in the United States
by Baker & Taylor Publisher Services